am i a normal parent ?

am i a normal parent?

EXPERT ADVICE, PARENTING TIPS AND
THE REASSURANCE YOU'VE BEEN LOOKING FOR

Sara Dimerman

Hatherleigh Press is committed to preserving and protecting the natural resources of the Earth. Environmentally responsible and sustainable practices are embraced within the company's mission statement.

PublishersEarthAlliance.org

PEA Member   Recycled Content

Hatherleigh Press
5-22 46th Avenue, Suite 200
Long Island City, NY 11101
www.hatherleighpress.com

CIP data is available upon request.

ISBN 978-1-57826-276-2

Am I a Normal Parent? is available for bulk purchase, special promotions, and premiums. For information on reselling and special purchase opportunities, call 1-800-528-2550 and ask for the Special Sales Manager.

Interior design by Maria E. Torres, Neuwirth & Associates, Inc.
Cover design by Michael Fusco, michaelfuscodesign.com

10 9 8 7 6 5 4 3 2 1
Printed in the United States

To my devoted husband, Joey, for choosing me to be your wife. Your words reassure, comfort, and encourage me every step of the way. I will cherish our love forever.

To my darling daughters, Talia and Chloe, for choosing me to be your mother. I will never know any greater honor.

Acknowledgments

I COULD WRITE a book of acknowledgements alone. Blessed with a loving family, both growing up and now, surrounded by exceptional friends and colleagues, I consider myself truly fortunate.

My husband, Joey, and I live by the motto "family first." He's not only an amazing father and friend, but my number one cheerleader. Supportive and dedicated, he's sometimes embarrassingly proud of my accomplishments. Knowing that he is in the wings to prompt me if I run out of lines center stage, to catch me if I fall, to listen and comfort me with reassuring words when I need them most, has helped me to realize my goals.

What I treasure most in life are my daughters. They are as proud of me as I am of them. When I shared my exciting news about *Am I a Normal Parent?* their genuine outpouring of emotion filled me with joy.

Every day, they teach me something new. I am in awe of them as people, am entertained by Chloe's expressions, quick-wittedness, playfulness, and impeccable sense of timing. I am impressed at her fluency with words at such a young age and her tenderness and empathy towards others. Her smile lights up a room and when she laughs, it's contagious.

I am moved by the caring and compassion that Talia shows toward her family and friends, admire her many artistic talents, attention to detail, her strong work ethic, morals, and tenacity when overcoming obstacles that have been thrown her way. I was so proud when the director of a day camp, where she has been hired to work this summer, told me that "Talia is like a ray of sunshine." She sat by my side and worked many long hours into late nights helping me sort through questionnaires and tabulate results. She patiently leads me through computer functions—formatting, fonts—anything other than the basics I know.

Throughout the making of this book, my family has recognized and valued my desire to complete my manuscript on time. For this, and so much more, I thank them.

My mother and I are more like friends. She is my confidante, my loyal supporter, and always there for me, no matter what or when. I inherited my passion and flair for writing from her. When we moved from South Africa to Canada, she spent hours at her electric typewriter filling the blank pages with colorful narrative to send to friends and family back home. Thirty years later, she continues to be a reliable correspondent, and her lucky readers beg her to write professionally. Instead, she lives vicariously through me. Her attempts at cajoling me to see or help edit my work in progress have been futile. I am looking forward to seeing my mom leisurely reading this beautifully bound final product. I know she will treasure it forever.

My father is one of my biggest fans, although he doesn't always know how to describe what it is that I do. That's okay. I sometimes forget which hat I am wearing, too. A graduate of the school of hard knocks, perseverance resulted in his success as a businessman. An entrepreneurial spirit and warm heart (he gives the greatest hugs) is what I have inherited from my dad.

My three younger sisters tell me how proud they are of my accomplishments and, along with my parents-in-law, my brothers-in-law and all of their families, near and far, I feel encouraged, loved, and supported. My acknowledgements of family wouldn't be complete without especially thanking my nephew, Josh, who is also my genius webmaster. He puts my cyber ideas into action and continues to amaze me with his technological talent.

When I first conceived of writing a series of *Am I Normal* books, I shared my thoughts with Kevin Hanson, a friend of my friend, Sharon, at her house party one evening. (Thanks to Alan for introducing me to Sharon!)I had heard that Kevin worked in the publishing industry and wanted his opinion. He was most encouraging. Despite his vote of confidence, it took a couple of years before I had the nerve to actually start writing a proposal. Despite many years of writing experience, knowing where and how to begin selling my book idea was very new to me. By the time I was ready to embark on my journey, Kevin was President of Simon & Schuster, in Canada. Despite his impressive title, position, and responsibilities, Kevin always makes time to talk and point me in the right direction. His support is unwavering. I will always be indebted to Kevin for his encouraging words and belief in me.

Along the road to being published, I met Leah Fairbanks, an energetic and talented editor at John Wiley and Sons in Canada. Leah was also very instrumental in helping me put my thoughts in the right order, refine my proposal, and pursue my dream.

Three-quarters of the way into my journey, with a couple of "great book idea but no thanks" responses under my belt, a guardian angel was sent my way. Dr. Susan Bartell was not an unfamiliar name to me. I had been recommending her books to my clients for years and had included them on the list of suggested readings on my website. One day, out of the blue, I received an email from Susan. She had written to ask if I could include her name next to that of her co-author of one of her books on my site. I apologized sincerely. Of course, I had not purposely omitted her name.

Through a series of further emails, Susan and I learned that our chance meeting was surely not so coincidental. We had both emigrated from South Africa in the same year, only months apart—her to New York and me to Toronto. Working in the field of psychology and sharing a love of writing were only two similarities on the list of startling parallels. It was Susan who ultimately introduced me to Andrea Au, editorial director at Hatherleigh Press.

And the rest, as they say, is history.

Once my contract was signed with Hatherleigh Press, I began wading through articles and other parenting books. I conducted research by reaching out and connecting with people who I had previously only read about. Well-known celebrities and authors such as Nanny Deb (who wrote the foreword and has been so supportive), Adele Faber, Lynn Lott, Kathy Lynn, and Mary Sheedy Kurcinka were willing and generous with their time. My writing was enriched by what they shared.

Other authors, writers, and publishers gave me their blessings to pluck from their books, articles, and pieces in which they were quoted. Thanks go to Jennifer Wise, Lynne Van Luven and Pat Touchie at TouchWood Editions, Rona Maynard, Dr. Scott Wooding, Dr. Nancy Freeman, Joanna Moorhead, and to Kim Paleg and Dr. Matthew McKay at New Harbinger Publications. Thanks also to Janet Chan and Caroline Connell.

Thanks also to Goldie Plotkin, Carroll MacIntosh, Dr. Ari Novick, Dr. Erik Mansager, Dr. Myles Blank, Romi Lassally, Patti Kirk, Leslie Chandler, Tracy Keleher, Howard Hurwitz, and Lana Feinstein for their words of wisdom.

And to a very important group of experts—over 200 parents who completed the parenting questionnaires—many anonymously. Their responses and reflections are a huge part of what makes this book relevant to other parents. To the parents I interviewed over the phone and in person—many of whom are quoted in the book—a very big THANK YOU for their time and honesty.

When my family and I travelled to New York in October 2007, we visited the Hatherleigh offices and met Alyssa, Andrea, Andrew, and Kevin. It was great to finally put faces to their names. I was sad to hear that Alyssa, my editor, was moving on but thrilled to have Andrea, Hatherleigh's editorial director, on my side. Special thanks go to Andrea for her patience, speedy responses to my endless questions, and for her expert editorial direction. Many thanks also to editor June Eding and Ryan Tumambing who stepped in at a crucial time to see this project through to completion. To Andrew Flach, Kevin Moran, and Mariel Dumas for their support and time spent in launching and promoting *Am I a Normal Parent?* To them and the rest of the gang at Hatherleigh and Random House—a million thanks for everything they have done in giving my voice a platform and for helping my dream of being an author become a reality.

And last, but definitely not least, thanks to a remarkable woman, Lynda Fishman, owner and executive director of Adventure Valley, in Thornhill, Ontario, and her exceptional daughter, Rebecca—for their enthusiasm and support of *Am I a Normal Parent?* and for partnering with me in announcing and celebrating its birth.

Contents

Foreword

by Nanny Deb of Fox TV's *Nanny 911*

When I was approached to write the foreword for *Am I a Normal Parent?* I was thrilled. This is a subject very close to my heart and a question that I am very familiar with. When I left Britain and started out as a nanny in Los Angeles, I had no idea that I would be become known as Nanny Deb on Fox's hit reality TV show, *Nanny 911*. For the first 26 years of my career, the agency with whom I was affiliated assigned me to various families in need of a nanny. Living in Hollywood, I landed amazing positions with great families, many of whom were actors and actresses in need of a surrogate parent for their children. I was very satisfied with my career and didn't go looking to be a big television personality. The opportunity came knocking on my door. Truthfully, at first I wasn't all that interested. However, it has turned out to be a wonderful experience, and I have met some amazing parents and children along the way, many of whom I have remained in touch with.

When I first meet with the families on *Nanny 911*, their lives are in chaos. They see me as a knight in shining armor coming to rescue them. It's a huge responsibility but the rewards are tremendous. One of the biggest things that I hear at the end of my time with the family is thanks for giving them their family back. This always makes me cry and gives me goosebumps just thinking about it. One little girl wrote me a letter that said she didn't like it when I took the television out of her room and that she thought that the rules that I implemented were going to be stupid. However, she went on to say that she realized that the rules had made her family happier, that she liked how I had made her daddy do homework with her and how her mom was acting more like a mom since I came into their lives.

I hope that everyone reads *Am I a Normal Parent?*—even if they're not parents. In fact, reading about the stark realities of parenting may be the best form of contraception around. That's what people said about *Nanny 911*. Once, when Nanny Stella and I went to do a book signing for *Nanny 911,* we were swarmed by a group of teenagers. They were screaming in excitement and came running over throwing skateboards and shoes at us asking us to sign them. They said that before watching *Nanny 911,* they hadn't realized that parenting was such hard work. They said they wanted to wait and be really prepared before they had kids. I was bowled over. High school and college teachers ask their parenting students to view *Nanny 911* because it opens their eyes and makes young people realize that taking care of a baby or child is not so glamorous and doesn't always make life better—especially if it's already rotten and you're just trying to fill a void.

Aside from helping prevent unwanted teenage pregnancies, I think that *Nanny 911* helps some parents feel that the dynamics in their family aren't as bad as they had thought. It also comforts other parents who may be in a similar situation with their kids and helps them learn new strategies for handling difficult behaviors. I think that *Am I a Normal Parent?* will have the same effect on parents.

I suspect that many parents would say that parenting is not what they expected. They think that they're going to have a baby and fall in love with the baby right away, that the baby is going to complete their family. I often remind people that they shouldn't just have a baby because they want a baby—they should also want children and teenagers. Babies grow up really quickly. Wanting only a baby is like wanting a puppy and then not wanting to keep it when it grows up to a be a dog and it's peed on the floor a few times. I recommend taking as many parenting programs, reading as many parenting books, and being around as many parents of newborns as you can before you have kids. When people ask the mother of a newborn about the delivery process, I can't believe a response about it being the most beautiful experience of her life. The truth usually comes out a while later when she shares the hell she really went through.

Am I a Normal Parent? will encourage parents to be more honest. I've been waiting for a book like this to be available so that parents can read the honest truth about parenting. I'd like them to realize that they are not alone when they feel that it's hard work.

Parents on and off the show often ask me if what they are doing is right. They often share their secrets about how they feel as a parent and ask if they are normal. They worry about sometimes feeling like they don't love their children the way they think parents are supposed to. They are concerned about not wanting to come home from work to see their children at the end of the day. I ask who they're measuring themselves against. I reassure them that there are probably people three doors down who feel exactly the same way—it's just that nobody talks about it.

In today's society, parents are often parenting for others and not for themselves. For example, there are trends about whether breast-feeding is best and whether you should sleep with your baby or not. And after years of advising parents to praise their children, the experts are now saying that constantly praising them creates praise junkies and is socially irresponsible.

Parents today expect so much of themselves. They'll say things like, "My mother managed to raise six kids without ever having help; my mom worked and had dinner on the table every night. I can't ask for help or people will see me as a failure." I remind those parents that they're raising their children in a different world. I also tell them that despite all the things in today's society that are supposed to make things easier, our lives have become too busy, and we're stretched too thin.

Parents have become so concerned with how they compare to others that they have forgotten to trust themselves. They have forgotten to ask themselves, "What is best for my family and for this child?" Whenever anyone asks me if what they are doing is okay, I ask, "Is it working for you?" If they say yes, then I tell them that it's okay. If they say no, then I ask them to consider why they are doing it and what they can do differently, even if it means that they do something "different" or "not normal."

From what I see, normal parents in America are those who love their children and love their family but whose priorities may be messed up. They often don't put their family first and don't seem to think about the consequences of their actions. Instead of going with their instincts, with what they feel is right, they allow society and peer pressure to take over. Many parents would rather hand off their children to the television or video games than spend time with them. I don't know if that's because working parents are too stressed or tired to deal with their kids or because parents are apathetic and think it's okay for their kids to watch TV because everyone else is doing it.

Once a parent recognizes how they are being influenced and how they may be parenting in a way that doesn't feel right, they need help figuring out how to change. Of course, not all parents fit into this definition of "normal," but many do. Reading books like *Am I a Normal Parent?*, attending support groups, and educating yourself as a parent is part of the way to go. Also, get back to basics. Think about what you want for your family, and then try to figure out if what you're doing is the best way to realize your goals.

Honesty is the start, not the end. We've got to learn to be supportive of one another and to reach out and to ask for help. You should be able to ask your neighbor to pick up milk if she is going to the grocery store.

This book will definitely be a wake up call for a lot of parents. They will say, "Wow, what's going on in other people's lives is not so different from what's going on in mine." That's a big start to being honest and acknowledging all the trials and tribulations that go along with parenting.

I am really and truly very excited about *Am I a Normal Parent?* I feel like buying one for everybody; maybe I'll just keep one in my handbag and recommend it to parents wherever I go!

Introduction

The "Am I a Normal Parent?" Questionnaire

Go on. Admit it. You wonder if you're normal. We all do. Not all the time, but often enough to make us curious about whether we stand alone. And interested enough to question how we compare to others in all aspects of life—but especially when it comes to parenting.

Sometimes, we're afraid to ask other parents whether they feel as anxious as we do about screwing up, as concerned about not spending enough time with their kids, as worried about being judged overprotective, impatient, or a pushover.

Lillian, a single mother of two girls, ages 10 and 8, worries about being immature around the kids. "At 45, I seem to be a lot sillier than other parents," she says. "I play practical jokes on people, but all in good fun. I find things like burping and farting amusing. I also wonder if I'm too open with them. I try not to tell them things that are inappropriate for their age, but I sometimes feel that I am giving them too much information. Where do you draw the line?" she asks.

Am I a Normal Parent? will answer your questions and calm your fears. No longer will you need to wonder and worry about how you compare. You may be surprised to learn that the thoughts, feelings, and behaviors of many parents are universal.

Am I a Normal Parent? is for you. It is filled with anecdotes and advice that will help you to learn and grow as a parent. Unlike other how-to parenting books, its focus is on you, not your child. You may read many other fabulous parenting books about acknowledging your child's feelings. *Am I a Normal Parent?* acknowledges *yours.*

Am I a Normal Parent? embraces *your* concerns about being judged and ostracized. Each chapter, like a mirror, will allow you to see yourself reflected in others' experiences. You will easily be able to identify with the emotional roller coaster that most parents ride. You will finally feel understood.

You will likely feel a renewed sense of peace at knowing that you are not crazy to think certain thoughts, invigorated by the knowledge that you are not the only parent on the planet ever to have contemplated running away—if only for one night. You will feel thankful to learn that many parents, like you, sometimes prefer one of their children over the others. You will feel grateful that you can easily fill the shoes of a normal parent, as defined in *Am I a Normal Parent?*

You may, on the other hand, decide that being a "normal" parent is not all that it's cracked up to be. You may wish to challenge and explore existing norms (since not all norms in society are healthy or positive) and decide to make changes. You may ultimately prefer to stand apart. You may not wish to be defined as a "normal" parent after all. "Normal" may not be good enough. You may realize that you are not typical of most and prefer to be different.

A VERY "NORMAL" QUESTION

Ever since I began working as a child and family therapist more than 20 years ago, "normal" has been one of the most common words I have heard in questions from parents. They ask, "Am I normal? Is my child normal? Is it normal to feel so guilty when I see my vegetative child sprouting roots in front of the television and do nothing about it? What is normal?"

When parents ask me if they are normal, I don't believe they are asking whether or not they fit the criteria for a diagnosis of abnormal behavior in a psychologist's manual. The majority of parents use the word "normal" in a very casual manner. They just want to know if they are typical of others. They want to know if they fit in, how they compare to most.

Writer/comedian Joe Ancis, who hung out with Rodney Dangerfield and Lenny Bruce, is quoted as saying, "The only normal people are the ones you don't know very well." My interpretation of this is that once you get beyond the superficial layers many people hide behind, you find that they too are no more or less normal than you or me.

Many parents are experts at keeping embarrassing or "abnormal" thoughts and feelings concealed. They take their masks off for very few people—a partner, child, close relative, or friend. I encourage parents to remove their masks and to share honestly with one another so that they can rejoice in the knowledge that they are not alone.

"What makes me *not* normal is that I am so unsure of myself as a parent," Cindy, a 43-year-old mother of two, told me when we first met. I asked her to repeat the sentence but to remove the "not." "What makes you normal, "I said," is that you *are* so unsure of yourself as a parent." It's the uncertainty and concern that parents feel about whether they're doing a good enough job, the guilt at thinking crazy thoughts about their kids and the fear that there isn't another parent on this planet that acts or thinks like them, that drives them to my office.

The privilege that comes along with being able to offer another human being a fresh perspective on an old belief is humbling. Cindy's expression changed and she began to cry. There were a few seconds of silence as I watched and waited. "I thought being unsure wasn't normal," she said. "I look around at other parents and they seem so sure, so confident, so all-together. They just go about the business of parenting without seeming to question themselves all the time."

Wanting to be normal is typical. Wanting to belong is part of what defines us as human beings. We commonly hang out with people who have similar values, desires, and cultural or religious beliefs. Human beings create families so they can "belong" to one another. We go to school, church, or synagogue so we can belong. We join book clubs, ski clubs, and dinner clubs so we can belong. Even those who prefer not to belong to the mainstream congregate with other like-minded people so as to define their own version of normal.

I believe that NORMAL is an acronym for No One Really Marches Alone. If you're ever in a situation where you feel as if what you are thinking or feeling is not "normal," comfort yourself by knowing that somewhere out there, next door or far away, another parent is feeling, thinking, and behaving just like you.

HOW *AM I A NORMAL PARENT?* CAME TO BE

Am I a Normal Parent? was conceived after many years of writing parenting columns and articles and counseling thousands of parents online and in person. Back in the late 1980s and a recent graduate of a postgraduate assessment and counselling program, I was asked to facilitate a parenting course at the Family Life Center where I worked. I hesitated at first as I certainly didn't have the confidence to run such a program. However, I was told that I had the skills required to lead groups, so I accepted the challenge.

I remember sitting on my living room floor with open books strewn all around me—a leader's manual, a parent handbook, and many parenting articles on various topics. I studied everything as if preparing for an exam. The only real experience I had, other than many years of babysitting other people's children, was with my then-8-month-old nephew (he's now 22). My involvement with him was more than the average aunt; he was being raised by my parents, and my husband and I were only too thrilled to assist. However, even this didn't prepare me sufficiently for the first time I led a parenting group with 10 eager-to-learn parents. I was terrified.

My biggest concern as a childless, newly married therapist in her mid-twenties was whether they would be able to look to me for answers. Some of the parents had children who were almost half my age. I started off by laying all my cards on the table. "Yes, I know what you're thinking," I said. "How can someone as young as me, with no children, help you with your parenting problems?" I tried to convince myself, and them, that I could remain more emotionally detached by not relating to their experiences personally. I later learned that without life experience, I really could not understand their desperate need to find quick solutions to their parenting problems.

Maybe it was the South African, British-sounding accent or my tool kit of successful strategies that convinced them to put their trust in me. That was the beginning of my love affair with parent education. A couple of years later I founded the Parent Education and Resource Center in Thornhill (Ontario, Canada), set up a private practice, and later passed examinations to become a member of the College of Psychologists of Ontario. This gave me even greater credibility in the field of counselling psychology.

Facilitating parenting classes was better than any other form of contraception for me. I heard the worst of the worst parenting woes and waited several years before having my first child. I now have two wonderful daughters, ages 8 and 16, who provide me with an endless source of stories to write about—often to their horror! I feel fortunate to have learned what I needed to know as I taught others. When I became a parent, I certainly had very realistic expectations.

Recently, my daughter, now in grade 11, had the opportunity to take a parenting course as part of her curriculum. I am convinced that this should be a mandatory course, and not an elective, for all high school students. After spending 48 sleep-deprived hours with her 10-pound computer-chipped baby girl, whom she affectionately named Michaela, she has decided that parenting is a lot more demanding than she had originally thought.

THE *AM I A NORMAL PARENT?* QUESTIONNAIRE

> If you've picked this book off the shelf, my guess is that you, like more than three-quarters of the parents who have already answered the questionnaire at the end of this chapter, wonder if you are a normal parent.

I created the questionnaire in order to identify what is most normal or typical in a variety of situations. The questionnaire is a compilation of 50 questions that cover many different topics related to our thoughts, feelings, and behavior as parents. The results are shared with you over the course of the book. For example, the question that asks if you ever do anything for your child that you know he or she is capable of doing for him or herself is discussed in more detail in chapter 10. The percentage of parents who answered yes or no is also shared so that you can compare your responses to the majority of parents'. In this way, normal or typical is defined.

If you flip to the end of the book, you will see a listing of the 50 questions. The chapter in which the results are shown is identified next to each question, so if you are interested in knowing more about particular questions, you can go directly to those chapters.

As part of my research, over 200 questionnaires were completed by parents, mostly moms, ranging in age from mid-twenties to mid-fifties. Their children ranged in age from newborn to late teens. The majority of parents were middle class parents from around the world. Most of the parents live in the United States. Others are living in Canada, South Africa, Australia, Israel, India, China, and England.

Their answers to the questions, plus my personal anecdotes and experience from over 20 years of counseling, and words of wisdom from other professionals, authors, and parents have been gathered here in one neat package. I take great pride and pleasure in delivering *Am I a Normal Parent?* to you.

Before you begin reading, take a few minutes to answer the questionnaire below. There are no right or wrong answers, so please be honest, even if your responses leave you feeling "sheepish" (as one parent said she felt). It should take between 20 to 30 minutes to complete.

So sit back, relax with pencil in hand, and begin. Keep in mind that some questions may not pertain to you, so you can skip over them. Also, if you have more than one child, you may find it helpful to answer the entire questionnaire with one particular child in mind. Then you might consider how you would respond differently to some of the questions with another child or children in mind. If there is no definite Y (yes) or N (no) response, then circle whichever you are leaning toward.

1. Have you ever asked out loud or of yourself "Am I a normal parent?"   Y   N

2. Do you ever resent being asked to put a project/activity on hold to accommodate your child(ren)?   Y   N

3. Do you ever threaten your child(ren) with punishment that you know you'll never follow through with?   Y   N

   Can you think of anything in particular?_____
   _____
   _____
   _____

4. Have you ever promised to take your child out for an ice cream, for example, and then not followed through?   Y   N

5. Have you had an argument with your child, had him/her go to bed angry at you, and then quietly kissed him/her as he/she slept?   Y   N

6. When angry, have you ever had thoughts/fears of hurting your child?   Y   N

   If so, how long did the thoughts last?_____
   _____

7. Do you feel that there are enough hours in the day to accomplish everything?   Y   N

8. Have you ever felt the need to protect your child(ren) from knowing intimate details of your life that might hurt them emotionally (e.g., diagnosis of illness, conflict in your relationship with your partner, personal use of alcohol or drugs?)   Y   N

9. Do you feel that your child's behavior is a reflection of you? Y   N

10. Have you ever told your child "I'll be there in a minute" but really taken 10?   Y   N

11. Have you ever told your child that you will stay close by while he/she is sleeping and then snuck away?   Y   N

12. Have you ever told your child, "If you don't stop hurting your brother/sister, I'm going to hit you"?   Y   N

13. Have you ever insisted that your child eat fruits and vegetables but not been responsible about eating them yourself?   Y   N

14. Do you always speak to older adults/parents in the way that you would like your child(ren) to speak/behave toward you?   Y   N

15. Would you leave a 3-year-old child alone in a car while you ran into a store for a couple of minutes?   Y   N

    If not, at what age might you consider doing so? _____

16. Have you ever worried that you were being "neurotic" in regard to your child's safety/wellbeing?   Y   N

17. Have you ever said something nasty to your child? Y   N

Regretted it later?   Y   N

18. Do you ever feel that of all the households in the neighborhood, yours could win the "Mornings from Hell" award?   Y   N

19. Ever feel that it is difficult to juggle all your responsibilities? Y   N

20. Have you ever disobeyed the law or rules in regards to your children (e.g., taken a child out a car or booster seat before the law allows)?   Y   N

21. If you're at a party with your children and your children are tired, do you leave even if you want to stay?   Y   N

22. Do you ever put your own needs ahead of your children's? Y   N

23. If you're at a pool party with other adults and children, do you change your behavior as a result of having children present (e.g., reduce drinking, dress more conservatively, censor your conversations with other adults)? Y   N

24. Do you ever feel that you like one of your children more than another? Y N

25. Do you ever feel that other parents are judgemental of your behavior toward your child(ren)? Y N

26. Do you ever feel guilty about how you prioritize your daily list of chores (e.g., laundry before lovemaking or paying bills before playing with the kids)? Y N

27. Do you ever feel that the boundary lines between work and home have become blurred (e.g., receiving business calls at home, working on a laptop for work-related duties while on vacation with the family)? Y N

28. Do you ever have long-winded conversations on your cell phone while in the company of your kids? Y N

29. Have you ever not shared a secret about your feelings or thoughts as a parent for fear of being considered not normal by others? Y N

Jot down any you can think of _____

_____

_____

30. Do you ever feel like running away from home, if only for one night? Y N

31. Do you ever long for life the way it was before kids? Y N

32. Do you ever wish that you were still a kid yourself? Y   N

33. Do you ever feel that, despite bending over backwards to accommodate your children, you are not appreciated by them? Y   N

34. Do you ever feel that you are being "abused" by your children? This may be in the form of swearing at you, kicking, hitting, pinching, biting, etc.   Y   N

35. Do you ever feel that you have lost the "power" or authority to get your children to behave in a way that you see fit? Y   N

36. Did you feel an immediate connection/fall in love with your child the moment he/she was born?   Y   N

37. Within the first few months of your child's life, did you feel that parenting was one of the most wonderful things that had ever happened to you?   Y   N

38. Have you ever felt that you weren't cut out to be a parent? Y   N

39. Have you ever regretted becoming a parent?   Y   N

40. Do you ever worry about the amount of time or the quality of time that you spend with your children?   Y   N

41. Do ever wonder if your rules are different than any other parents? For example, insisting that your children wash their hands as soon as they come into the house or not allowing them to have friends up to their bedrooms?   Y   N

Share any other rules that you think are unique to your family?_____
_____
_____
_____
_____
_____

42. Do you feel that your sex life (i.e., frequency, quality) has changed since you had children?   Y   N

43. Do you ever attend parenting classes or seminars?   Y   N

44. At what age do you feel that it is appropriate for your child to?

_____ Walk to school alone

_____ Tell you, rather than ask your permission to go out

_____ Date

_____ Go to a mall/movie or public place with friends

_____ Own an iPod/cell phone

_____ Stop sleeping in the same bed with the opposite sex parent

_____ Stop bathing/showering with the opposite sex parent

_____ Be left alone in the house

_____ Be allowed to drink alcohol at home

45. Is your confidence as a parent higher, lower, or not applicable when compared to your confidence in your career?

_____

46. How influenced are you to change your behavior as a result of how you perceive others regard you as a parent? Please circle one of the following:

Very   Not Much   Very little

47. Is parenting what you expected it to be? Y N

48. Do you ever give your child what he/she wants as a result of his/her nagging as a way of shutting him/her up? Y N

49. Do you ever give in to your child because he/she says that other parents are letting their children do what your child is requesting of you—even though you would have preferred not to have consented to that activity? Y   N

> **50.** Do you ever do for your child what you know he/she is capable of doing for him/herself (e.g., cutting food at table, helping with toileting)?   Y   N
>
> Any other examples:_____
> _____
> _____
> _____

You may have been surprised at your responses to some of the questions or challenged yourself to respond more candidly than you would with another person. You are likely curious as to how other parents responded and how you compare. So read on . . .

1

Define Normal

"A normal parent is someone who is not a total clean freak."
—Chloe, age 8

IN RESPONSE TO Chloe's definition, I asked my daughter whether she considered me "normal" then. "Well, not normal in that you always want everything in it's place."

Our children may be harsh critics, but they are also very forgiving and accepting. Chloe's comment is simply a statement. In fact, if she were to conduct a survey amongst her friends, my guess is that many of her peers would say that their parents were also "not normal" if they were to agree with Chloe's definition.

. . .

WHAT DOES "NORMAL" MEAN ANYWAY?

The more families I meet, the more I realize that there is no such there as an absolute version of "normal."

> Take Susan and George, for example. Now 62 and 59 years of age, their children are all grown at 31 and 26. After the kids were born, says George, "I still fooled around with other women, my wife still fooled around with men. We were into sex, drugs, and rock and roll."

When I asked Susan whether she thought of herself as a normal parent, she answered that although she doesn't believe that that there is one definition of normal, she's sure that her normal is not the same as others—especially not the same as the way in which she was raised. "There wasn't the openness, my parents just did things and you followed along because you were told to. You didn't question. When I did rebel, they kind of looked at me as if to say, 'This is a weird stage that she's going through and she'll come out of it.'"

When I asked George the same question, he responded with, "No. It doesn't matter to me if I am normal. I've seen what normal is and I'd rather not be that."

"What is normal?" I inquired.

"Living your life by society's norms," he says. "Having the Levi's jeans when they're in, wearing MAC lipstick. Things that are dictated by advertising and branding."

"What is normal parenting?" I ask.

"Having 2.3 children, two cars in the driveway, a nanny or a cleaning lady once a week." He says he's not interested in that lifestyle.

He says he'd rather have a "big mouth, talk about forbidden things, and easily break taboos."

Susan met George when she was 17 and says he was a big influence in her life. "Until George, I lived what you might call a 'normal' life. Then I started questioning all kinds of things."

Susan and George were married in 1970 and about 5 years later, their first child was born.

Susan remembers that "George used to play bridge with his friends, and our 2-year-old daughter would sit on a chair beside them and hold their cards while they passed dope around her. They would be drinking beer, and she would be slugging back beer in the bottle, and I would think that she must be getting high from the fumes."

The kids accepted that their parents smoked marijuana almost every day but they knew, as Susan says, as they grew older, that "what happened in our home stayed in our home. The majority of our friends had the same lifestyle, so our kids were okay with them, too." Even though their kids knew that they were not typical when compared with most of their friends' parents, this was their normal; when they were younger; they accepted their parents the way they were.

As the children grew into teens, Susan says that a lot of her daughter's friends thought that they were "cool" parents. "We would sit on our loveseat in our bedroom with our window open. Her friends would walk by and ring the doorbell and say, 'Oh Mrs. K, Mrs. K, it smells so nice,' and I would thank them and then close the door because I wasn't going to offer them any."

When I asked how their fully grown children feel about their lifestyle now, they say that their daughter, in particular, thinks that they're a couple of immoral hippies and is sometimes embarrassed by them. "She's quite conservative," Susan says. Their son, on the other hand, smokes dope even gives his mother names of "coffee shops" to visit in Amsterdam.

George's philosophy is "Children do not grow up on account of us but in spite of us."

NORMS OR STANDARDS

Norms or standards are determined and defined, to a great extent, by what was passed down through the generations and how you were raised in your family of origin. They are also defined by societal laws, the community in which you live, and your religious, cultural, or ethnic heritage. Some parents adopt the norms that they have been exposed to. Others, like Susan and George, rebel against those norms and create their own definition of normal.

I am interested in how parents from other countries and cultures adapt to life and redefine themselves in North America. I see that while some parents assimilate quickly and willingly, others hold onto their beliefs and mostly congregate with other parents from the same culture, religion, or country as themselves. In doing so, they continue to uphold and encourage the conventions inherent in their upbringing and culture and maintain their version of normal within their family and community.

Perhaps my interest in this stems from having been raised in another country, South Africa. Although my parents' lifestyle was not that far removed from the one we settled into in Canada, there was certainly a period of re-evaluation and adjustment as they accepted some and rejected other aspects of the North American way of parenting.

Chapter 6 is devoted to how culture and religion defines us as parents. I was fascinated to learn, for example, that it is not uncommon for working parents in China to enroll their children in residential boarding schools as early as 5 years of age so that they can learn social skills and be taken care of while their parents work. In America, it's shocking to think of separating such a young child from his parents for even a week at a time.

When parents arrive in America after being raised in another country or culture, it is sometimes difficult for them to know what is expected of them if they want to appear normal. They have to familiarize themselves with new rules and conventions. This is discussed in greater detail in Chapter 2, Conventional Wisdom.

DELUGE OF ADVICE

However, it's not just newcomers who are sometimes confused. Parents who have been born or raised in North America often feel overwhelmed by the deluge of advice from relatives, media, peers, and parenting experts. As a result, many struggle to define normal. I recommend that instead of only looking outwards for our definition of normal, that we dig deep inside of ourselves to explore what normal means to us, why we want to be normal, what the consequences of following the masses are, and what we need to change in order to feel that we are the best we can be—regardless of societal standards.

Lillian, the 45-year-old single mother of two daughters, ages 8 and 10, believes that society's standards are always changing. "Normal back when our parents were raising us was totally different. Back then it was spare the rod, spoil the child. Children should be seen and not heard. I think that really affected me, personally. I didn't want to parent that way," she says. "I'm the kind of parent who listens to my children, there's nothing that we can't talk about." However, trying to replace her parents' approach with something new is not always easy. "I sometimes turn to professionals or people that I trust or admire for their help."

CHANGING DIRECTION

Dr. Ari Novick, a licensed marriage and family therapist and parent educator in Laguna Beach, California, established www.onlineparent class.com to provide online parenting classes for parents who want to refine their parenting skills. He's also the father of a 3-year-old and an 8-month-old. Dr. Novick says that parents want a barometer or benchmark on what's normal. He contends that it's hard to come up with an exact measurement of what normal looks like because "what is normal in your family of origin might be different to what's normal in someone else's." He says that without meaning to, we often end up parenting our kids in the same way we were parented—even if we swore we never would.

For example, if you were raised in a community that condoned beating your kids when they were badly behaved, then you might think this type of discipline is normal. Of course, in the United States and other industrialized countries there are child abuse laws that don't allow parents to discipline in this manner. However, a parent may be lost when coming up with another approach if this was their "normal" growing up.

Clementine, a 46-year-old single mother of a 15-year-old son, has chosen to turn away from the way in which she was raised. "My old definition of normal," she says, "had a lot to do with my upbringing. I was raised in a very strict Italian household—we weren't allowed to do too many things and had lots of rules. Although I try not to follow my upbringing, I am influenced by it." She says that her definition of normal now is "when I act or behave in a way that is, for the most part, consistent or similar with other parents who have children the same age as mine."

THE MEDIA'S INFLUENCE

Other than your family of origin, another strong influence in defining normal is the media. Open any parenting magazine, for example, and you'll see ads with glowing pregnant women and captions that read, "It's the most beautiful time in your life" and other images of adoring mothers gazing down at their sleeping babes. No wonder moms-to-be anticipate that the first months of their child's life will be blissful. Little do they know that the mother's gaze is more the catatonic look of a sleep-deprived parent.

Caroline Connell, editor in chief of Canada's *Today's Parent Magazine* agrees that "certainly the idealized image is everywhere." She considers it her responsibility to balance those types of ads with articles that recognize the realities of being a parent. "Not that we want to make parenting seem scary or gloomy," she says, "but at the same time, we want to be realistic and acknowledge what it feels like."

Leslie Chandler, a bookseller at Toronto's Parentbooks and a parenting and childbirth educator, says that less obvious than the ads in magazines are the "television sitcoms where families create problems that are resolved in 20 minutes, parents have skin and makeup that is perfect, their nails and hair are done, and they're all driving great cars. And they're sitting with kids in clean clothes. These pictures are insidious," she says, "because they build the imagery we have of what we're supposed to look like as mothers. More realistically, I'd like to see a mom in her jeans and t-shirt and looking as if she hasn't washed her hair for a while, her nails aren't done, and I'd like to see a pile of dirty clothes in the background."

LOOKING FOR ANSWERS WITHIN

She believes, as do I, that we "tend to look at others as a guide for whether we are normal or not." We sometimes do this on a conscious level and other times not. She says that she tries to "encourage parents to tap into their intuitive selves" even though she realizes that at first they look outside for reassurance and validation.

Ever since the explosion of information on the internet, parents have turned to various websites for reassurance that what they're doing is normal. Nitin is married and the father of a 1-year-old. As first-time parents, he and his wife Reena often wonder if their response to their son is typical of other parents. They don't lose sleep over it, but they are concerned about doing the "right" thing. Nitin is quite comfortable checking things out with co-workers and peers. However, he says that "the internet is often the first place I go to check out whether other parents are doing the same as us. In other words, are we normal?"

For example, when their son wasn't sleeping well during the night, "we didn't know if it was right to let him cry it out or go to him. You hear so many things from so many different people. So I went online and Googled 'nine month old and sleeping' and came up with so many chat rooms—people talking about the same thing as us. So, I said to my wife—see, it *is* normal—everybody's going through it. It made me feel reassured that we weren't crazy or doing anything wrong."

After doing their research on the internet, Nitin and Reena no longer worried about whether they were responding normally to their son's sleeping issues. Often, first-time parents such as Nitin and Reena don't trust their intuition and rely instead on the opinions and advice of peers and professionals. In this age of the expert, it's easy to get lost in the mountain of available advice. Add the opinion and advice of well-meaning internet moms and dads, and you're left with an often even more bewildered parent.

Nitin realizes that there is a lot to wade through when looking for information on the internet. He says that he looks at different responses, weighs which are most common, and then decides what will work best for their family. Nitin admits that part of the allure of the internet is to find arguments that support what they would prefer to do. Although they had read Richard Ferber's *Solve Your Child's Sleep Problems,* they just couldn't "ferberize." "It didn't matter to us if everyone else thought it was a great method. For us, standing outside the door and listening to our baby cry felt inhumane." They found like-minded parents on the internet, and this encouraged them to follow their hearts rather than the masses.

HANDLE INTERNET INFORMATION WITH CARE

Caroline Connell, editor in chief of Canada's *Today's Parent Magazine,* agrees that "the internet is huge for parents. If your child is not sleeping at 2 a.m., you can just Google to find at least 10 possible reasons why." However, she advises parents to treat internet information with care. "There are a lot of great sources out there with a lot of solid information, but you need to make sure that your source is reputable."

DEFINING YOURSELVES

Family of origin, religious and cultural beliefs, outside influences such as television and magazines, observing and talking to peers, reading books and articles, consulting with parenting professionals, and understanding the laws that govern society all play a role in helping a parent define normal.

As I pull back the layers to reveal what parents are *really* thinking, feeling, and doing, I know that you will feel encouraged to shed your superficial skin and to confess your secret fears of not being defined as a normal parent.

2

Conventional Wisdom

⸻

WHEN I WAS growing up in the 1960s, my parents adhered to the norm that children should be seen but not heard. "You can sit with the adults for an hour before you go to bed," I was told, "but only if you don't make any noise or interrupt our conversation." Oh, how things have changed. Today, parents are comfortable with and even encourage their children to be heard loud and clear. We want our children to be visible and acknowledged so as not to damage their self-worth. We have moved from an authoritarian style of parenting to one which is more democratic, sometimes even permissive. We have family meetings so that everyone can have a say, and mutual respect between young and old is encouraged. Some say that the pendulum has swung too far– that children have too much say and that parents of today are allowing their children to call the shots.

CHANGES IN TRADITION AND THE FAMILY

Lynn Lott, mother, grandmother, parent educator and author in California, says that "when I had children, what was normal was to spank your children, punish and reward them—that was the conventional wisdom. I thought a lot about that and decided that it was incredibly disrespectful and insulting to assume that children were mindless objects and that we had the right to manage them in that way." Several of her co-authored books, such as *Positive Discipline A-Z*, offer parents countless strategies for dealing with difficult behaviors by using a natural and logical consequence approach. This approach, in keeping with a democratic style of parenting, is much more fitting of contemporary norms. The belief is that rather than arbitrarily imposing unrelated rewards and punishments, you choose a logical consequence (because your homework is not done, I will ask your teacher to keep you in during recess to complete it) or let a natural consequence occur. (For example, when you allow hunger to act as a reminder that failure to show up for dinner at a specific time means going without food until the next meal is served). Lynn recalls that when she was raising her kids, "it was normal for women to stay home and for men to have a whole other life." She says that although she still works with women who buy into that belief system, "there is a whole part of our culture in California where the men are just as involved with their kids as the women. It's delightful. Things are no longer so role-dominated; just because you have a penis doesn't mean that you only take on certain tasks."

Nitin, the 37-year-old father of a 1-year-old, went back to work within two weeks of his son being born. He says that he didn't feel guilty about it, "just bad about leaving my wife, and I missed the baby. I used to think that if she made more money than me I would stay at home. Then I stayed at home for one day and I didn't feel that way anymore. I wondered how women across the world do it—it was just so draining."

Joe, age 30 and father of two young children, was raised in a traditional home. He says that growing up "as a boy in an Italian household, I didn't do much. When I got married, my wife expected me to do dishes. When we had children, she expected me to change diapers. My father would never have gotten off the couch to change a diaper. I remember when we were little kids and my Dad was on his way home. My mom would remind us to keep it down because Dad was tired. Things are so different now. When I come in through the door, I have a baby thrown into my face with 'here, it's your turn.'"

FAMILY STRUCTURE

Along with the new normal in parenting styles and roles, there are changes in family structure. As the percentage of marriages that end in divorce in the United States continues to grow, I no longer assume that most children are being raised by both parents in the same home. It has become more conventional for same-sex couples to have and raise children, and the number of grandparents in the United States raising their grandchildren has increased to over two million nationally. What was convention decades ago is no longer normal in the twenty-first century.

CONNECTING AS A FAMILY

Unfortunately, some of what is new may not be improved.

> For example, 60 percent of parents who answered the questionnaire admitted to having long-winded conversations on their cell phones while in the company of their kids.

I was curious about the age at which parents felt comfortable with their children owning a cell phone or iPod.

> When parents responded to the questionnaire, the majority identified the youngest age to own a cell phone or iPod as 10, the oldest, 18.

Walking through the airport a few weeks ago, I scanned the crowds in the waiting lounges. At least half of the people, both adults and children, were plugged in. Not to one another, but to a screen or other technological gadget. Even those who appeared to be traveling together were not engaged in conversation. Many were multi-tasking, one ear connected to an iPod, the other to a cell phone. Where has downtime gone? The opportunity to unwind, to give our brains a rest or to be contemplative? The opportunity to connect with other human beings?

In an effort to stay connected to one another, one of the rules we have tried to establish in our family is no iPod use or cell phone conversations while in the company of others. I was pleased to hear that other parents have implemented guidelines due to similar concerns. One mom told me that she did not allow her children to hang out on the computer as an activity when their friends were over, another that she did not allow the use of the phone during dinner or before 8 p.m., and another that she did not allow any television or electronic gadgets during the school week.

We recently implemented "the 10-minute rule." Up until then, there were barely 2 minutes between my older daughter's arrival from school and her connection with the computer. Although the addiction is difficult to break, we have asked our kids, and ourselves, to take at least 10 minutes for one another when we come home from school, work, or being out socially. I won't lie and say that the rule is always adhered to, but with regular reminders, we're hoping that it will be the trick to staying connected in an often disconnected (to human beings) world.

CREATING OPPORTUNITIES FOR CONNECTION

As parents, we need to ask: "Do we create opportunities for connection? Is being together as a family a privilege, or do the kids see it as a punishment?" A sad reflection of what is normal in today's family is that each member is often off doing his or her own thing. Too often I hear of 13-year-olds refusing to go on family vacations and even younger children not accompanying their families on outings because they'd prefer to hang out with their friends. Although I recognize the increasing pull that peers have on kids as they grow, I believe that children are moving away from their families too soon and that parents are allowing it to happen.

As a way of preventing this from happening, make sure to have fun as a family. Although it's great to eat meals together, if they turn into an opportunity for a lecture on the virtues of healthy eating, your children are going to find excuses to leave the table quickly or make up stories about stomachaches. Similarly, if a recreational swim turns into an intense lesson on proper breathing and stroke technique, your kids aren't going to look forward to being with you. However, if you genuinely enjoy your time with your kids, play board games that are fun for everyone, and make mealtimes opportunities for sharing, then you may find that your children want to spend more time with you.

SARA'S SUGGESTIONS

The shape of families and the way in which we interact and discipline our children has changed over the years. Despite these changes, our role and responsibility for maintaining a healthy family environment still exists.

SUGGESTION

It is a parent's responsibility to create guidelines and boundaries for their children and to make sure that they are followed.

Sadly, I see that parents are sometimes afraid to implement and uphold rules at home. They may feel that they have very little control and fear that their children will be angry or rebel if there are too many limits set. In order to avoid conflict and confrontation, they turn a blind eye even when they become aware that a rule is not being adhered to. They easily give in and conform to what they believe others are doing.

I was reminded of this when I attended a dinner party where I was introduced to a mom who believed that her 14-year-old son was entitled to all the freedom he desired. "Now that he's 14, he has a life of his own. All the kids of his age are the same," she said. It was 9 p.m. when she looked at her watch and realized that they had not connected the entire day. She said that she had left the house early that morning "with him sleeping, as usual" and that he was "supposed" to call to "tell" her where he was headed once he had woken up but hadn't. Earlier, she had tried to reach him on his cell phone but couldn't. Several hours later, whilst sipping her café latte, she still had no clue as to his whereabouts.

Seemingly unworried by this, she went on chatting and checking her text messages until someone reminded her that she had wanted to reach her son. She finally did locate him—by calling his friend's cell. She learned that they were partying in the park and that he'd get a ride home by midnight. She seemed fine with this and went on conversing with the mom beside her. My evening had taken a turn. No longer was I able to remain quiet. I asked where the park was; she did not know. I asked who would be driving him home; she did not know. Later, I asked how old she felt children should be before "telling" rather than "asking" permission.

She said 18.

> Of the parents polled, the average age at which some thought a child should be able to "tell" rather than ask was 17.

Until I pointed it out, she did not realize that she had just been *told* by her 14-year-old son that he was partying with friends and that he would not return until *he* was ready. "Well, what am I supposed to do?" she asked rhetorically, not really wanting or expecting an answer. Even if she had wanted to explore options, this was not the time nor the place.

Conscious parenting takes a tremendous amount of strength, courage, and effort. I recognize that it is often easier to let your children do as they choose. There is less friction, less arguing and negotiation, less work. I also would have said that in the long run, she was not doing her a son a favor by letting him set his own curfew and schedule. I would have suggested that they sit down to discuss rules or guidelines for the family to live by and set logical consequences if the rules were broken or not taken seriously.

Dr. Scott Wooding, Canadian psychologist, parenting expert, and author of several books including *Rage, Rebellion and Rudeness,* writes that "many parents are just too busy with work and leisure activities to control their kids. Discipline takes emotional energy and will. A large percentage of modern parents don't have this energy because their priorities are their careers and making money. Their focus is on paying for their huge home, their two cars, and the many other assorted toys that are so prevalent in our consumer society. These parents come home from work tired and stressed, and all they want to do is rest and relax. The result is that they avoid disciplining their teens whenever possible. They just do not want the tension that results from these confrontations."

You might be surprised by the number of teenagers I meet in my practice who wish that they had more restrictions placed on them. They say that they would feel a sense of security in knowing that their parents cared enough to work at setting rules and making sure they are followed. One teen shared that he felt like running away and was sure that his parents wouldn't even know that he was gone. When I asked what would be left undone in the house if he left, he said, "Nothing. Sometimes I wish they would even ask me to take out the garbage. At least then I would know that I was making a difference to the family."

One of the questions I asked parents related to the age at which they felt comfortable with their teenagers dating and drinking alcohol. Although the age at which a teenager is legally allowed to drink alcohol varies depending on where you live, some parents allow their older children to drink alcohol at home.

> The ages between which most parents who com-
> pleted the questionnaire felt that it was appropri-
> ate for their kids to drink alcohol at home were 18
> to 21.
>
> The youngest age at which parents felt that it was
> appropriate for their child to date was 12 and the
> average was 16.

SUGGESTION

Model. It is the key to lifelong success.

If your children see you disobeying the law by parking in a no parking zone, jaywalking when the traffic light is red, or driving without
a seatbelt, for example, they will quickly learn that it is okay to
break rules.

> Thirty-six percent of the parents who completed the
> questionnaire admitted to breaking laws that affected
> their children, such as removing their child from a
> booster seat sooner than the law dictates.

I become incensed when I am driving next to a car in which I see
a young child, obviously not strapped in, jumping around in the back
seat or with his head out of the window. I'm infuriated by parents

who don't insist that their children put on their seatbelts (or buckle themselves in) with comments such as "I'm just going around the corner, nothing bad will happen."

If you do not set a good example by following rules, then your children may rebel against the rules you have created at home. If you model the behavior you want to see, such as respecting established laws, offering a seat in a bus to an elderly person, opening a door for someone, and saying please and thank you, then your children will follow in your footsteps.

> Of the parents who completed the questionnaire, the majority (almost 60 percent) said that they spoke to older adults or parents in the way that they would like their children to behave towards them.
>
> And 34 percent of the parents who responded to the questionnaire admitted that although they insisted on their children eating fruits and vegetables, they were not very responsible about modeling the behavior themselves.

SUGGESTION 3

Parenting means putting your children's emotional, psychological, and physical needs ahead of your own.

And most parents do that. Most of the time.

> Almost 70 percent said they would act more conserva-
> tively, drink less alcohol, and censor their adult conver-
> sations if their children were present at a party. Eighty
> percent said that they would be considerate of their
> children and leave a party if their children were tired.

When parents decide to divorce, for example, they recognize the impact that this will have on their children. When they consult with me about how to break the news, I know that they are likely struggling with their decision to put their needs ahead of their children's—for the short term, at least.

When I write about putting your children's needs first, note that I mention children's psychological, emotional, and physical needs in particular. I am not suggesting that parents put certain "needs" ahead of their own as in "I 'need' to go to the mall now." These are often "wants" and not needs. Try not to feel guilty, therefore, when you put your own need to take a break over their need to be on the go.

SUGGESTION 4

Understand that the rules in every home are different.

> Over half (58 percent) of the parents who responded to
> the questionnaire said that they wondered how their
> rules differed from others.

One of the rules in our home is that we wash our hands ("with soap") whenever we come home and before we eat. My sister thinks this rule is crazy. She thinks germs help build immunity.

In some homes, turning off the light as you leave a room is expected. In others, brushing your teeth before coming downstairs for breakfast is mandatory. One mom said that her children have to wash their feet if they are dirty from being outside, another that her children have to shower every day, must say good morning to everyone in the household, and are not allowed to eat food anywhere other than the kitchen.

More than one parent said that shoes had to be removed as people entered the home. Several talked about rules pertaining to television programs that could or could not be watched and the times at which they were allowed. One mom said that in order for her children to use the computer, they must first take a walk or a bike ride. One mom wrote that she does not allow her children to "hide" behind closed doors. Another mom said that although she was not happy about buying "junky" cereal, she agreed to on the condition that her children would only treat themselves to it on weekends.

Kathy Lynn, a Canadian parenting speaker, columnist, and author, says, "When I was being raised, there were certain expectations, and I didn't have to worry about whether I was in my house or the neighbor's house—I knew what was expected of me. Nowadays, every time children go into somebody else's house they have to find out what their rules are because they may be so different. When my children were little, we didn't allow guns and we insisted that whenever kids came into the house that they show respect by saying hello to us." On one occasion Kathy Lynn says she even "had to tell a kid not to swing on our doors."

While it may be perfectly reasonable to gently reprimand a child who is being destructive or out of line in your home, there is an unwritten code of conduct about disciplining another child when his or her parent is present.

SUGGESTION 5

It's best not to discipline another parent's child.

Most parents prefer to discipline their own children, successfully or not, rather than being undermined by another person who thinks that he or she knows better.

I remember a time when I was having a telephone conversation with a friend when my then 6-year-old daughter came bouncing into the room and asked to whom I was speaking. I motioned for her to wait and be quiet by placing a finger to my lips. Determined to find out sooner than later, my daughter pushed the hands-free button on the phone. Then I gave her what she wanted. My attention. I asked my friend to hold while I turned away from the mouthpiece, clicked the button to its original position, and asked my daughter to leave the room.

We all know that children command attention when we're occupied, especially on the phone, and this day was no different. My daughter persisted and I ended my conversation so that I could attend to her. I talked to my daughter about how annoyed I was by her behavior, and we talked about consequences for future behavior of the same kind. All was resolved and I put the incident behind us.

Apparently, however, my friend had not. Later that week, when she saw my daughter, she talked directly to her about her inappropriate behavior and asked her not to do it again. When she finished, she could see from my expression that I was not happy. "I hope that was okay?" she inquired, knowing full well that it was not. I didn't want to respond in front of my daughter, so I said nothing. Later on, when the kids were in bed (I certainly did not want a repeat performance), I called my friend to talk about the incident. I shared that my daughter was upset by it and that I had already handled the situation in a way that I saw fit. My friend, realizing her error in judgment, apologized. I was glad that I had politely asserted myself.

As a parent, it is normal to be taken off guard when another person steps in to take over. It is also normal to feel undermined and judged as an ineffective parent. Many parents freeze and don't know how to react. Unless the other adult is being too harsh or saying things that you feel may be detrimental to your child, it may be okay to stand back for a few moments before responding. However, if you feel that the intervention is entirely inappropriate, it is also okay to gently steer your child away from the other adult.

A client shared her annoyance at a parent she met while in the park with her child. Apparently, their two young children were playing side by side. After witnessing my client's child's refusal to share his truck with her child, my client watched in surprise as the other parent approached her child and chastised him for not sharing. As much as she wanted to confront the parent for interfering and disciplining her child, she felt frozen. Before she had a chance to say anything, the other parent had removed her child from the sandbox and was preparing to leave. My client asked me if it was normal to feel such resentment toward another parent for approaching her child without permission, and I assured her that it was.

SUGGESTION 6

Young children should never shoulder their parents' problems.

> Seventy-three percent of parents who completed the questionnaire had felt the need to protect their children from knowing intimate details of their life that might hurt them emotionally.

Some of what parents hid related to financial stress, personal anxieties, a diagnosis of illness, conflict in a relationship, or personal use of alcohol or drugs.

Lana, a 48-year-old mother of three children ages 12, 18, and 22, believes that in the ideal world, "children should see you as a person first and then as a parent," but in reality, "I don't think that a child really wants that."

With this in mind, Lana didn't tell her 12-year-old son that she was having surgery following her diagnosis of ductal carcinoma in situ. She even put on a brave face during her period of recuperation and despite how weak she was feeling, traveled to his overnight summer camp to spend time with him on visitor's day.

She says that "when I first found out that I had cancer, I protected my children. Originally, I removed the word carcinoma or cancer because I didn't want to create fear in them." In addition to coping with her diagnosis and treatment, Lana was still coming to terms with the breakup of her marriage. At this time in particular, "my kids needed me in their lives and I didn't want to create further anxiety in them. They needed to focus on their lives and school. I didn't want to be a burden on them. I gradually gave them pieces of information as things unfolded. I didn't want them to think that I was hiding things and lying to them, but at the same time, I didn't want to shock them. Ultimately, I got a very positive prognosis."

Sheer internal strength and determination to put her children's needs first motivated her deliberate delivery of specific information. At a time when she so easily could have turned to her children for support, she found the strength to separate her personal needs from her parental responsibilities.

Lana recognizes that her behavior may not be typical of every parent in her situation. "I think that some parents would want to tell their children everything—especially if the kids are older," she says. "I didn't want my children to play that role for me."

SUGGESTION

Familiarize yourself with the child protection laws of the state or province within which you live.

After Lana and her husband separated, her 12-year-old son wanted to sleep in her bed, and she found it quite comforting to have him there. Then a therapist said it was absolutely wrong. Lana felt that he was lonely and scared and needed to know that he wasn't alone. She went against her intuitive sense of what he needed because of what she was told by the therapist.

When Lana spoke to other friends who had gone through breakups in their marriages, she was comforted by knowing that they too had their children sleep in their bed at various times—at even older ages such as 14 or 15.

> When parents responded to the questionnaire in regards to the age at which they felt it appropriate for a child to stop sleeping in a bed with the opposite sex parent, the average age was 6 and the oldest was 15.

Howard Hurwitz, Director of Children's Services at Jewish Family and Child Services in Toronto, says that from a child protection agency's perspective, if an older child was sleeping with his or her parent, "we would want to assess the reason behind a parent's behavior when it was deemed to be outside of what would be considered an appropriate child-care behavior given the child's age."

If there was a death in the family or some other crisis or trauma, for example, they would take this into account. "If a parent feels that that they need to comfort his or her child and it's for a time-limited period, and someone can explain why it needs to happen and how beneficial it will be to the child, then we certainly wouldn't have a problem with that," he says. This would be far different, of course, than a child of 12 who was sleeping between his parents every night or had never slept alone.

> The average age at which parents answering the questionnaire felt it was inappropriate to continue bathing or showering with the opposite sex parent was 5, and the oldest was 11.

Hurwitz says that "If a parent was bathing a 10, maybe even an 8-year-old, that would be problematic. A parent might want to be in the bathroom supervising but not actually washing the child." He says that their role would likely be to educate the parent around the appropriateness of boundaries and developmental abilities of an average child. Hurwitz says that parents are often not purposely going against the norms. For example, they may be immigrants from other countries that have different child protection laws.

I remember counseling a mom who, without realizing the impact of her behavior, mentioned within the context of a story she was sharing, that she drove her husband to the train station every morning as her 8-month-old baby lay asleep in their apartment. When I talked to her about the consequences of doing this, she seemed surprised. She hadn't realized that it was entirely inappropriate to leave a baby alone for any length of time, nor had she taken into account the possibility of being in an accident and not being able to return home. After she became more aware of the possible dangers of leaving her child alone, as well as her parental responsibilities, she promised to never leave her baby unattended again.

Other behaviors that may cross the line and warrant investigation by a child protection agency include corporal punishment, failing to properly supervise young children, not providing children with food and shelter, or exposing children to alcohol or drugs.

There are rules and norms dictated by the laws of the society within we live, norms that are established within our communities, and others that are peculiar to ourselves and our children. Along with paying attention to conventional wisdom, take note of your common sense. The late Samuel Taylor Coleridge; English poet, critic and philosopher, wrote "Common-sense, in an uncommon degree, is what the world calls wisdom."

3

True Confessions

———

MY CATHOLIC FRIENDS tell me that it's very cleansing to spill their guts to a priest in the safety of a confessional booth. My clients say that they too feel a heavy burden lifted off their chests after sharing their innermost thoughts out loud. Every year, I attend the Kol Nidre service at a local synagogue on the eve of Yom Kippur. This precedes a day during which Jews confess our sins, atone for them by fasting, and ask God for forgiveness.

This year, the rabbi's sermon touched on people confessing secrets on the internet. He talked about an American man by the name of Frank Warren who several years ago randomly handed out hundreds of postcards to people at various locations. He asked people to record a secret never shared with anyone before and mail the postcard back anonymously. It didn't take long before Warren was inundated with tens of thousands of postcards from around the world. Four hundred of these are compiled in his book, *PostSecret: Extraordinary Confessions from Ordinary Lives.* Others are posted at www.postsecret.com, which is updated weekly. The posts range from incredibly sad to outrageously funny.

> When asked if they ever wished that they were still kids themselves, 41 percent of the parents who responded to the questionnaire said yes.
>
> Seventeen percent said that they had, at one time or another, regretted becoming a parent.

PARENTS IN CYBERSPACE

Sitting at one's computer, surrounded by other virtual parents in cyberspace, it's so much easier to share unsettling thoughts and feelings. On September 1, 2007, Canada's *National Post* ran a story entitled "Mind if I Air Some Dirty Diapers?" The article, by Sarah Bancroft, is headlined "True Mom Confessions" and features www.truemomconfessions.com, a website for "tired, cranky mothers" founded by Romi Lassally, a 43-year-old mother of three. When I called her in Los Angeles, I confessed my guilt at not having enough time for my kids while writing a parenting book!

Of course, I hadn't just called to confess. I wanted to know more about how her website had come to be. "It came to me about 6 months ago when my son, who was then 6, woke up in the middle of the night, stumbled out of his room and projectile vomited all over the carpet," she said. "I was of course exhausted at 3 a.m. and I decided, after bathing him and myself and washing the linens, to leave the goopy vomit on the carpet, hoping the dog would eat it." (He didn't, and it was worse the next morning).

She went on to say that this "followed a weekend of parental misdemeanors and was the proverbial straw that broke the camel's back." She said that she had tried various unsuccessful parenting techniques with her kids, "dealing with their sibling rivalry and whining and just being spoiled brats. It just pushed me over the edge. What directly preceded the site's inception was telling somebody I had left the vomit on the carpet overnight. I didn't just live with my dirty little secret. I felt such relief in talking about it, and I saw this other mother, after she was done wincing in disgust and laughing, nod in response and then tell me her own story. Confessing on a website literally unlocks a whole myriad of emotion—including guilt and anger and longing."

Although the True Mom Confessions site is just for moms, Lassally has founded several other websites, including www.truedad confessions.com for dads and www.truemilitarywivesconfessions. com. The link between these sites is that people can go online and say things that they are thinking but afraid to say out loud, such as:

- ➤ "I'm so glad she came out looking like him and not that other guy!"
- ➤ "I'm too busy parenting to enjoy my kid. That sucks."
- ➤ "Mr. Rogers is on TV on the kitchen . . . and my children are all at school. Just hearing his voice makes me feel like everything is going to be okay."
- ➤ "I had sex with someone and it's not my wife."
- ➤ "My kids wouldn't come in from the backyard so I mooned them from the deck. The neighbors saw so I mooned them."

➤ "I just found out my dog has cancer. I have no idea what to tell my kids."

As I read through the confessions online, I laughed and cried. Many were totally relatable.

Anonymity can open up the floodgates of emotion. Lassally says that she hears a "tremendous amount of guilt and ambivalence from moms who say that they spend more time on the computer than with their kids, that they put their kids in front of the television for hours and hours and hours because they're exhausted, that they don't pay enough attention to their husbands, don't initiate sex often enough, and don't keep a clean house."

Bite-sized absolution

There is an explosion of confessional websites for people looking for "bite-sized absolution," as Lassally puts it. She's hoping that, like herself, people will view their lives differently after reading some of the confessions on her sites. She says that she sometimes thinks, "Thank God my life is not that bad. I should be grateful and shut up." Other times she thinks, "Oh good. That thought I had isn't completely evil. I'm not alone and I'm doing the best I can.'

Popcorn for dinner

Kathy Lynn, author and one of Canada's leading professional speakers on parenting issues, says that "If parents yell at their kids, they're always relieved to know that somebody else does too. They're also relieved to hear that somebody else actually gave their kids popcorn for dinner one night because nobody had any energy to do anything else. So they popped some corn and cut up some apples and called it dinner."

A NEW MOTHER CONFESSES

Robin's story

Robin, 34, is the mother of a 4-month-old. Before her daughter was born, Robin worked as a registered massage therapist and loved it. Although she planned on returning to work within a couple of months, her yearning to get back to her old life began much sooner than she had anticipated.

Now that she is back to work a couple of days a week, she feels better and is grateful to be getting a break.

"From what?" I asked.

"From boredom," she said. "It's like a combination of being busy but bored at the same time."

Robin said that after the dust had settled following the birth of her first child, and there weren't as many visitors around, she began to feel lonely and isolated. She started to feel that she was the only person in the world sitting at home with a baby.

UNWANTED THOUGHTS

When you're a parent to a newborn, unwanted thoughts may creep into your head more easily. When you're tired, your mind sometimes plays games with you. Becoming a parent to a newborn reminds us of how immense our task is. As we gaze down at a tiny, vulnerable baby, we are reminded of how vital we are for that human being's survival. This can feel like an overwhelming responsibility, especially in the first few days or weeks.

Some parents confessed to disturbing thoughts, such as, "What happens if I leave the baby in the water for a second while I answer

the phone (which of course you should never do) and he drowns?"
Or "What happens if I let go of the stroller and it goes down the
hill and crashes into a car?" Or "What happens if I drop my newborn?" If you think thoughts like these often and for lengthy periods, it may be wise to speak to a therapist who can help you figure
out why they keep popping into your head and what you can do
about them.

SLEEP DEPRIVATION

Patti Kirk, co-owner of Parentbooks in Toronto says, "We get a lot of
sleep-deprived parents in their first year of parenting in the store. As
a result, they can't think clearly and they're at their wits' end. I think
in North America we have a very poor idea of what parenting is going
to be. People think that they're going to have their nights off. In a lot
of other cultures there is a lot more co-sleeping and more family support. In North America, people feel that they have to get back to their
real life, whatever that is."

Patti went on to say that "even I had this idea that I would go
back to work after the twins. I would have them in nice little bas-
kets and the babies would sleep and I would work. What a joke.
Maybe there is one in 6,000 babies who sleep when their mother
wants them to. Some days you can't even take a shower. Parenting
can be exhausting. And you think you're tired in your first trimester
of pregnancy!"

Shouldn't this be more fun?
After Robin's baby was born, she wondered if she was normal.
She asked herself, "'Shouldn't this be more fun? Shouldn't I love
this?' My friend who has a baby of the same age summed it up

perfectly. She said that after her child was born, she thought that a switch was going to go off and that she was going to just love being a mother and know exactly what to do, but she didn't. She felt such a disconnect with her baby when he first came home from the hospital that she called him 'the baby' and not by his name. I can't even tell you what a shock it was to hear this because she is the perfect little mom to me. I could've just hugged her, it was such a relief," said Robin.

Robin felt even more at ease after reading a book, *I Was A Really Good Mom Before I Had Kids,* written by Trisha Ashworth and Amy Nobile. While reading it, she learned that there are so many mothers thinking the same things as her.

Robin says that when she was pregnant she pictured herself sitting on a picnic blanket in the summer having the best time with her baby. Her dog was with them and she envisioned thinking that everything was just perfect. That she couldn't be any happier. "But of course it's not really like that," she says.

Robin asked if I had ever conjured up similar fantasies before I had kids. I didn't want her to feel alone, but I honestly hadn't and gently told her so.

"You are so much smarter than me," she said.

"No," I responded. "I was teaching parenting courses before I had children, so I had a very clear idea of what was in store for me. I knew that parenting was not going to be glamorous."

Robin, however, is not alone.

> 40 percent of parents who completed the questionnaire felt that parenting was not what they expected it to be
>
> And 30 percent felt that they weren't cut out to be a parent.

Robin said that before her baby was born she would look at pictures in magazines of smiling mothers holding their smiling babies. "When you're pregnant, you think they're going to pop out and smile and look right into your eyes. That didn't happen for a few months, and even then my baby looked right through me."

REALITY HITS

Robin also realized that she couldn't just sit and enjoy every moment with her baby and ignore other things that needed to get done "like paying bills and dealing with the ever-growing pile of dirty laundry."

Robin continued to ask me questions, wanting to make sure that she was normal. "Were you shocked at all after you had a baby?" she asked.

"I was surprised by the overwhelming responsibility and the isolation," I said, "but again, I don't think that I had any misconceptions about crying babies or sleepless nights. I didn't have any illusions that it would create a stronger bond between my husband and I, and I knew that the changes would take some time getting used to."

I reassured Robin that even if she and I were not able to share the same experiences, that were many other parents who would be able to relate to what she was feeling and thinking.

She remembered being at a gathering attended by a lot of other parents and young babies. "I knew that I just had to move away from this one mother with a 5-month-old because she was doing that 'Isn't being a mom just the most amazing thing that you've ever experienced in your whole life,' and I'm thinking 'No, not really.' Then there was another mother that I totally clicked with. I think she rolled her eyes when her baby cried and said, 'Shit.' I knew that I could have a conversation with her. I felt that I could have talked with her for ages because whatever I said she responded with 'Yeah, I felt like that, too' or 'that happened to me, too.'"

I asked Robin how she would feel if the majority of parents felt that having a baby *was* the most wonderful thing that had ever happened to them.

"Scared," she said "because I would think oh my God, maybe I'm not going to be good at this. Right now, even though I have these feelings, I feel that I am a good mom and will be a great mom. If I knew that everyone else thought that parenting was just fabulous, I would be scared."

> In fact, just over 70 percent of the parents who responded to the questionnaire did say that they felt, within the first few months of their child's life, that parenting was one of the most wonderful things that had happened to them. Only 20 percent of the parents said that they did not feel an immediate connection or fall in love with their child the moment he or she was born.

There are so many other thoughts and feelings that parents have a difficult time admitting to. Nanny Deb of the *Nanny 911* television show, a nanny for many years and the writer of the foreword for this book, says that "one employer was really honest and admitted that she couldn't bear being with her child for more than an hour at a time without feeling like she was losing her mind. Most people are not that honest. They'd rather say something like 'I've got stuff to do' and give the baby to me."

It takes courage to openly admit what you are feeling.

"There are the internal thoughts and feelings that parents want reassurance about," says Caroline Connell, editor in chief of Canada's

Today's Parent Magazine, "but there are also things such as the way that they approach discipline and nutrition, for example. Also bedtime, as in 'Oh thank goodness my child is not the only one who stays up until 10:00.'

> Almost 60 percent of the parents who completed the questionnaire admitted to threatening their children with punishments that they knew they'd never follow through with. Many parents did not follow through with groundings, time-outs, or threats to cancel birthday parties, play dates, and extracurricular activities. One parent admitted to threatening to throw away her 5-year-old's "blankie" even though she too didn't know what she would do without that scrap of fabric.
>
> Forty-nine percent said that they had made a promise to their child that they had not kept.

OH GOOD, THEY'RE SLEEPING

Joe, 30, a hairstylist in the Toronto area, is the father of two children, ages 2 ½ and 3 months. He often acts as father confessor to his customers. His personal confessions include how overwhelmed he felt when his first child was born and he took on the role of Dad. "I thought I knew how to do the right things after reading books, but I started realizing that I didn't know how to handle a lot of things— like the unpredictable schedule and when the baby wasn't pooing or was crying nonstop. We were constantly worried about things.

"After the birth of my second child, there was no time for us a couple at all. I thought that it was going to be easier because I had already been through it with my daughter, but then I realized that it's a totally different ball game."

Joe says that he often feels guilty about wanting to stay at work late to avoid dealing with his kids. "When I get home and they're both sleeping I think 'oh good.' When I do come home early and I've already had a stressful day, it's a battle. Everything is coming at you. The baby is crying and my daughter wants to play, I haven't eaten dinner so I try to eat it as fast as I can, then my wife needs a break so I'm with both of the kids. Sometimes all I'm thinking is 'please let's put them to bed.'

"Don't get me wrong. I love my kids and I do want to spend time with them, but there are times when I miss those days of being a bachelor. I think that every parent wants a day off."

> A whopping 62 percent of parents admitted that they had thought about running away from their responsibilities at home, if only for a night.
>
> And 34 percent said that they had, at one time or another, longed for life the way it was before kids.

Join the club. Confess your true thoughts and feelings so that you can help others release what they may have been concealing.

4

No Time for Me or We

⟋⟍

NO TIME FOR LICE

The week I sat down to write this chapter was a perfect lead-in to the topic. Perhaps there was some divine power that bestowed it upon me. By surviving one of the most grueling experiences of parenthood, I was certainly in the right frame of mind when writing about parents being challenged by so many responsibilities and so little time.

It began on Tuesday morning, a day I had set aside to write without interruption. My 8-year-old stumbled downstairs on a school day morning complaining of an itchy scalp. At first I thought nothing of it, thinking that it was likely a reaction to the new brand of shampoo we had used the night before. However, as I stood making the kids' tuna sandwiches to take for school lunch and noticed her scratching with increased fervor, I thought I'd better do some further exploration. I couldn't deny what lurked in the back of my mind. My suspicions were confirmed when I spied a tiny translucent nit attached to the shaft of her hair.

"Shit!" I exclaimed out loud, remembering what we had gone through when my older daughter was her age. I called a friend with lots of experience to give me a second opinion, and my fears were realized when she sympathetically delivered the news. Not only did my daughter have lice, but so did I. Gone were the hours I had envisioned at my computer composing great prose. The next few hours and days were spent saran wrapping our oil-drenched hair, precisely removing nits and sitting patiently as my husband pored over my head.

I was just about ready to shave our heads—especially by day 7 when the cat threw up all over the carpet and my older daughter needed help on an important homework assignment. I broke down crying after two weeks of washing sheets, vacuuming couches, sterilizing hair brushes, and still finding nits after I thought I had gotten the buggers.

Finally, at midnight, days after planning to write this chapter, here I am. Such is the life of a parent. The good news is that, as crazy as it sounds, I enjoyed spending time with my daughter and combing through her hair. It's a luxury she barely allows me now that she is older and can do it "herself." I also feel oh-so-very prepared to write a chapter on trying to juggle career, family, and kids and everything else that is required of us as parents.

> Forty-seven percent of parents felt that of all the households in their neighborhood, theirs would win the "Mornings from Hell" award.

NO TIME TO PEE

Most parents can relate to the crazy-making schedules we often bring upon ourselves. Who says a child has to partake in so many activities? Who says that she has to take horseback riding lessons just because she loves horses? However, we all know the guilt associated with not exposing our children to everything—just in case they miss out on the one program that reveals a special talent. Come 3:30 p.m. you're likely heading back out the door, kids waiting in the van, double-checking to make sure that you've remembered the paraphernalia required for that afternoon's activities. You might consider a mad dash to the bathroom but decide against it. Who has time to pee? You're almost late to pick one kid up from school and drop the other off at a dance lesson.

Sandwiched between meeting the demands of work schedules, kids' schedules, homework, and extracurricular activities (multiplied by the number of offspring), you may often feel overwhelmed, frazzled, and out of breath. Often, we are required to actually make time for downtime, to literally mark off time in our busy electronic day timers for our kids, ourselves, and our partners. What you do in that time can be varied but at least if it's scheduled, you may be more inclined to put that time to good use.

Tamara's Story

Tamara, a 33-year-old nurse and mother of a 4-year-old son and 9-year-old daughter, was in tears when she arrived at my office. Her usually evenly-controlled emotions were no longer in check, and she wanted to get my opinion as to whether she was clinically depressed or going crazy. Despite her years of experience in working with others' medical and emotional needs, she worried that her negative feelings toward her son were not normal. She had gotten to the point where she could no longer tolerate his whining, aggressive behavior towards her, his infantile temper tantrums, and his unwillingness to accept "no." She was so afraid of her possible reaction to his behavior that she had asked her husband to step in and take over for a while so that she didn't need to be close to him. Along with their housekeeper, they were getting him up in the morning, making his breakfast, and taking him to and picking him up from camp.

At night, when he was calmer, she was willing and able to take part in his night-time routine, something they had always enjoyed together. Tamara said that prior to handing over the reins to her husband and housekeeper, she had especially dreaded waking her son up for camp in the morning and picking him up at the end of the day. From the moment he entered the car, he began nagging. Despite an 8-hour day of heat and activity, he appeared raring to go. "Can we go to the toy store?" was a typical request before she could even ask any questions about his day. Anything other than a "yes" from her would bring about kicking on the back of her car seat, refusal to buckle himself into his seat, and other oppositional behavior. This, combined with the incessant arguing between him and his sister, made Tamara want to crawl under her seat and cry.

As we began to dissect his day and hers, though, Tamara was able to explore his behavior from a much more comfortable position on my couch. Tamara realized that an 8-hour day in the heat, without the afternoon nap that he was used to having at school, sent her son into overdrive. By the time she picked him up, he was completely exhausted. As a result, he could not be reasoned with. Once Tamara realized this, compassion and love replaced anger and frustration. She was once again able to embrace the little boy she had previously been concerned about harming.

This was only part of the puzzle, though. Tamara, like so many other working moms, was up and getting ready for work at the same time as her children. She left them eating breakfast with the housekeeper while she grabbed an apple and dashed out the door most days of the week. It had been a while since she had shared breakfast time with her children, so I asked if she might be able to go into her office later in the day at least 2 days a week. We also explored the possibility of not working on Saturdays or perhaps taking her son out of camp for a day or two to reconnect with him. We discussed starting out slowly with an hour's trip to the mall or an evening building a Lego castle on the floor or a morning having breakfast and not changing out of their pyjamas until noon. After our first hour together, Tamara slumped back and sighed, "What I'm hearing is that even before I begin to consider dealing with his behavior, I need to change how I'm conducting my life." I nodded. Two days later I received the following email:

> Dear Sara—Thank you again for your advice. The very next morning I woke up extra early to have breakfast with the kids, we kept Cody home yesterday, and probably will do so for the rest of the week. His behavior has dramatically improved in one day! We also already have a plan in place for me to start working less.
>
> Best regards, Tamara

"YOU CAN HAVE IT ALL.
YOU JUST CAN'T HAVE IT ALL AT ONCE."
(OPRAH WINFREY)

Rona Maynard, journalist and author of *My Mother's Daughter*, was quoted in Canada's *National Post* in September 2007 as saying that she belongs "to the first generation of women who were told 'we could have it all'—and then, in the frenzy of doing it all, we were forced to choose between domestic graces (homemade dinners) and workplace rewards. I later managed the daughters of women like me. Intent on 'balance,' they wanted what we had rejected—part-time hours and designer laundry rooms. I see disgruntled young women packing up their Palms and going home to their kids."

> Over 80 percent of parents who responded to the questionnaire in the introductory chapter said that they felt that there were not enough hours in the day to accomplish everything and that they had difficulty juggling all of their responsibilities.

WORKING PART-TIME

Anna, a 42-year-old part-time teacher and mother of a 4-year-old son agrees that there is "no way that you can get done what you need to get done during the week and work full-time—I don't know how people do it." She said that she would worry about working full-time and having her son looked after by caregivers. "I know that a good number of children go to day care 5 days a week, 8 hours a day or longer, and that becomes the norm and so it becomes okay, but is it?"

Anna feels better that her little guy is not in day care full-time but does appreciate his being out of the house for short periods even when she's not working. Anna says that when she's at home she feels "kind of torn and cheated and frustrated when I am trying to do stuff—the chores—and he wants my attention. I don't want to stick him in front of the television so that I can get on with my projects. And if I don't get them done, then I feel irritable. If he's away for part of the day and I get a chance to catch up on chores and projects, then I am calmer when I pick him up, and we have a good time."

> Almost 50 percent of the parents who responded to the questionnaire felt resentment at having to put a project or activity on hold for their child.

WORKING AWAY FROM HOME

There are some parents who prefer to go to work than be at home. Many can't wait to return to work—often full-time—after being at home with children. Lynn Lott is a mother, grandmother, family therapist and has been a parent educator in the United States for the past 35 years. She is also the bestselling author of books such as *Positive Discipline A-Z* and *Chores without Wars*.

She thinks that some "women who work still think that they are being terrible and hurting their children and are embarrassed about it, especially if they enjoy going to work and leaving their kids. I think they feel guilty and want to hide it as opposed to saying, 'Woo-hoo, I get to exercise a whole different part of my brain.'" She reminds parents that they are people first and that being a parent is only one of their roles. Lynn realizes that working all day and then being a parent when you return home is exhausting. However, she also works with parents who stay at home but somehow manage not to spend most of their day interacting with their children. Instead, they say, "'Well, I could play with you after I've done the laundry or after I've washed the dishes.' They're irritated because the kids are bugging them and they don't know how to set boundaries for the kids or for themselves."

> If you're like the 52 percent of the parents who admitted that the lines between work and home have become blurred, then rest assured that you make up the majority. However, being normal in this regard may not—should not—make you feel settled.

"In that way I don't think that I'm a normal parent," Gail says. She is a 38-year-old single working mother with an 8-year-old daughter. She works long hours and sometimes has to take business calls at home. Gail feels that her daughter overreacts to the time she takes to respond to work related activities. In fact, the opposite is true, Gail says. She is especially sensitive to not being away from her daughter too much. "So, I generally don't have a life," she says. "I don't go out with friends after work, and everything I do on the weekends includes her unless we have made plans for her to be with a friend."

When she compares herself to other parents, Gail says that she spends far more time with Jessica than her friends do with their kids. Gail believes that she has set the bar high, and Jessica has come to expect her mother's undivided attention when she's at home. "Sometimes she'll complain if I don't want to play with her dolls or if I don't want to go on a ride with her at an amusement park. However, when I ask if her friends' parents always play with their kids and go on all the rides, the answer is usually no," says Gail. "And when we revisit our time together over the weekend and she realizes the amount of time we've spent together, it gives her a different perspective, but it doesn't stop her from complaining the next time she wants me to do something."

OPTING OUT

*Watching parents juggle so many balls
can be overwhelming.*

Jennifer Wise opted for a career without children. An author, artist, and associate professor of theatre history at the University of Victoria in British Columbia, Canada, she knew by the age of 6 that she'd "rather be a hobo" than have children. "At least there'd be a change of scenery from time to time." Her essay entitled "Who Wants to Be a Mommy" was published along with a collection of 21 essays and a poem in *Nobody's Mother: Life without Kids*, edited by Lynne Van Luven and published in 2006, and is part of a compilation of stories shared by women, mostly writers, who have not given birth to their own children.

Wise writes, "For as the experience of my sisters, friends, and colleagues made clear, an ordinary person who tries to combine work and motherhood will soon be a gibbering wreck. The sleep deprivation. The total lack of privacy, sex, and quiet. The constant demands to do and say the same things again, and again, and again. The relentless questions. The loss of control over one's routine, the inability to fulfill one's own needs."

Creating boundaries

It has become the norm to see parents looking like aliens with those metallic earpieces permanently located in the hollow of their ear. It's bad enough when you're in the company of other adults and carrying on a conversation with someone else, but even worse are parents talking on their cell phones or responding to text messages while in the company of their kids. This has also become the norm, but that doesn't make it any less rude.

It teaches children inappropriate social skills and makes them feel as if they are not as worthy of attention as the person at the other end of the line. We regularly tell our kids not to interrupt our conversations but then interrupt their time with us the second our phone rings. We have become slaves to our ring tones and God forbid we should ignore call waiting and let the call go to voicemail.

Furthermore, by carrying on different conversations, responding to incoming calls and multi-tasking, we are teaching our kids that it's okay to operate in a frenetic environment rather than to focus on one thing at a time and give it—and them—proper attention.

Janet Chan, editorial director for the Parenting Group and editor in chief of *Parenting* magazine in the United States, says that on weekend mornings, "my husband and I—and my daughter, when we can drag her out of bed—take walks through Central Park in New York, and I can't tell you the number of moms and dads who are pushing a stroller while talking on their phones. I don't mean that they have to be talking to their child at all times, but they may as well be pushing a shopping cart."

Technological devices have allowed us to be more mobile and work from home but have also broken down important boundaries that used to exist—now when you are home, you often have your work there, too.

I believe that modern technology has become more of a curse than a blessing. Although I couldn't be without my computer and internet, I have made a point of not getting caught up in the madness of being reliant on gadgets and gizmos that seem to rob us of any quiet time.

PRIORITIZING

Whether working full or part-time or staying at home with the kids, some parents use chores as an excuse to hide from their kids. Others genuinely feel the need to keep from drowning under their ever-growing list of things to do.

> At almost 70 percent of parents admitted to feeling guilty about how they prioritized their daily responsibilities.

At least with household chores, most parents feel that they are being constructive. However, if they ever sit down to read a book or to indulge in a cup of tea, they worry about being accused of or feeling lazy or unproductive. That is, if they have enough time to worry before being called to attention by one of their children.

THE LION'S SHARE

> Even though many moms may feel that their lives have changed more significantly than their partners after their baby is born, 60 percent of the dads who responded to the questionnaire also felt that it was difficult to juggle all their responsibilities after their children were born.

Some people might say that dads aren't adding parenting into the equation when considering what they have to take care of, but I have seen a marked increase in the number of involved dads over the years.

* * *

Robin, the 34-year-old mom of a 4-month-old, says that although she doesn't feel resentment towards her husband, many of her female friends with young babies do. "They think that their husbands get away with a lot and just march on with their lives," Robin says. "They say that their husbands continue to work, go to the gym, and go out with their friends. They are continuing their lives as they were before the baby was born, but the women are tied to their babies. Many ask, 'What about me? When I am going to get back to my life?'"

Robin says that after their daughter was born she felt embarrassed about how she looked when her husband came home from work at the end of the day. She hated him seeing her not put together, especially on days that she hadn't even had time for a shower. "I wanted my husband to have this image of me as a beautiful mom taking care of a beautiful child." Robin believed that her husband thought she could take of everything, and she was letting him down. "I hated having to tell him that I didn't have it all together. He tried to convince me that what he was seeing was no different than what he expected. I know moms that rush around the house and straighten up 15 minutes before their husbands come home so that things look normal," she said.

As well as feeling physically unattractive, more tired and overwhelmed by having to keep it all together, many parents, (moms in particular) feel resentment and anger towards their partners if they feel they are not as involved in parenting. If a mom feels that she is parenting alone, angry that her partner's life has gone back to "normal" and hers hasn't, or that her partner is responding to the children in an abrasive manner, she will often disconnect from him emotionally.

Even though I feel blessed most of the time for having chosen such a great person to father my children, there are times when I feel resentful that he so easily climbs into bed with a book when he is tired while I'm still running around at midnight washing out sandwich containers for the next morning and sorting through a pile of papers. I think that dads know when to call it a day, whereas moms continue to push themselves beyond their limits.

PLAN AHEAD

I always suggest that before a baby is born—in fact, even prior to the conception or adoption of a child—that a couple have in-depth discussions about the way in which they want to structure their lives after they become parents. They might consider discussing whether they would prefer a more traditional arrangement where the mom is the primary caregiver or if they would prefer an alternate arrangement. They might want to discuss their views on other caregivers for the child and who will be responsible for all the different child-care needs such as diapering, feeding, and taking to medical appointments. Children do not make a weak marriage stronger but can make a couple drift apart if they are not on the same wavelength.

TAKING TIME OUT

A mom of a 2-year-old admitted that she looked forward to time away from her daughter. "Sometimes I just want to breathe. At first I felt guilty for wanting this, and then I reminded myself that it's okay to relax and take a break. I look forward to and relish the time that I have to myself—even if I just vegetate for an hour to watch Oprah. Actually, I think that it makes me a better parent because I recharge my batteries."

Most parents can attest to the guilt they feel when they sneak off to play a mindless game of poker on their computer while their kids are at home or when they spend extra time on the toilet so that they can read the daily newspaper.

> Of the parents who completed the questionnaire, 66
> percent worried that they were not spending enough
> time or quality time with their kids.

Many parents ask my opinion on how much time is too little.
There is not one absolute answer. However, I do believe that a minimum of 20 minutes of one-on-one time with your child every day
can go a long way towards fostering a greater bond.

Adele Faber, bestselling author of several parenting books,
including *How to Talk So Kids Will Listen and Listen So Kids Will
Talk*, shared some candid stories with me from her home in New
York. She remembered a story she had shared in one of her first
books, *Liberated Parents, Liberated Children*, about making friends
with your own limitations. "It's important," she says, "to realize that
sometimes when you're being horrible to your kids, it's because
you're trying too hard to accommodate their needs and not tuning
in to your own."

Once, when she was a young mother, she sat down on the sofa,
happy to finally have a minute to herself. She'd folded the laundry,
put away the dishes and was just happy to have 5 minutes to flip
through a magazine. Suddenly her kids came charging in with
"Mom, Daddy promised to take us for ice cream and now he says
he can't; he has to finish paying bills." She didn't want to disappoint
them, so she dug herself out of the nice warm sofa. Then "she was
awful to them," she remembers, snapping "things like 'how long
does it take you to get into the car?' and 'so what if they didn't have
the flavor you wanted?' And she remembers being "vile" to her kids
because she was so tired and irritable and wished that she was still
relaxing on the sofa. In her book, Faber recounts her "long journey
to becoming as tender and kind and compassionate" to herself as

she was to her children.   In the process, she learned to ask herself questions such as "do I have it in me to do this now and if not, am I able to just say—kids, I hear how disappointed you are. I wish I had the energy to just spring off the couch and take you, but just now I don't."

TIME AS A FAMILY

Some of the best times with my husband and kids are when we go away together. It doesn't have to be a fancy or expensive vacation. In fact, camping (if you don't mind bugs and sand in the tent) may be one of the best ways to get back in touch with one another. When we go away, I carry my cell phone for emergencies only.

We take old-fashioned board games like Scrabble and Monopoly with us. I know it sounds corny, but we play charades and make each other laugh. There's no greater feeling in the world than to catch yourself in that moment, to feel gratitude for being able to connect with your kids in such a back-to-basics way, and to really feel a deep connection to each family member. Those moments can, of course, be captured at home during regular Sunday family game nights or family meetings where everyone has the opportunity to come together and vent. However, there's something about being away from the computer, telephone, laundry, and daily chores that makes coming together so much easier.

Another great time to connect with your children is at bedtime. After reading a book to my 8-year-old, we turn off the light and lie together. It's amazing what stories are shared in the dark. I learn more in 10 minutes of snuggle time than I do in the hours after school when there are so many other distractions. I've even learned not to fall asleep before she does.

This time of day, I have been told many times, is a source of frustration for many. Instead of focusing on your child, it's normal for us to be agitated as we think about all the other mundane must-dos like returning phone calls, preparing for the next work day, and checking bank balances online. However, I recommend that, as much as possible, you free your mind of all those thoughts and indulge in that time alone with your child. It's an opportunity to let your mind and body relax for a few minutes, and it's times like these that your children will remember. This quality time will give you a lot of mileage towards enriching your relationship for the future. My daughter recently turned 16. I miss lying in her bed at night, stroking her hair and hearing about her day. Most of the time she is still awake when I turn out my light (and I don't go to bed early), but occasionally she will lie down on my bed, kiss me goodnight, and tell me how much loves me.

TREASURE THESE MOMENTS

As I count on one hand the number of years we may have with her living under our roof, I feel my eyes fill with tears, and I am reminded of an excerpt from Kahlil Gibran's poem, "Children," from his book *The Prophet:*

> Your children are not your children.
> They are the sons and daughters of Life's longing for itself.
> They come through you but not from you,
> and though they are with you, yet they belong not to you.

We can't wait for our children to move through one stage and onto the next, but time is fleeting and one day, when your children have moved out and there are no more knapsacks and coats cluttering the hallway, you may look back and wish that you had spent 5 more minutes snuggling with your child, holding her hand, and sharing in special moments together. There will always be laundry to fold, bills to be paid, and errands to run, but your time with your children is brief.

TIME WITH FRIENDS

Having said this, don't neglect yourself or your relationships with your partner or friends in the process. When the children have moved on, that's what will be left. Having your kids see you taking care of yourself and nurturing relationships with other adults is important, too. Unfortunately, when juggling self, children, and career, the relationship with your partner is often overlooked. Aside from not having enough time to nourish your relationship, parents are often too tired to give of themselves to another person.

TIME AS A COUPLE

> Although some parents don't readily admit to their sex lives being that much different, 72 percent of the parents who responded to the questionnaire said that their sex lives had changed—both in quantity and quality—since they became parents.

Many couples have confided in me that although they fantasize about being intimate more often, their reality is that they have sex as infrequently as once a month or less.

Leslie Chandler, a parenting and childbirth educator and bookseller at Parentbooks in Toronto, says that she felt like her sex life and sex drive was really abnormal after she had a child because no one ever talked to her about it—that nobody ever explained to her about the effects of breastfeeding hormones on her sex drive or helped her anticipate how tired she would be. "Who wants to go bed and have sex with someone when you're feeling tired and angry and resentful and feel like you haven't had a moment to yourself? I felt I wasn't normal at that point because I had such a strong sex drive before.

"For women there is a lot of body image stuff," she said. "Their bodies have changed, they're softer and bigger and some places never go back to the way they used to be." Leslie believes that for men there is often a deep hurt because they may not understand the changes and they really miss the physical connection with their partner. Before the baby is born, Leslie notes, couples get that warm nurturing touch by holding hands and having sex, for example. Once you have a baby, a mom has that need for touch fulfilled all the time by the baby—"plus the baby is peeing and pooing on her all day so that at the end of the day she doesn't want anything else on her." Leslie says that she spends a lot of time talking about these changes in her prenatal classes. "I really think that couples are vulnerable during the first few years [of their child being born]," she says.

Joe, a 30-year-old father of two young children, says that he hates all the interruptions when he and his wife are trying to be intimate. "Sometimes we start and then the baby starts to cry. Then she goes to tend to the baby and then we start to fool around again. Then the other one comes in. After a while, we say 'forget it, we'll try again tomorrow.'"

Reena, 27, has been married for 4 years and is the mother of a 1-year-old. She says that she and her husband go on "dates" in their living room and watch a movie. "My husband is not very demanding; he is very easy going. It's insane how good he is—I'm so lucky because all of my energy and all of my love is on my son. I know that a lot of husbands would feel jealous, but not mine." Now that her son is in day care, she looks forward to going on dates with her husband during the day.

And as the children grow older, become teenagers, and stay up later than you, being intimate with your partner becomes more awkward. You often feel as if you have to sneak around the house behind your teen's back in order to get some loving. My husband and I celebrated our twentieth wedding anniversary this year. Instead of spending the night at a hotel as we sometimes do for special occasions, our children slept over at their grandparents' house and we had our house to ourselves. We ordered in Thai food and my husband set up four tall, fiery, mosquito-repelling citronella bamboo sticks, "Survivor"—style, around our hammock. Then underneath the stars, we lay together for at least an hour and reminisced about our years together. Then, for a change, we settled into the guest bedroom for the night.

Sharon, a 46-year-old mother of three, says that teenage kids can be a "huge damper" on a couple's sex life. She told me that she and her husband wished that they had slept with their door closed while the kids were growing up. Now, if they close the door, the kids will know that something is up. However, with all three kids at camp all summer, she is rekindling her relationship with her husband. "We've made love in every room in the house," she said.

BALANCING ACT

There's no doubt that taking time for yourself, your kids, your partner, and your family takes a great deal of coordination and work. At times you will feel like a rubber band stretched to the limit and about to snap. I find that making lists really helps me to deal with one thing at a time. If I make a list of things to do the night before I have to do them, I can cross them out as they're taken care of and not have to think about what comes next. The important thing is to take time to enjoy each moment and to try not to allow your mind to race ahead.

SLOW DOWN

I was recently sent an email entitled "Slow Dance." This poem was apparently written by a terminally ill teenager in a New York hospital:

SLOW DANCE
Have you ever watched kids
On a merry-go-round?
Or listened to the rain
Slapping on the ground?
Ever followed a butterfly's erratic flight?
Or gazed at the sun into the fading night?
You better slow down.
Don't dance so fast.
Time is short.
The music won't last.
Do you run through each day
On the fly?
When you ask, How are you?
Do you hear the reply?
When the day is done
Do you lie in your bed
With the next hundred chores

Running through your head?
You'd better slow down
Don't dance so fast.
Time is short.
The music won't last.
Ever told your child,
We'll do it tomorrow?
And in your haste,
Not see his sorrow?
Ever lost touch,
Let a good friendship die
Cause you never had time
To call and say, "Hi"
You'd better slow down.
Don't dance so fast.
Time is short.
The music won't last.
When you run so fast to get somewhere
You miss half the fun of getting there.
When you worry and hurry through your day,
It is like an unopened gift . . .
Thrown away.
Life is not a race.
Do take it slower
Hear the music
Before the song is over.

5

The Electronic Umbilical Cord
. . . Keeping our Children Close

"Making the decision to have a child—it's momentous. It is to decide forever to have your heart go walking around outside your body."

—E. Stone

> The majority of parents worry about whether they are being neurotic when it comes to their children's safety and wellbeing.
>
> In fact, 60 percent of the parents who completed the questionnaire admitted to feeling this way.

IT'S NORMAL FOR parents to feel uncomfortable about sharing anxieties related to the safety of their children. Some parents even allow their children to participate in activities or take on certain responsibilities too soon because they want to appear "normal" to others. Most parents recognize the value of allowing their children greater independence as they grow. Inwardly, however, many prefer to keep them wrapped in a cocoon for longer than the time at which their children choose to emerge as butterflies.

Not only may you be influenced by what you believe your peers are thinking about you, you may also second-guess yourself. When your child accuses you of being a "worry wart," you may even put aside what you intuitively feel is best and go with what she wants. I know that it is sometimes difficult to confidently assess the difference between your intuitive self sending messages that are based on personal anxieties versus rational thought, but not listening to yourself for the sake of pleasing your child or others may put your child at risk.

PERSONAL ANXIETIES

I sometimes reflect on whether my personal anxieties about letting my children "go" are reality-based (real danger exists) or whether they are irrational and may impede my child's emotional and psychological growth. For example, I'm first to admit that I felt panicked when my daughter was younger and liked to play hide-and-go-seek between the racks at a clothing store. Although I knew that she was close by, not being able to see her, even for a few seconds, was terrifying. I also dreaded school field trips when the kids were younger. I had horrible visions of them getting lost in the crowds and never being found.

Other thoughts are more rational. For example, I believe that it is not safe for young children to go to public washrooms on their own. I have always insisted, therefore, that my 8-year-old take a "buddy" or an adult with her. I believe that it is best for me to know the parents of my younger daughter's friends (and even to introduce myself to my 16-year-old's friends' parents), and therefore will not allow her to play at the home of a child whose parent I have not yet met. I also will not let my 8-year-old stay alone in the house until she is older and more mature.

> The average age at which parents who completed the questionnaire felt comfortable with their children being home alone was 12. However, one mom said that she was comfortable leaving her 7-year-old alone and another not until she was 18. Five percent of the parents who answered the questionnaire said that they would leave a 3-year-old alone in a car while they ran into a store for a few minutes. The majority of parents said that they wouldn't leave their children alone in a car until they were at least over the age of 10.

GAINING INDEPENDENCE

It's hard for me to believe that my 16-year-old daughter is old enough to become licensed to drive a car. Although she is excited at the prospect of doing so, I'm in no rush for her to sit behind the wheel of a hunk of metal. Actually, I think that 16 is too young to be operating such a dangerous piece of equipment. When people ask me which university or college she plans on attending and whether she will live away from home, I tell them that is not an option—my umbilical cord doesn't stretch that far.

When I look around, I see that my teenage daughter has followed a different path from many of her peers. I am so proud of the person she has become: mature, responsible, caring, and an excellent decision maker. I used to worry that perhaps I had held her back too long. I saw that many of her peers were more streetwise than her. When they were walking to school at the age of 13 or younger, we were still driving her there and back.

> Of the parents I polled, the youngest age at which a parent felt comfortable having his or her child walk to school alone was 8, although most ranged between 12 and 14, and the oldest was 18.

When her peers were hanging out at malls at the age of 12, we insisted on an adult being present. When she was 14 and started high school, we bought her a cell phone, our electronic umbilical cord. She was thrilled and so were we, knowing that we could reach her at any time. This worked well for us. However, I have heard stories from many parents whose experiences haven't been as positive. For example, many kids monitor their incoming calls and choose when to answer. Although a cell phone can be an amazing tool for communication, it's not foolproof.

I now applaud my daughter's independence. When she goes to the mall with a friend and uses her well-earned money from working part-time to buy an outfit or pair of shoes, I rejoice in her ability to stand alone and to make great choices. I can finally say with great conviction that I'm glad I waited to give her the independence she is now so ready to handle.

When our children are young, we often don't realize how lucky we are to hold them close, choose their friends, and be a big part of their decision-making. As children grow, it's normal for them to want more autonomy, some sooner than others. I notice that my 8-year-old is pushing our limits far sooner than her sister did. I think this has something to do with being second-born to a much older sister. I think it also has something to do with her spirited nature, self-assuredness, and impressive awareness of the world around her. I can already tell that I will likely be okay with her gaining greater independence sooner than my 16-year-old did. I am able to recognize her readiness. I am also not as anxious a parent as I was with my first-born.

Paula is a 52-year-old mother of a 21- and an almost-16-year-old. She recently faced a dilemma. Her teenage son's friend, who had just been granted a driver's license, asked that her son join him as a passenger. Paula was torn between allowing him to join his friend or standing firm in her belief that a new driver shouldn't be driving his friends around until he is more experienced. She worried that she would alienate her son from his peers by setting limits that were too different or extreme. In the end, she let him go while she stayed at home and counted the seconds until his safe return.

WORRIED SICK

Selena, a 37-year-old mom with two young children, says that she is an extremely anxious parent. "I worry so much," she says, "I feel I may be sick. I worry that someone will take my child away from me, and I think that I am the only parent who feels like this. I always imagine the worst." She wonders if the way in which she was parented has created her fears. "When I grew up, my parents always checked up on me. Even when I was working, they asked that I be home by a certain time, and even if I was a half hour late they were angry. So I was afraid to be late."

Ava, a 49-year-old mother of a 12-year-old daughter, also worries that she is not normal to feel so afraid about something bad happening to her child. She asks, "Am I alone? Do others feel the same thing? Are my thoughts rational, or not?" A social worker by profession, Ava knows that her thoughts of her daughter being abducted are irrational. Ava believes that part of the reason she is so fearful of losing her daughter is because she is such a "huge commodity." She went through a long process of fertility treatments before finally becoming pregnant.

Ava admits to having irrational thoughts about her daughter "vanishing into thin air" since she was born. However, she says that they are getting more elaborate as her daughter grows older and more independent. "So now this thought is becoming too real. I'm thinking that she's going to be in the mall with other people and this thought may become a possibility. Have you heard about this before?" she asks me with a half laugh, embarrassed to be looking for reassurance that she is not crazy. "You and my husband are the only ones that I've shared this thought with," she says.

"How would you feel if you knew that other parents had thoughts like this?" I asked. "I'd feel very comforted," she responded. "When you're amongst a group of people who share the same or similar thoughts, you feel more normal."

Clementine, a 46-year-old single mother of a 15-year-old son, is "envisioning him driving when he's 16" and has "already started stressing out about it." She doesn't think that "the average parent worries about something that isn't even happening yet." I assure her that they do, and she is relieved to hear it. She continues by sharing that "when he travels with his dad, I start to feel freaked out because he's going on a plane. This week he was on a boat and I told him to make sure to wear a life jacket. His comment to me was 'Oh, I shouldn't have even told you.' He thinks that I worry far too much and it's caused him to withhold things from me. So I try to change some of what I ask, but I can't help it." Clementine and I discuss ways for her to ease her anxieties when her son is away from her. One idea is that instead of reciting a long list of what he should or should not be doing, it may be better to ask him what he plans on doing in order to keep safe. If a parent is lecturing, she doesn't know how much her child is absorbing. If a child shares what he knows to do, however, the parent may be more comforted.

Separation anxiety

Bruce is a 48-year-old father of a 4-year-old son. He says that when his son was around the age of 3 and going to home day care for the first time "he was nervous because I didn't want him to feel abandoned. The degree of attention that we paid to reassuring him that we would return made me wonder if we were normal." Bruce wanted his son to "see concern in our eyes, but wondered if he could also see our fear and anxiety."

"There was an early morning child-minding center where we would leave him before the actual day care began. I didn't understand why he didn't want to go, but he would hug me very tightly and squeeze me very hard when I said goodbye. I'd remind him when I was coming back and the woman there was very nice, but she had a lot of little babies to attend to. One day, we walked in and one of the babies started wailing. My son put his head down on a chair, and I heard a kind of helpless cry or whimper. I felt terrible and my wife thought that I was taking it a bit too hard. I tried to comfort him and he said, 'I'll be brave, Daddy' and then he asked me to read a story. Even though I knew I'd be late for work, I stayed and read the story and he seemed to feel better. But soon after that I made plans for him to not go there anymore."

NEVER LET THEM FALL

Canada's Kathy Lynn, parenting speaker, columnist, and author of books such as *Who's in Charge Anyway?* believes that "parents are overprotecting children to a level that is stultifying them. We run the risk of raising a generation of kids who are going to be so afraid and so incapable of taking any action on their own because they never have." She says that she sees "parents who run around behind a toddler who is trying to learn how to walk" because they don't want to "let the kid ever fall down." She believes that the world is just as safe as it used to be but that our perceptions have changed and encourages parents who are afraid of harm coming to their kids to "take a look at the real statistics of whatever it is that they're afraid of."

For example, she says that "something like 75 percent of missing kids are runaways, and the largest majority of the rest are custody disputes; yet we have this vision of pedophiles running around snatching kids every day, which just doesn't happen." She suggests that parents take action toward being less overbearing. "A 7-year-old, for example, should be able to walk a few blocks by himself. Streetproof and then let them go," she says.

LETTING GO

As parents, we are bombarded with messages from experts to "let go." However, I don't believe that letting go should be an opportunity to shirk parental responsibility when it comes to keeping our children safe. Letting go may mean allowing our children to venture away from us, slowly and steadily, as they are ready. Letting go does not mean abandoning your children by the age of 12, thinking that they are old enough to make decisions that are suited for a much older child.

Barb, a 42-year-old parent, says she doesn't care what others think about her wanting to protect her 5-year-old. She prefers to be her own expert. Barb works 3 days a week as a community mental health nurse. She says she is more of a "just flowing from the gut kind of person and if something feels right, I go with it. I've found that the few times I've pushed my intuitive feelings aside and gone with the masses, I've learned a hard lesson. For example, we were in the park a couple of years ago when my son was 3 and he was climbing on something that I wasn't comfortable with. All the other moms were saying, 'Oh, let him go.' And I'm thinking 'but I know my kid and I know that he doesn't have the same strength and agility as their kids'. I could tell what the other moms were thinking: 'Well, that's why he's not doing it well. You're smothering him. Why not let him fall so that he can learn the hard way.' Even though that's the way that lots of parents operate, I say that they're just so bloody lucky that nothing really bad has happened to their kid. Now when somebody makes a comment, I say something like, 'Well, that's really great for your kid, but my kid is not going to be climbing this.' I'm far more assertive with that.

"Now he's climbing on equipment in the park that other kids were climbing on two years ago, and I let him. I know he has the coordination and the strength. If he falls, he'll not fall like a rag doll like he used to."

PEER PRESSURE

Many parents feel pressured into pushing their safety concerns aside. Instead of standing up for what they believe in, they allow their children to venture into situations that make them uncomfortable. They do this out of fear of being called a neurotic or overprotective parent. They reluctantly allow their 6-year-old to sleep over at a friend's house even though they know that she's not ready and ship their child off to sleepover camp by the age of 8 because their friends say that it's good for a child and his parents to have some distance. I say, why so soon?

Childhood is fleeting, and children have many years to experience life. I have seen too many parents who have allowed the use of makeup and sexually provocative clothing for their children, even at around the age of 11 or 12. I have seen too many children who were taken to teen idol rock concerts at the age of 10. Too many children have televisions and computers in their bedrooms and don't have to wait their turn because their bathrooms are en suite. Too many children who have never had to delay gratification turn into bored teenagers looking for excitement.

I am suggesting that parents work at preserving their children's innocence and maintaining consistent rules in regards to their children making decisions and engaging in activities that should be reserved for when they are older. I am still shocked when I overhear children as young as 10 or 11 accusing their parents of being paranoid and overprotective for not wanting them to go to the mall, for example, with their friends.

> When parents completed the questionnaire and responded to an age at which they felt comfortable with their child being in the mall without adult supervision, the youngest age was 8 and the oldest was 20. Most parents stated ages between 12 and 15.

I don't believe that 10,-11, - or even 12-year-olds should hang out at the mall or other public places with their friends. They usually don't have the life skills to deal with unusual situations that may arise.

One parent shared her story of being in the mall with her 11-year-old. Earlier, they had gotten into an argument about the child going to the mall with a friend instead. While her daughter was in the changing room, a siren went off in the store alerting the customers that there had been a robbery and that they were trying to apprehend the thief. Soon after, an iron gate closed the store off from the rest of the mall and the customers were asked to remain where they were until the police arrived.

In the end, they caught the thief and the store returned to normal. The parent and her daughter were quite shaken and left. Afterwards, the child thanked her mother for insisting on being there with her. This incident gave the mother an opportunity to share some more streetproofing tips with her daughter. It also reinforced the mother's belief that her daughter, at 11, was not yet old enough to be without adult supervision.

CYBER SAFETY

Sadly, our children are sometimes safer outside of our houses than when they are in front of a computer behind the closed door of their bedroom. Even computer-savvy kids get caught up in the power of the internet. They are lulled into a false sense of security by thinking that they are protected by their familiar four walls. They often don't grasp the enormity of the world they are stepping into by exposing so much of themselves, often unintentionally.

As parents, we need to become better educated about the cyber world and set very clear limits about which sites our children are free to enter. One mom of a 7- and 8-year-old shared that her family had created a list of "safe" sites and taped it to the computer. Any other site that the child wanted to visit had to be discussed with the parent first.

PRIVILEGES WITHOUT RESPONSIBILITY

Many young teens believe that they should have all the privileges of adulthood without any of the hardships. They expect freedom and privacy without responsibility. They accuse their parents of being crazy for wanting to know whose house they are going to and whether there will be adult supervision. I say to keep asking and knowing. As the old adage goes, it's better to be safe than sorry. Although you need to be respectful of your child's need for autonomy and aware of the potential embarrassment he might feel as a result of having you involved in his life, it is still your right and responsibility to keep your children safe, even when they think that they're old enough to make their own decisions.

LOVING LIMITS

Children equate limit setting, which is a form of protection, with love. When a child's behavior becomes intolerable and a parent gives up by giving in, the child suffers and does not feel loved. When a parent gives up on her child because he has become too difficult to manage, the child usually suffers rather than benefits from being let go.

Despite what your teenager appears to want, she will thrive best when firm, loving limits are set and adhered to. Dr. Scott Wooding, Canadian psychologist, parenting expert, and author of several books including *Rage, Rebellion and Rudeness* writes about teens' need for limit setting. "The teenage years are the most insecure of a person's life. Teens need many obvious signs that their parents care about them, and when these signs are not clear enough, they become angry and resentful." He goes on to say that "they need to know that their parents care enough about them to take the time and energy to set and enforce limits."

Goldie Plotkin, a rabbi's wife, educator, and mother of eight children, looks to the Torah for answers about protecting her children. "The laws are very specific and were created to prevent, God forbid, things such as molestation and rape. Little girls older than 3 are not allowed to be alone with a member of the opposite sex, other than a brother or a parent. Statistics show that children are mostly molested by a cousin or someone that they know. God really put this into effect to protect our children—our daughters, our sons. A little boy 9 or older is not allowed to be kissed or touched by anyone that is not his mother or grandmother, sister or aunt."

Goldie says that when "children are 15, 16, and older and want to go out with a group of friends, you might consider letting them go if you know that they are able to make the right choices. But what about these little 11- and 12-year-olds whose parents are allowing it?" she asks. She answers herself with "I think its all part of this 'everyone else is doing it' attitude. I will never forget when I was 11 years old and I wanted to go out on a Saturday night with a group of friends to an activity that my parents didn't think was appropriate for me as an Orthodox girl. I told my parents I was going with a specific girl, and my father was shocked because her father was one of the great rabbis in Brooklyn; he said that he was going to call the father. He called and the father had thought that his daughter was going someplace else. So this girl had told her father that she was going somewhere that she was not. My father put a stop to it. I realize now that someone has to sometimes check out where everyone is going and to ask if all the parents really agree. Even then a parent has to put her foot down if she thinks that what her child wants to do is wrong. When I say no, I explain to my children why it's wrong; this is the perfect opportunity to mold your children for life. You explain the challenges, the problems, the dangers, ask them what they think. This is where communication works."

CALCULATED RISKS

Michelle, a 41-year-old mother of an 8-year-old daughter, says that when her daughter was 7, stable on her bike, and only had a small side street to cross, that she let her cycle around the block on her own. "I thought of what I was doing at her age and how I trusted her and then I let her go. I stayed outside and calculated how long she would take. When she came home, she wanted to do it again and I said okay. However, this time she was gone for what seemed like forever. So, after about 10 minutes I started to walk in the direction she had gone and she appeared. She had stopped to talk to some friends from school. I told her that in the future she should tell me if she was going to visit friends." Michelle says that living in Toronto makes her slightly more nervous than if she was raising her daughter in Halifax, where she was raised. Michelle believes that "most of the people I spend time with are overprotective. So the question is," she says, "are they overprotective or am I not protective enough?"

Lillian, a 45-year-old single mother of two girls, believes that many parents are overprotective and that she is "normal." She says that tries to give her girls "enough training and the right amount of freedom for their age. I let them go out alone on the street in our townhouse complex as long as they stay together. I allow them to call on friends without me constantly keeping an eye on them. I feel that I've given them the skills necessary to be safe. I do feel that at ages 8 and 10, they have the skills necessary to play outside together for a few hours."

Beth, a 46-year-old mother of three children, ages 14, 13, and 10, says that she is not overprotective. "I'm fairly liberal and trust my instincts." She doesn't think that there's an age at which children should cross the street by themselves. "I believe that you will know it when they're ready. Only now is my 10-year-old son ready to ride his bike around the block. Before I let him, I drove my car beside him, I watched and then I let him free. My 14-year-old takes the bus. I trust my instincts on that. I try to be realistic about safety—I don't focus on the bad things that can happen."

TEACHING CHILDREN TO TRUST THEIR INSTINCTS

Adele Faber, co-author of many parenting books including *Siblings Without Rivalry*, shared a story of being in a supermarket and standing at the checkout line behind "an adorable child and her mother. She's looking at me and grinning, and I grin back at her and ask her a funny little question. Then her mother gives me that 'don't speak to my child' look, the child catches it too, looks away from me and thinks of me as a menace." Although neither child nor parent can say for sure whether a stranger is good or bad, we may have gone too far in frightening children not to trust in people they don't know. It seems reasonable, for example, for children to be able to engage in limited conversation with a stranger when they are with their caregiver. At the same time, it is important to teach a child to trust his or her intuitive response to others.

As an example, Adele recalled a story in her *Liberated Parents, Liberated Children* book. It was about a 9-year-old girl who had gone to a community pool with some friends, and they were all playing water tag with a teenage boy. At one point, the boy said to her, "C'mon, let's go to where the trees are and I'll lick your toes." She thought that this was really strange, so she left the pool, returned home to her mother, and told her what had just happened.

Instead of panicking, the parent acknowledged her daughter's intuitive sense of danger and praised her for responding appropriately by returning home. Since parents can't be with their children every minute of the day and can't anticipate every situation they'll be in, Adele also encourages parents to teach their children to trust their feelings.

TRUST IN YOURSELF

When parenting, listen to your intuitive self and you will be able to make important decisions about when to let your children spread their wings. Along with this sense, you will likely take many other factors into consideration, such as his age and level of maturity. Even more important than deciding at what age you are comfortable with your children walking to school alone, going to movies without adult supervision, taking public transit, crossing the road, and staying home alone, is looking at their level of maturity, insight, ability to reason, problem solve, and make appropriate decisions and choices.

Unfortunately, too many parents approach me when their teens are already in trouble. They want to know how to rein them in and get control back. Unfortunately, if a child has been given too much freedom too soon, the struggle to regain control is like trying to walk up a slippery slope. Although it is never too late to try make a bad situation better, it's best, if possible, to give your children greater freedom over a more protracted period.

EDUCATE YOURSELF

Lana is a 48-year-old mother of three children ages 22, 18, and 12, and the director of development at LOVE (Leave out Violence) in Toronto. She says that "the at-risk youth that I work with have educated me about what it's really like in their world of clubs and parties. For me to know that my daughter has gone to a party is of little value in terms of her personal safety. What I think is most important is to remind her how valuable she is and how loved she is and that when she is in a situation where there are drugs and alcohol, to be very careful.

"For example, you might educate your child that if there is marijuana at the party and if she is going to try it, to make sure that she knows the source and that she is in a safe environment. I'm not advocating drug or alcohol use," she says, "but you need to be realistic and prepare them to make safe and healthy choices. If we get information so that we really understand the world our child is in, and we create an open dialogue with our child and make sure that they know that they are valued and loved, we can more realistically help him or her navigate through their teenage years."

To those parents who believe that their personal anxieties are impacting on their child's move towards independence: Comfort yourself by looking at the real statistics, face your fears by talking to other parents and professionals if necessary, and don't allow your children to be crippled by unrealistic fears.

To those parents who believe that children should have freedom of choice by the age of 12 or 13: Keep in mind that children thrive on loving limits, and many do not have the skills or maturity necessary to always make good decisions or to be engaged in certain activities.

To those parents who have worked through their own kinks and struck a balance between allowing autonomy within appropriate boundaries: Keep going.

To all parents: It's normal to worry. Some worry about being overprotective, others worry about not being protective enough. The trick is learning how to protect without going overboard. Few have struck a perfect balance.

6

Conform to the Norm?

⁓

WHEN I WAS 15, I left my friends and grandparents in South Africa, and moved to Canada with my parents and siblings. Although we had to get used to some changes, the transition was not that huge. After all, English was our first language too, and our lifestyle was quite similar to North Americans.' This is, however, not the case for many families who have moved from non-English-speaking countries or from places where children are raised far differently.

Dr. Nancy Freeman, associate professor of early childhood education and research director of the Child Development and Research Center at the University of South Carolina, wrote an article on "Early

Education in China," which was printed in the *Early Childhood Education Journal* in 1988. In it she compares "child-rearing practices in modern America with modern mainland China." Following a visit to China with a group of early childhood educators, she writes about "the popularity of residential programs for 2- to 6-year-olds who are separated from their parents for a week at a time." She says that "this practice dismayed our group of American early childhood professionals who questioned the advisability of enrolling children in boarding school during their preschool years when week-long separations may have a detrimental effect on important mother-child and family bonds."

Dr. Freeman explains why working parents in China often choose boarding schools for their children. Instead of being overindulged by doting parents or grandparents, being lonely, and lacking in social interaction, parents believe that they are doing her children a favor by sending them to school to socialize them. By the end of her journey in China, Dr. Freeman concluded that "it was important that we consider how parenting practices reflect cultural norms, values, and expectations."

The Best Dads in the World?

Most moms dream of sharing the joy of breastfeeding with their husbands—especially at 2 a.m. In an article printed in U.K's The *Guardian* in 2005 entitled "Are the men of the African Aka tribe the best fathers in the world?", Joanna Moorhead writes that "Professor Barry Hewlett, an American anthropologist, was the first person to spot male breastfeeding among the Aka Pygmy people of Central Africa. According to the data he began collecting; Aka fathers are within reach of their infants forty seven percent of the time—that's apparently more than fathers in any other cultural group on the planet."

Moorhead goes on to quote Hewlett as saying that "there's

a big sense in our society that dads can't always be around and that you have to give up a lot of time with your child but that you can put that right by having quality time with them instead." After living with the Aka, Hewlett is not so sure about that. He believes that fathers should spend more time with their children, holding them physically close more often.

Hewlett's personal beliefs about parenting, according to Moorhead, were changed after spending time with the Aka tribe. He believes that a lesson we can all learn from them is "how precious children are and how lucky we are to have them in our lives." Hewlett, in his conversation with Moorhead, said that "we've strayed into believing that kids are a burden rather than a blessing and that's something the Aka never do." To the Aka, your children are the very value of your life. The idea of a child as a burden would be incomprehensible there—children are the energy, the life force of the community."

For most parents in our society, breastfeeding fathers would not be considered normal. In Moorhead's article, she writes about Jack O'Sullivan of Fathers Direct (a national information center on fatherhood) who was invited onto several chat shows after Hewlett's report went public. Apparently, "some fathers phoned in to say they'd let their child suck their nipples—they said that it often just happened when the baby was lying on their chest in bed," O'Sullivan was reported as saying. Moorhead went on to say that "some people were disgusted—the words 'child abuse' came up more than once which points to interesting cultural differences when you think that, to Aka folk, much of the way we raise our kids would count as child abuse to them (babies being left to sleep alone in a different room from their parents, for example)."

There's no doubt that cultural norms affect our style of parenting.

Selena, 37, her husband, and their daughter, then 1 year old, moved from China to Canada seven years ago. I was privileged to chat with her about her experiences growing up in China. I was interested to learn whether or not she had been influenced by her cultural norms.

Selena's Story

Selena and her family were happy to arrive in North America but had a difficult time adapting to the differences between their culture and ours. Several years after arriving in Canada, Selena gave birth to another daughter, a privilege she would not have been allowed had they remained in China, where the government has mandated that each family have only one child in an effort to combat overpopulation.

Selena's parents moved to Canada for 6 months so that they could help with child care. When they returned to China, Selena's parents-in-law took their place. "Because I always have grandparents around to help take care of the kids and we all live together, my husband and I always felt like *we* were kids. My parents helped to take care of my eldest daughter for 6 years, so I didn't realize that I was a mother. I took care of myself first because my parents were there for my child. When I got home from work I sat down to read the newspaper. I think that is why my first daughter and I are not as close, but I hope she knows how much I love her."

Selena says that "When my parents were here, my mom said, 'We knew we were wrong when you were little.' She asked me not to push my daughter too much with practicing piano, to be nice to her and talk to her. I know that it is not good to be so strict but I have to do it—I can't control myself.

If she does something wrong, I get so angry. I think that she has to be good. I also now appreciate my parents. Even though they beat me, I know now that they wanted me to be good too."

When asked, Selena says that they don't beat their daughter. "I know that in Canada it's not allowed. My mother told my daughter that if we beat her, she can call 911." I encouraged Selena to help her child behave appropriately through encouragement and not intimidation. I told her that it was best if a child could stand up for herself, that she could be strong and polite at the same time. This way of thinking is sometimes foreign to new immigrants, especially if their culture condones physical discipline and compliance without question.

Some other parents of Chinese heritage have told me that they expect their children to be passive, compliant, and respectful. Selena expects this too. As a result, she has a difficult time when her daughter asserts herself. She says that her daughter "has her own mind."

Despite this, Selena realizes that for a child her daughter's age, her behavior is quite normal. Selena admits that "when I was little, I was the same. My father wanted me to study all the time—mathematics and writing and reading. I had no Saturday or Sunday, and I was so tired. From grade one up to middle school, from ages 7 to 16, I had no time for play. They were very strict with me and they wanted me to follow their will. I was not allowed to do anything I liked—not even read a novel. The reason that my eyes are so bad now is because I would read under the covers at night. I used the flashlight and had to hide my books because if they found them, I would be beaten. My father was bad-tempered.

"Now I know that they loved me and wanted me to be good, always be number one. Back then I thought that I was not their daughter. I thought that I was adopted. I cried at night and wrote in a diary and I was always so sad when I was little. I have one younger sister who lives in the United States, but they treated her nicer because she listened to them. She was more compliant."

Selena says that for Chinese parents, "education is the most important thing. When I was in grade one and I wanted to do knitting and sewing, my mother said, 'No, you don't want to be a housewife.' My father said that math, physics, and chemistry were the most important subjects. So I had to be very good at that, and I felt a lot of pressure. At school we had pressure too. They told us which number ranking we were and it was posted for everyone to see."

Although Selena realizes the pressure that she felt, she has a hard time behaving differently towards her daughter. While other kids take it easy over the summer months, her daughter practices piano for 2 hours a day. Selena says that a year ago "she refused to do any practicing and she was very angry and I almost gave up, but my mother didn't. She very nicely asked her to play again and again—she was very patient and then she did gradually, and now she is used to that kind of life."

Selena says that in China "I don't think I would push her so much. In Canada I feel much less secure—about my future, jobs, kids, everything. It's not my country, not my home. Even though we have a home, we still feel unsettled. In China, if something happens we know how to deal with it, we know where to find help. Here we don't know anything. Even if we are sick and we need to go to the hospital, we don't know what the system is about and how the doctors work with you. It makes you feel very insecure."

Selena says that it is because of her insecurity that she

puts more pressure on her daughter. She wants her to be able to "stand on her own in the future, to be the best she can be. Even if isn't number one, we want her to be in the top 10 in the class. In school they don't learn a lot compared to kids in China. It's all play, play, play. If you learn piano, at least you have one more skill."

When Selena's daughter compares her lifestyle to that of North American kids at school, she is not always happy. She realizes that her parents' expectations of her may be higher and that she is practicing piano far longer than anyone else she knows—aside from a couple of friends whose parents are also Chinese. Selena organizes most of their family get-togethers with other Chinese families whose parenting values and expectations match theirs. When Selena's daughter spends time with their children, she can feel more of a kinship. Being around these friends, Selena feels that she is a normal parent.

Selena says that she feels strongly enough about her approach to stick with it, despite what other parents expect from their children. She does realize, however, that her daughter may feel that she is different than her peers. Kids sometimes have a difficult time if they are raised seeing one world inside of their home and another outside of their home. They are often torn between feelings of duty and devotion toward family versus wanting to be more like their friends. This may cause them to rebel.

This past summer, Selena's daughter spent 8 weeks at home with her grandparents and younger sibling while her parents worked. Selena reluctantly enrolled her in 2 weeks of day camp at the encouragement of a Canadian friend and was glad she did. This was her daughter's first experience at any kind of summer program. Even though Selena was afraid of her daughter being exposed to too much sun, drowning during swim lessons, and not eating enough lunch, she realized that "it is too boring at home. This is a big step for me. I'm trying to be normal."

Selena is confronted by her new normal every day. She is very conscious of that which she wants to hold onto and that which she knows she has to change in order for their family to fit in.

When asked to discuss what was normal in China as compared to North America, she says, "In China, kids are more protected. We prefer that grandparents take care of our children." She also says that most Chinese children sleep with their parents until they are 5 or 6, but that this is often because space in their homes is at a premium.

Another difference she has noticed since arriving in North America is that Chinese people don't express their feelings very much. "We are very reserved, even with our children and husbands. My parents never said 'I love you' when we were young, so I don't tell my children that I love them either. I love my daughter so much in my heart. I feel sad because I love her so much but I'm not used to expressing feelings—either good or bad. Now that I see other people being more emotional, I'm trying to show more emotion. When she plays piano, I sit with her and try to encourage her. I sometimes hold her and kiss her and say, 'You are good, I like you, I'm so proud of you.'"

Selena's daughter, having grown up in North America, may be more comfortable with expressing emotion. When she says "I hate you" to her mother, Selena is deeply hurt and feels that she is not a good mother. I shared personal experiences with her that helped her realize that she was not alone. I also offered my opinion about reading between the lines. I suggested that instead of being upset by her daughter's words, she could say something like: "You're angry at me for not giving you a cookie before supper. It's hard to be a kid because there's often an adult standing in your way."

I was deeply moved as Selena shared her story with me. Despite her reserved façade, she was quite tearful at times. It was enlightening for me to understand more about her journey towards establishing new norms in her adopted country and culture.

Sushma's Story

Sushma is 37 years old and has two children, ages 12 and 7, both born in North America. She was born and raised in Delhi, India, moved to Canada in 1999 and then to New York in 2006, where she is requalifying as a dentist at New York University.

When Sushma and her family lived in Toronto, we were neighbors, and I became spoiled by her delicious Chai tea, the likes of which I have not since tasted. Recently, we spoke long distance about her definition of normal and how her upbringing differed from the way in which she and her husband are raising their children.

Sushma believes that "most parents in India today are a little less involved in the upbringing of their kids, especially in the metropolitan cities. They are busy working and have the resources to have full-time nannies. The families have become nuclear, so I see a shift there. I was raised differently in that my mom left her job to raise her family."

Sushma has chosen to weave strands of her upbringing and culture into her children's lives. Both children speak English and Hindi and follow religious and cultural observances with their parents.

Sushma's children never slept in a crib, but instead slept in their parents' bed with them. Even as they grow, children are not rushed into their own bedrooms. "There are a few Indian families I know, influenced by Western trends, who are starting to put kids in cribs when they are born but in my experience, it's rare. Another thing is that we never sleep back to back with our kids, we always have the kid's back towards our belly or our face towards the child—that way the mother has her eye on the child all the time."

When it comes to eating, Sushma says that "the mother, father, or grandparents will feed the child for a number of years. It's a way of showing love and making sure that the child has good food. Kids are lazy when it comes to eating; at the first feeling of being full, they want to shove the plate away. So I'm not aware of Indian parents encouraging kids to eat on their own for quite some time. It's acceptable to hand or spoon feed your child for at least the first 4 years of life, but we also wouldn't think twice if the child was 6 years old and we had to feed him or her. At first, I was surprised when I noticed a North American parent giving a spoon to a child when he was only 1 year old. He was sitting in a high chair, which is something we wouldn't even use. The child would be on our lap."

I asked Sushma how she would feel if someone made comments about her child sleeping in their bed or being spoon-fed. "I would still feel comfortable that I was doing it. I would just accept it as a difference in the way that we choose to parent. I don't let many things influence me when it comes to bringing up my kids. Actually, I see a lot of my peers acting as confused parents; they change themselves so suddenly when they move here and then they complain that the kids are not behaving as they think they should or as they want them to."

"For example," Sushma said, "one of the women I know was very happy buying her daughter the skimpiest dresses when she was little. Now that the girl is older, she is comfortable wearing that type of clothing, but the mom is not comfortable because modesty is stressed in India. If friends or family visit from back home, she does not want her daughter to dress that way." But it may be too late. In an effort to fit in, to conform to the norm, this parent may have tossed certain values aside. When she wanted to go back, even temporarily, her child was not willing to comply.

MODERN TIMES

As tradition is filtered down through the generations, so parenting the way of one's parents and grandparents becomes more and more diluted. Reena, a 27-year-old with a 1-year-old, was born in Canada. Her mom and dad were born in India. When asked how she was planning on raising her son, she said that she is "raising him more Canadian than Indian." Reena said that when she was being raised, it was normal for Indian parents to give their babies pureed adult food at 3 months. "My mom and mother-in-law encouraged me to do the same, but all the Canadian books say 6 months, so I decided to stick with what I read and what my doctor said."

Asked how her parents deal with their daughter not following tradition, Reena says that "they understand but don't agree. I do make Indian food for my son, I just don't put salt in it, even though they say I should." Unlike Sushma, who was born and raised in India, this first-generation Canadian mom has her son in a crib and uses a high chair.

STRONG RELIGIOUS CONVICTIONS

Along with exploring how culture affects norms, I was interested in knowing more about how children who have been raised by parents with strong religious convictions grow up to parent their own children.

Carroll's Story

Carroll MacIntosh and her husband have been ministering in churches all over North America and in England for more than 25 years. They are now pastors just north of Toronto, Ontario. They have three grown children and three grandchildren. Carroll's father was a pastor, too. "We were called PK's or preacher's kids," she said.

Carroll didn't like growing up as a PK. They lived right beside the church so people had access to their dad 24 hours a day, and she felt like she was under a microscope. "Everyone expects the pastor's kids to be perfect. Dad felt the pressure too. I know that because he made it look like we were the perfect pastor family—like we were children who were totally obedient and said, 'Yes, father, whatever you say.'"

When she became the wife of a pastor, something she swore she would never do, she didn't want her kids growing up feeling as she had. "I was very clear with our congregants that my kids were just like their kids—they'd do goofy stuff and get into trouble. I asked that they not place expectations on them that they had to be perfect role models for all the other kids, although of course I hoped they would be."

Carroll's normal was having "my father's friends come over and spend hours of the day in prayer. I remember wondering as a kid what they had to pray so much about, and yet when one friend in particular got up to minister, you'd think it was God standing there. I've seen pupils forming in eyes; blind eyes open, deaf and dumb people begin talking. My own father had leukemia, and the doctors gave him 2 months to live; this friend came up, and he rebuked the spirit of leukemia in Jesus' name and it left—the doctor called it an instantaneous remission. That was 41 years ago, and Dad will soon be 85."

Being exposed to many "miracles," Carroll says that the "fear of God was put into me." She says it's a good fear because it keeps you out of trouble. "Even when I wanted to be rebellious I couldn't rebel against God because I saw and knew too much." Carroll prays for guidance when being challenged as a parent. She recalled "a few years back when my son was visiting a new youth group, and my husband went to pick him up and couldn't find him. I prayed to God to show me where he was and I found him. I was able to see a staircase at the end of hallway and my son necking with a girl with dark, curly hair under the stairway. When I confronted him about it later, I told him that the girl had a seductive spirit and to stay away from her because she was bad news. He was so scared that I had seen so much that he agreed. I wish that God showed me more things like that!"

When Carroll speaks about her children, she says "I don't own them. I am only a steward. One day I will stand in front of God, and he will ask me what I did with these kids." Carroll's strong religious convictions lead her to parent the way she does. Her parenting practices are based on the way in which she was raised and the lifestyle she has chosen. Not everyone she knows follows the same path when parenting and, of course, her normal may be different than theirs. She says they hang out with other religious families a lot "but even within the same church, parents can vary a lot in how they parent. We knew a mom who thought that it was the Holy Spirit's job to raise her kid, and so she wouldn't discipline her kids herself.

They were crying out for boundaries but she said, 'No, the Lord can speak to them and change their heart.'" Carroll was very upset by this and tried to convince her to act differently.

Carroll takes her job of parenting and grandparenting very seriously. She believes that a lot of parents appear to think of parenting as a hobby that they do in their spare time. She says that she and her husband chose to live very simply so that she could stay at home with the kids. "It isn't just about having babies—it's about raising good people, which takes a lot of time," she says. "Those foundational years that the kids don't remember are like the foundation of your house. You may not see it, but it's holding the house up."

When asked about her definition of a normal parent, Carroll says that she sees a lot of parents feeling pressure to be like everybody else. "They often go into major debt when they first get married. They buy a big house and fancy furniture and cars. They're both working and when the kids come along, they don't have much time for them. They miss the joy of every single day. I say that every day is a gift—that's why they call it the present. You have no guarantee of tomorrow with your kids."

Carroll's normal is to "train up a child in the way he should go and when he is old, he'll not depart from it. That's scripture," she says. And she isn't departing from her beliefs and values either.

Goldie's Story

Goldie was also raised by parents with strong religious convictions.

Goldie Plotkin grew up in Brooklyn, New York in a very observant Jewish home. She was one of 10 children. Today she is married to a rabbi and together, they lead the Chabad Markham congregation and help their community in Thornhill, Ontario, just north of Toronto. As well as being an incredibly inspirational speaker on parenting and marriage, she is also director of their preschool and involved with adult education. She is also a devoted wife and mother to her eight children and a role model to many who are fortunate to know her. When I asked Goldie if she had ever wondered about being a normal parent, she said, "I wouldn't wonder about that because I have incredible role models, so I'm very confident with what I am doing. I also have the Torah, which is my very definite guideline; when I open up the code of Jewish law, Talmud or Customs, God is very clear about the role of a parent and the role of a child, and it takes a lot of the guesswork out. When you don't have doubt, you can be very confident."

I then asked about the Torah's definition of a parent. "A parent," she says, "is given the responsibility to raise children to be moral, ethical, and godly people in this world, and a parent has to be that compass to guide their children to fulfill their potential. Each one of my eight children is very different, and I believe each one was brought into this world to accomplish something different. My husband and I have the responsibility to look at each as a whole child and recognize each of their abilities and strengths. God gave them personality, character, and capabilities. Along with what God gave them, we as parents have to bring out their best."

She also shared that the Torah says that children should only see pure and holy things; she says, "that means that the pictures up in their room should be pictures of things that are precious and kind." I thought of the *High School Musical* posters stuck to the wall of my 8-year-old's bedroom when Goldie talked about a poster of a heartthrob on the wall of her friend's teenage daughter's room. "So when she lies in bed, this is what she sees. How healthy is that?" I felt guilty for a few seconds before reminding myself that although I fundamentally agree with what Goldie is saying, my family's normal is quite different than hers.

When Goldie offers premarital counseling, her focus is on communication. She and her husband believe that if children are brought up in a home where the parents have a strong relationship, good communication, respect, and love for one another, then children can overcome any obstacle. She believes that during the first few years of a child's life, in particular, they "need a lot of physical love and attention, a lot of eye connection—like looking through to the soul of the child. No matter how wonderful a nanny or a babysitter can be, they don't love your child like you. Yes, the child will be diapered and fed but the vitamin L, the love, they can't get that like they can get from a parent."

As the mother of eight, Goldie doesn't have time for "manicures, pedicures, or going to movies." She says that her existence as a mother is maybe more selfless. "I have to devote more time to homework and giving my children private time every night. During the day, if I have an extra hour, I'll pick up one of my kids and take them out of school for lunch. We each have 24 hours in a day, and some of us waste it away."

Goldie believes that our role as parents is to raise kids who are "productive, honest, caring human beings. We're not here just to amass wealth or to go to the gym. Our number one job is to bring up our children." She says that some parents who have a lot of outside interests ask how she has time for eight kids. She thinks the question is "What are you making time for? For your own needs or for the kids?" Goldie may not fit the norm in that she is one of the most selfless parents I have spoken to. This does not concern her, though. With religious convictions and a very specific view of her role, she is not swayed by the thoughts or actions of other parents around her.

Goldie says, "when I look at the children in the Western world, I am never tempted to change my ways. Instead, I look at them and say, 'Oy vey.'"

It appears that parenting with firm religious or cultural beliefs often helps a parent feel less doubtful and more self-confident. North America is a melting pot for people from many different countries and cultures. Whether you are an immigrant or were born here, embrace or abandon your parents' religious or cultural beliefs, or find a way to harmonize the two, it's important to keep an open mind. What may be normal to you may not be to others and vice versa. The questions that often remain are: do you feel as if you belong and if not, why not? Are you willing to cast aside what you believe in so that you can feel a greater sense of belonging, or would you prefer to surround yourself with people who are like minded or accept who you are? I hope that you will find your answers while reading this book.

7

Being Judged

~

THIRTY YEARS AFTER being separated, my mother and her best friend, Gayle, were reunited. Gayle came to visit from South Africa and we spent hours catching up. I was only 15 when we left South Africa and knew Gayle through the eyes of a teenager. Now grown, I was able to fully appreciate the depth of her wisdom, both as a person and a parent to four grown children.

Sitting at my kitchen table, discussing the trials and tribulations of parenting, Gayle said, "Society is quick to point an invisible finger at parents. Sara, it's time that someone stood up and defended parents—moms in particular, who are always blamed for everything that goes wrong with their children but are never given credit when things go right."

> When I asked parents whether they ever felt that other parents were judgmental of their behavior towards their children, more than half the respondents (59 percent) said yes.

One parent reflected on her attitude and recognized that although she did not like being evaluated by others, she realized that "when I think someone is being too relaxed as a parent, maybe they see me as too anal. Maybe I am too uptight and they are just right. So when I am pointing a finger at others, I guess I also need to look at myself."

Janet Chan, mother of two, editorial director for the Parenting Group and editor in chief of *Parenting* magazine in the United States, agrees that "most moms don't think that they are judgmental, but I think we all are. I also think that most moms feel that they are being judged by others. It starts when you're pregnant. Your belly is an invitation for people to lean over, give you unsolicited advice, and to tell you what the right answer is—the right stroller, the right diaper, the time to put your child to bed, or whether the child should sleep with you."

Although clients often ask me to evaluate or give my opinion, I tell them that I am not a judge. I am a listener, a facilitator, a guide. I work hard at remaining neutral. Sometimes this is difficult—especially when I feel a negative reaction to something a parent has shared with me. Even then, I try to respond in a caring, compassionate manner. I ask questions to help my clients self-evaluate rather than expressing my opinion. No one likes to be judged, especially when they are looking for support and understanding.

PERSONAL REFLECTION

I am not immune to being concerned about being judged. Living and working in the same community has its pros and cons. It's great living within walking distance of both my office and my daughters' schools. However, there's rarely a week that goes by that I don't bump into a client outside the school, in the park, at the local supermarket, hairdresser, or bookstore. I prefer to hang my professional hat on the door of my office so that when I bump into clients, it's as a neighbor.

I must admit, though, that I am sometimes self-conscious about how I appear in public and wonder whether others are looking at me and my children to see how we behave. I do not expect my children to be angels. I expect that my 16-year-old will sometimes give me attitude and that my 8-year-old will sometimes plead and whine. If this behavior happens to emerge in the company of a client, I remind myself that I too am human and that my clients likely appreciate seeing that like all parents, I am sometimes challenged by my children.

Dr. Ari Novick, a licensed marriage and family therapist and parent educator in California, agrees that it is normal to be concerned about what others are thinking of you. He feels, like me, that parents trained in the mental health or parenting fields may be even more self-critical. He comforts himself with reminders that he "can't be an expert in every parental situation. No one can. I've lost my temper with my son, felt badly after I'd raised my voice and wished I hadn't." Despite this, when he asks himself, "Does this make me a bad father?" his answer is, "Absolutely not. "

OUT IN PUBLIC

Dr. Novick says that in everyday life he tries not "to judge other people's parenting because you never quite know what the situation is with their particular child. For example, sometimes you'll see a mom or dad scolding a child in a restaurant and you may think to yourself, 'Oh, that's so awful. They're being so mean.' But you never know what the rules are or what happened before you looked in."

Restaurants are often a great source of stress for parents, especially if they don't cater to families. As much as you may want to teach your children proper etiquette at fancier establishments, it's often not worth the price you pay—and I'm not talking about money.

Supermarkets are equally unnerving for many parents. Please-can-I-have-items that are purposely placed at the height of a 5-year-old just to drive parents crazy. A supermarket manager I recently spoke to said that their store had actually created candy-free checkout aisles for parents who want to whiz through without having to deal with meltdowns. And which parent hasn't felt eyes burn a hole into her back as strangers stare aghast at the child who is lying on her back, screaming at the top of her lungs and refusing to budge because her parent has refused her demands for the latest and greatest gadget?

IT'S ALL RELATIVE

Next to total strangers, our relatives are the harshest critics. Once, when my teenage daughter stormed off mid-conversation, slamming the door behind her, my father was quick to ask how I could *allow* her to get away with that sort of behavior. He said that he thought that I should know better.

Our parents often parented from a more authoritarian approach that included sentiments such as children should be seen but not heard and wait until your father gets home. Today's parents tend to be more democratic, sometimes even permissive. Our parents may take exception to us raising our children in a manner that is quite different than the one in which they raised us. They may feel personally offended by this and judge us because they think that their way of raising children was the right way and the better way. After all, they remind us, we turned out alright!

Conversely, our parents may not be impressed if we treat our children more harshly than they did and may want to protect their grandchildren. If your parents side with your child, you will likely feel angry at them and resent their involvement. Their alliance with your child will likely make you feel undermined and humiliated.

One of my adult clients is a single mom who moved into her parents' home with her child shortly after she and her husband separated. She found this very difficult and said that her son had a hard time knowing who to join forces with because his mom and grandparents' approaches to parenting were so different. There was so much conflict between my client and her parents that she realized she had taken him from one unhealthy home to another. I helped her to establish clear guidelines and boundaries with her parents.

She explained that even though they didn't always agree or approve of the way she parented, she would appreciate their support in front of her son. She also agreed to remain open to their suggestions about parenting him when he was not around to hear what they had to say. I assured my client that her resentment and anger at being harshly criticized by her parents was very normal. It is often difficult to move back in with one's parents, especially when you have children of your own.

In the same way you asked your mom or dad if they liked a picture you had drawn as a child, you want their approval for the way in which you have raised your child. When you don't get it, and especially if you get their disapproval, you will likely feel as if you are not good enough. As a way of seeking approval, some adults will parent differently in front of their own parents than when in the company of peers, for example. A client once shared with me that although he normally allowed his children to drink soda at meals, he refused their requests at his parents' home and told them to drink water instead. He realized that he did not want to be put down by his parents for giving his kids something he knew they disapproved of. This confused his children, he said, and often led to disagreements. We talked about ways in which my client could assert himself so that his behavior would be more consistent and so that his children felt supported by him.

Dana, 42, is the mother of a 9-year-old daughter. She says that she doesn't usually let her family's opinion affect the way she parents her daughter. "The only thing that I care about is when they judge me because my daughter is overweight. They think that I should control every little thing she eats." So even though Dana is a very educated and aware parent, she has begun to second-guess herself every time her daughter eats something that is high in calories.

Dana says that other people pass judgment about her daughter's weight too. She says that "when there are people around, I find it especially hard because I see them watching me let her eat an ice cream sandwich, for example, and I know they're asking, 'Why would that mother let her child eat ice cream?'"

When you feel evaluated and judged by others, especially those closest to you, it's very normal to be hard on yourself. Even the most confident parent is prone to second-guessing herself. Sometimes all it takes is a look or a comment from a friend or family member to hit you where you're most vulnerable. Normally, the first response to any form of criticism is to feel anger or resentment toward the judge.

Reena, at 27, is the mother of a 1-year-old. When he was 7 months old, her mom said that she should begin toilet training him. Reena did not do as her mom suggested. She says that if she was raising her son in India, which is where her mom was raised, she would be judged for not doing her job well. Her mother-in-law, also raised in India, realizes that toilet training in North America is different. Reena says that she will not allow herself to be judged and pressured by tradition.

Her husband Nitin supports her. "I always ask Reena if she feels good about what she is doing, and I encourage her not to worry about what other people are saying," he says. "There will always be a thousand people telling you different things. I'm not afraid of being judged as long as I feel good about what I am doing."

INFLUENCED TO CHANGE

> When I asked parents how influenced they were to change their behavior as a result of how they perceived others regarding them as parents, the majority of parents said "not much" or "very little." And when I asked parents if they had ever not shared a secret about their thoughts or feelings for fear of not being considered normal by others, three-quarters said no.

Some of the concealed secrets from those who were concerned about being judged as not normal included one mom being worried that her son would some day be gay, another admitted to finding playtime boring, and one mom said that she sometimes yelled at her baby to stop crying.

JUDGING OTHERS

Pam, 41 and mother of a 3-year-old, says that she is usually not a judgmental person but is often critical and can't relate to parents "who don't seem to care if their children get bruised by falling because they want them to learn by trial and error. They just seem so casual in their approach." Those other parents may, in turn, judge Pam for being overly involved.

Pam admits that there are "probably fewer parents like me around but I have connected with some like-minded parents. I've learned to separate myself from the pack mentality of parenting and to not feel bullied. I do feel that I come across differently when I'm part of a group of parents."

"I was recently at a company picnic for parents and their kids. We were near a big park near a pond and the ocean and there was a kid running far, far away over a hill, near the pond. The mom was nowhere to be found, so I chased after this kid and herded her back. I was running as fast as I could to catch up with her and when we returned, I found the mom sitting down eating her lunch with a 'whatever' attitude. I didn't blame the child for the mom's indifference and I tried to engage her in play with my child. When she pushed my child I tried to help them talk about their feelings. I didn't want to discipline the child, but the mom was totally nonresponsive and didn't say a word. The child was looking at me as if I was really weird—you could tell that negotiation wasn't something that her parents did. Then my son, who was trying to make things better between them, picked some dandelions and gave them to her. The final straw was when she grabbed them, threw them to the ground, and stomped on them. I can't understand parents who are so removed. They'd rather hang out with their friends and let their children run wild than get involved."

Pam says that on another occasion she was leaving the parking lot of a grocery store and "watched a guy in a pick-up truck pull into a parking space and then leave his two little kids in the car while he went into a beer store." She watched and waited for him to return before she left. Although Pam believes that we, as parents, should all watch out for each other's children, she feels that she is in the minority.

Parents stand in judgment of their peers for many other reasons. One mom wrote to tell me that she has seen many mothers "who are nonmaternal, and I don't consider them 'normal' parents. I don't think that they care about their kids. One didn't help her young adolescent girl through her period, another didn't send lunches to school for her young son, and another didn't dress her son warmly enough on a very cold day. I feel that many parents are too occupied with their own activities. It makes me wonder why they had children. I feel sorry for the kids. I hate to see a child hurting or in need when the situation could so easily be avoided with a different attitude by the parent. But it would be tricky to get involved, so I just watch and get upset and angry."

WHEN OUR CHILDREN JUDGE US

Next to our parents and peers, our children are often harsh critics. When they are really young, we can do no wrong. We could commit a crime and they wouldn't seem to mind. As they grow, children see the world and us through different eyes. An older child, for example, may show anger or disapproval if she feels that her younger sibling is being parented differently than she was at that age. "You never let me do that!" she may protest. It's true that parents may discipline their children differently, sometimes because of differences in the children's personalities, their position in the family, or as a result of a shift in one's approach to parenting.

Although children's perceptions are often quite accurate and valid, it is also important to remain true to yourself and stand firm depending on the situation. Children often find very clever ways to manipulate their parents into changing their minds. An old trick is trying to convince you that you are a mean, bad parent because every other parent has allowed their child his request.

> When I asked parents "Do you ever give into your child because he or she says that other parents are letting their child do what your child is requesting of you— even though you would have preferred not to have consented to that activity", 33 percent said yes.

So, if you feel that you are sometimes being manipulated, you are in good company.

In fact, upon further exploration, you may find that the other parents are in exactly the same boat as yourself. If you really would prefer that your child not go to a party or to the mall, for example, remain firm but fair. If you give in to avoid being hated by your child, you run the risk of sliding down that slippery slope to the land of no return where children don't tolerate limits and you're angry at yourself for being a pushover parent.

Young or older, experienced or not, we are all vulnerable to the comments and criticisms of our peers, parents, relatives, children, and strangers. The people whose opinion you value most will affect you more. You may be able to allow the opinions of strangers to let slide off your back.

If you are a more experienced parent or a parent who has had children later in life, then you may be less likely to let others' opinions affect you as much. If you have taken parenting classes or been educated in a field that is related to child development, you are more likely to have realistic expectations of what is normal when parenting and again, more inclined to be your own judge.

Next time you start to judge something that a parent is saying or doing, remember the words of my dear friend Gayle who shared a message with me that her grandmother passed down to her. "You never know a person until you've eaten a bag of salt with him or her . . . and it takes a lifetime to eat a bag of salt, one pinch at a time."

8

Feeling Bad When You're Mad

(and Other Guilt-Ridden Emotions)

⟋⟍

YEARS AGO, WHEN I first began creating book titles in my head, I came up with *Guilt and the Working Mother.* I ultimately moved on to other topics, but I often think back to the day I sat in a doctor's waiting room and wrote down chapter ideas. Truth be told, guilt is probably one of the feelings most often experienced by a parent.

Parenting and guilt go together like cookies and milk. There's guilt for:

- having to leave the kids with a nanny to make it to work in time

- leaving your crying toddler at day care
- not making it in time to see your son's launch into stardom on the school stage
- not remembering to send a dollar to school for cupcake day
- not setting a good enough example
- going out for the evening and leaving your kids at home with a sitter
- not working enough hours to contribute your fair share to the household expenses
- going for a massage instead of helping your daughter with her homework
- snapping at your child because you've had an exhausting day
- overreacting to spilled juice or crumbs on the floor
- being impatient, explosive, or saying something you didn't really mean
- wondering what life would have been like without kids

So much guilt, guilt, guilt. But why? As parents, we often feel torn between being available to our children 24/7 versus taking care of ourselves.

> About half of the parents who completed the questionnaire said that they put their own needs ahead of their children. But when they do, their guilt meter often enters the dangerous red zone.

Putting our own needs ahead of the kids is not the only reason we feel guilt. In fact, whenever we experience internal conflict about something we feel we should not have done, or not done something we should have, we feel guilt. Feeling guilty has some merits. First, it says that you have a certain code of behavior that you like to live by, and when you fall short of that, you are not happy with yourself. Guilt may help you rethink your behavior and make changes for the better. Second, guilt means that you are sensitive to the feelings of others, that you are remorseful if you feel you have hurt your child's feelings, for example. This too can encourage positive change.

Although feeling guilty is perfectly normal (psychopaths usually lack feelings of remorse or guilt), too much or too often is not a great thing. Some people are naturally inclined to feel guiltier than others—they may be overly concerned about making other people, their children included, happy. Some parents were raised in an environment where guilt was used as a form of manipulation. For example, if you were raised with comments such as "So you'd prefer to go out with your friends than stay at home with your mother who will be all alone," you may be more inclined to feel guilty for going out and leaving your children at home.

HOW TO MANAGE GUILT

So how do you deal with feelings of guilt? Sometimes, just talking about things out loud can help you realize that your guilt is illogical. For example, when you talk about feeling guilty for not being at home 1 night a week to tuck your child into bed but then remind yourself that you are at home the other 6, you may be able to stop feeling so guilty. Other times, guilt may motivate you to look at making positive changes—adjusting your work schedule so you can share breakfast time with your kids, for example.

Parents often feel guilty when they say something to their child that they don't really mean or when angry words are exchanged. One mom admitted to regretting saying "If you don't shape up, I'll ship you off to boarding school." Other examples included "What did I ever do to deserve a child like you?"; "You're a lazy slob"; and "Don't touch me with those dirty hands" when her child tried to embrace her.

It's true that nasty words or a sarcastic tone can feel as harsh as a slap across a face.

> When parents responded to the questionnaire, 75 percent said that they had, at one time or another, spoken angry words and regretted them later. And when asked, "Have you ever had your child go to bed angry at you and then quietly kissed her as she slept?" almost 65 percent of the parents who responded to the questionnaire said yes.

YOU'RE SO MEAN

Sometimes, the wires between our head and our heart get scrambled. Even though we're smart enough to know that it is wrong, we retaliate in a way that reduces us to our child's level. I'm sure you can think of many times when your son or daughter has pushed just the right (or wrong) button to elicit the worst possible response. For example, when a child says, "I hate you, you're the meanest mother in the whole world," you may want to get even by saying something like "well I don't like you a lot of the time either."

It is best to acknowledge your child's feelings with a response such as "You're really angry at me right not for not allowing you to do what you want." However, we're not always in the right frame of mind or had enough sleep to respond the "right" way.

Ava, a 49-year-old mother of a 12-year-old daughter says that "if I snap at her, I feel guilty." Ava recognizes that she often says things because she is feeling tired or cranky and not because of anything that her daughter has said or done. "I have made it very clear that if

I say things that are inappropriate, that I own them. She is not accountable for how I feel. I tell her that if I say something like 'Leave me alone, I don't want to talk to you now,' that I am sorry and that I know that it is my problem."

INTENSE ANGER

A friend once said, "I hate being around him, he's such a prick." At first I thought she was talking about her husband, but then realized that she was referring to her 5-year-old son. She said that her anger was so intense that she had to lock herself in the bathroom for 10 minutes for fear of what she might do to him. She found it hard to believe that she could feel such mixed emotions toward her child over the course of a day.

Caroline Connell, editor in chief of Canada's *Today's Parent*, said that their magazine ran a piece a few years ago about a woman in British Columbia who was doing some work on mothers and anger. "The mother used some very strong language to describe her feelings—the words 'fuck you' were in there." Connell said that the mom may not have said it out loud but thought it towards her toddler. "We printed this and the response was amazing. Moms were saying, 'So I'm not the only one, thank goodness, how do I get in touch with her, I'm so glad you printed that.'

APOLOGIZING

Kathy Lynn, a Canadian parenting speaker and author, says that parents often ask her if they should apologize to their kids for what they have said or done. She says yes. She also reminds parents that everybody blows it from time to time and not to worry so much. However, she says that if they find themselves apologizing a lot, then they need to consider what else is going on. Kathy says that perhaps they're not rested enough to respond appropriately or there's something else going on in their lives.

While we're on the subject of apologies, keep in mind that it is not a good idea to go on bended knees and plead for your child's forgiveness. Although there may be times that an apology is in order, it is important that children not see their parents demeaning themselves. For example, if a parent were to say to her child, "I'm a really bad mommy, aren't I? I would understand if you didn't think I was doing a very good job," then the child may be frightened by the position that his parent has taken. Children need to know that they are being taken care of by competent, confident parents— even if we don't always feel we are.

When parents come together in a support group, the conversation inevitably turns to concerns about how to manage their anger. At one such group, a dad admitted to the insanity of screaming uncontrollably at his 6-year-old about restraining her temper. Another mom admitted to having grabbed her daughter's hair and holding onto it as her daughter tried to run away in the grocery store. "I feel terrible when I lose my patience with my daughters," said one mother. "I worry about the impact I have had on them for a long time afterwards."

FEARS OF HURTING A CHILD

As the child and family therapist expert at www.canadianparents. com, I am often sent detailed questions from concerned parents looking for reassurance that they are normal or doing the right thing. One post entitled "Please help me with this child" was from the mom of a 4-year-old who had been very "rambunctious" since the age of 1. The mom wrote that she felt that his behavior was getting worse. Toward the middle of her message she wrote, "He gets me so angry and so upset . . . sometimes I feel like I can hurt him and then I doubt myself as a parent and I ask why am I feeling this way about my child? Why am I thinking hurtful thoughts? Why am I contemplating giving him up for adoption?" The mom went on to say that she did not want to continue feeling this way. Her pleas for help sounded desperate.

As cute and irresistible as babies can be, most parents know that as children grow, there sometimes seems to be a monster living inside them. At times like these, there are no logical words to calm that demon. Try as you might to use humor, pleading, consoling, or consequences, nothing works. It's times like these that parents often have an overwhelming desire to take drastic action—like shaking their child or using their physical strength to force compliance.

One of my clients admitted to feeling that she was not normal to think negative thoughts about her kids. She felt especially different because of her extended family members' reactions. They say, "Oh no, we've never had those feelings." So are hateful, angry thoughts normal? Of course.

> In fact, over 30 percent of parents who answered the questionnaire said that they had thoughts or fears of hurting their child. Most said that these thoughts were only fleeting—lasting only a few seconds. Some said that they lasted from 5 minutes to half an hour, and one parent said that her thoughts sometimes lasted for days.

Beth, a 46-year-old mother of three children ages 14, 13, and 10, shared a story about the time when her eldest child was 12. Beth says that "she was being so completely belligerent and would not go to her room when I told her to. So I literally pushed her upstairs and into her room and then afterwards I was sick about it. She was crying and shouting that she was going to call 911, and that's when I thought, 'I'm not a normal parent.'"

I asked Beth what it was that made her feel not normal. "My anger," she said. "Sometimes I don't feel that I have enough control over my anger." Beth compares herself to her friends who seem so much more easy going. "Then again," she says, "their kids never go to bed. Maybe they're too relaxed. Our household has many more rules than theirs." Beth believes that her children's defiance is "normal, but it's my anger and the way that I deal with things that may not be."

Dana, a 42-year-old mother of a 9-year-old, shared how badly she felt about losing her patience with her daughter when they were out for dinner and she was eating with her hands and blowing bubbles in her milk. "I feel even worse when I reprimand her when there are other people around," she said. "I sometimes wonder if I'm too hard on my child. Should it really matter if a child eats food with her fingers?"

DO YOU LIKE YOUR CHILD?

Recently, a parent and her 11-year-old son came to see me. She had called because her son was getting into fights at school. When I observed them together, I noticed that they did not seem connected. They sat on opposite couches and the mother didn't show any empathy towards her child. Instead of listening to his story about a disagreement he had with a friend at school, she interrupted with questions such as, "What did you do to make him cry?"

After half an hour, I asked the child to wait outside the room so that I could talk to his mother alone. When I asked her to describe her son, she was only able to do so with negative adjectives. I asked,

"Do you like your son?" She looked at me as if I was crazy. "Of course. I love him. He's my child."

"You may love him," I continued, "but do you like him?"

She seemed stunned and sat without speaking for a few seconds. I broke the silence by saying that not every parent likes her child. Slowly, she relaxed against the back of the couch, started to cry and shared feelings of disappointment and resentment about her only child. Afterward, she told me how relieved she was to have shared her feelings out loud.

PARENTS SHARE MORE STORIES

David, a 36-year-old father of a 4-year-old son, works with children in the mental health field. He shared a story about when he was at a restaurant with his son. "I was getting really angry at him for tasting and then refusing to eat the blintzes he had asked for. Then when I took a little taste, I realized that he was right. I apologized and said, 'Daddy made a mistake, you were right, the cheese is sour.'"

Molly, a 55-year-old mother of three children, ages 19, 17, and 13, says that she feels "bad when I get angry over a situation like the kids not doing their schoolwork and wanting to play computer games or watch TV instead." Molly has learned that it is sometimes best to remove herself from the situation before it escalates. In fact, putting yourself in "time out" is often what I recommend to parents. Not as a form of punishment, of course, but as an opportunity to compose yourself and return to the scene from a different perspective.

Natasha, a 33-year-old mother of two children, ages 9 and 6, says that "I feel guilty about not being able to control my anger better at times. I have lost control and hit my oldest son on a few occasions when he has pushed me to the edge. When he hits me or hurts me physically, it triggers anger going back to my childhood. It reminds me of when my brother used to hit me, and I would go into a rage and not be able to control my actions."

"Through lots of parenting courses, therapy, and self-will, it has not happened in a long time, and I hope that it will never happen again. I understand that it does not work and does not set a good example. We have worked very hard to teach him not to be aggressive, so we have to be good role models."

> Almost 25 percent of parents who responded to the questionnaire admitted to telling their children that if they would hit them if they didn't stop hurting their brothers or sisters.

However, I am sure that many realize that modelling aggression only encourages more of the same behavior in a child.

Ilana is a 47-year-old mother of five children between the ages of 3 and 22. She says that "when my son was about 8 years old, I used to end every day in tears because of my relationship with him, and it used to make me feel like an evil mother. Every night I would vow to myself that tomorrow I would not hit, smack, insult, or pull at him, but I just couldn't stick to it. He used to push all the wrong buttons with me."

"Now that he is 19, we are wonderful together; I am no longer mad at myself for being angry or short-tempered with him or, call me barbaric, for smacking him at times. What I would love to erase is the shame I carry for letting him feel that he was disappointing me. I will have to live with that huge mistake. We have had many discussions on that issue, and I hope he understands that I was young and a bit immature and didn't realize what a gift he was."

LEARNING AND GROWING

Normal parents are often quick to show temper, impatient, moody, easily frustrated, annoyed, and hurt by their children's behavior or words. Part of growing as a parent is learning how to think before we talk or act and figuring out how to respond to our emotions in a way that is not harmful to our children and leaves us feeling proud of ourselves.

An excellent resource for helping us learn more about ourselves, our anger, and how it impacts our kids is *When Anger Hurts Your Kids*. Co-authored by Matthew McKay, Kim Paleg, Patrick Fanning and Dana Landis, the authors write that their book "is a result of a two-year study of 285 parents—normal, regular parents much like you, with normal, regular, infuriating kids much like yours." They found that "two-thirds of the parents reported feeling anger to the point of shouting or screaming at their children an average of five times per week. These were normal parents with normal children, but the majority had an intense anger episode nearly every day." Following their research, the authors put together a "master plan for anger control," which is laid out in their book.

PERSONAL REFLECTION

I was recently reminded of how my emotional reactions, triggered by my child's behavior, can lead me down a path I hadn't intended to wander. It was late on a chilly evening and our family was driving home from an evening out with friends. I had chosen to sit in the back seat of the car to keep our 8-year-old from falling asleep. The windows of the car were slightly frosted, a perfect palette for little children to trace patterns and words. When I looked over at my daughter, I noticed the letters "I L."

Remembering that we had just cleaned the car, I opened my

mouth to ask her to stop what she was doing so that smudge marks would not be left on the window. Something stopped me, though. I bit my tongue and boy, am I grateful I did. I watched as she continued to write "I LOVE YOU." "Look, Mom," she said, not realizing that I had been watching all the time. "I wrote this for you." Had I interrupted her for the sake of a clean window, I would not have been touched by three of the most precious words a parent can hear from her child. What a valuable life lesson I learned.

9

I'll Be There in a Minute
(and Other Lies We Tell Our Children)

PARENTS OFTEN ASK me why their children lie. Although my answer may be different for each family, there is a common thread between most. Children lie because they are afraid of the consequences when telling the truth. The same is true for parents.

I recognize that there are all sorts of lies—big black lies like denying an extramarital affair, gray lies like calling in sick to work and then spending the day at the casino or denying that you smoke when your 12-year-old accuses you of doing so, and smaller white lies such as when you tell your child that you're out of chocolate to avoid a temper tantrum when you deny her request for more.

Within the realm of being afraid of telling the truth, most lies fall into the following categories: protecting your children from the truth, trying to keep peace (by avoiding conflict or confrontation), and evading the truth.

PROTECTION FROM THE TRUTH

Do you like my picture?

Most parents can remember a time when their child asked for their opinion about a hand-drawn picture. Even if you didn't think that your child showed a great deal of talent, your instinct was most likely to say something like "I love it." Children are very wise and know when you are not being genuine. In response, your child might have said "But you didn't even look!" And he may have been right.

One way to help your child trust in your response would be to take a minute or so to really look at the drawing and then, instead of commenting on the final product, say something about the process. For example, you might say "I like the way that you drew a black circle around the yellow sun to make it stand out. I also like the red shirt on the boy in the picture. It reminds me of the shirt you wore to your last birthday party." This will help your child feel like your response was not a lie or a brush-off, but an honest reflection of what you have seen.

Even if you don't really like the overall look, you can usually find one or two details to comment on. I call this the "needle in a haystack approach." By focussing on what you genuinely feel are strengths and ignoring the overall effect, you will not be lying, but rather encouraging future creative endeavours.

Mommy, are you going to die?

A mother of a 6-year-old shared a story about a time when her husband returned from work and told her that a colleague's husband had died. Their son walked into the room and, seeing his dad's sad expression, asked, "What happened?" The mother responded, "Daddy's friend is very sick and in hospital." She didn't feel that it was appropriate for him to know the real story. Similarly, when he asks, "Mommy, are you going to die?" she says no. She says that she prefers to keep his 6-year-old innocence. She says that will tell him the truth one day, but not at 6.

When then? There is no magical age at which a child is 100 percent ready to hear the absolute truth to this question. However, it is typically around the age of 6 and up that children ask questions about mortality. As children grow older and become more aware of the cycle of life, such as when they experience the death of a pet (raise your hand if you've ever replaced a goldfish to prevent your child from suffering the loss of his beloved pet), they may be more ready to hear truthful, age, appropriate responses to this delicate question.

Some parents shared that when the time was right to tell the truth, they softened the blow with something like, "Yes, I am going to die one day, but that is not going to happen for a long, long, long time." Sometimes, that's all a child needs to comfort him.

Is the tooth fairy real?

Most parents respond with "Yes, of course she is."

Children (and many adults) love fantasy, things magical and extraordinary. The tooth fairy, Santa Claus, ghosts, and goblins are all part of this. One tradition, generally passed down through generations, is to place a fallen baby tooth under one's pillow and leave it overnight for the tooth fairy. In exchange, the child is left with money or a small gift. When I was growing up, it was a mouse that took our teeth. My 8-year-old not only receives money but a letter and certificate from the fairy. I think she is more thrilled by the letter than anything else and often leaves a response for the fairy in our mailbox. The elaborate scheme we have to plan in order to retrieve the note and respond to it turns this exercise into quite an event. Only recently has she begun to question whether a tooth fairy actually exists.

"Tell me the truth," she says. "I don't think she's real, is she?" Many thoughts go through my mind as I imagine her response to knowing the truth. On several such occasions, I have come very close to telling her the truth, but I just can't bring myself to. I don't want to shatter the relationship that she has created with the tooth fairy (aka her sister)—at least not until all her baby teeth have fallen out!

By not telling our children the truth about who really leaves them money and notes in the middle of the night, we preserve their image of the fairy and her kingdom where teeth are polished and carved to make castles. We preserve a tradition passed down through generations and don't let them down by acknowledging that we have been lying for years!

On the other hand, by not responding honestly when our children are already on the brink of knowing the truth, we are denying what their intuition, heightened awareness, and intelligence is telling them. We are also opening up the possibility of them not trusting us on future occasions when they beg us to validate if what they are feeling is correct or not.

I suggest that you teach your child to trust herself by acknowledging that she must be feeling unsure, asking what caused her to feel this way and then perhaps telling her the truth. I certainly would not advocate breaking the news before your child initiates the conversation.

You love him more than you love me.
If you are raising more than one child, you will be familiar with this accusation.

Parents will typically respond with "No, I don't. I love you both the same."

Parents feel incredibly guilty if they like one of their children more than the other or if they prefer being with one of their children over the other.

> However, almost 40 percent of the parents who responded to the questionnaire felt that at times, they liked one of their children more than the other.

It is also very normal for a parent to feel that he or she is more compatible with one particular child over the other or that their temperaments are a better match. I have yet to meet a parent who is brutally honest when faced with this question by her child, nor would I recommend it. Can you imagine responding with "Yes, I do prefer your brother"? No matter what your true feelings are, this response would be extremely hurtful and could potentially cause long-term damage to your relationship with your child.

Keep in mind that if your child is asking this question, she has likely picked up on something you are feeling. Children are incredibly intuitive, and her sense of your bias towards her sibling may be true. When she brings it to your attention, your first response is likely to deny what she is feeling. However, this may not comfort or reassure her. In fact, she may then feel that you are not only favoring her brother, but a liar too!

When you are asked this question, you might consider responding with something like: "I love you both differently. You and I get into more arguments, so maybe you feel that I don't love you as much." Or you could respond, "You feel that I might love your brother more than I love you. Can you tell me what I do to make you feel this way?" Depending on her response, you could talk about her feelings right away or ask for some time to reflect on what she has said.

If, after reflection, you conclude that she has just cause for perceiving the situation as she does, you may acknowledge her feelings and say something like, "I've had some time to think things through, and I can see why you sometimes feel that I love your brother more. I can understand why you felt that way when I took his side during an argument that the two of you were having or when I chose to buy chocolate ice cream for him at the supermarket even though you prefer vanilla. Next time, I promise not to blame you just because you are older. I'll let the two of you figure things out unless you need my help. I also promise not to choose the chocolate ice cream just because he and I both prefer it but to flip a coin to make it fair. Even though it may seem that I can relate to your brother more because I was also the youngest in my family and prefer chocolate ice cream, there are many things that I love about being with you. I love the way you make me feel when we laugh at silly things, how kind you are to animals, and how you help me when I cook. You are both special to me in different ways. Next time you feel that I am favoring your brother, please tell me. Even parents make mistakes."

KEEPING PEACE

When your child asks if he can do something, have something, or go somewhere that you'd rather he not, you may lie to avoid temper tantrums, conflict, and confrontation. For example, if your child asks "Can I go on the internet?" and you'd prefer he doesn't, then you may say, "No, the internet is down," when it really isn't!

Sometimes it's easier to come up with an excuse that lays blame on an inanimate object than to take a firm stand and deal with the fallout. However, you run the risk of always having to come up with creative, plausible excuses that lay blame on external sources rather than being able to set limits and deal with your child's reaction. This can be rather exhausting and may not always work. Also, this may only work with younger children. Once he realizes that you have not been truthful, he may not trust your word in other situations.

It may be best to learn strategies for more effective limit setting so that you are prepared to deal with your child's reaction to being told the truth, even if he doesn't like it.

EVADING AND AVOIDING

It's all in the presentation

My friend Barb regularly reminds me that "it's all in the presentation." In other words, we can influence people, our kids included, by the way that we present information to them. We may embellish or leave out certain details to make our argument more convincing. Manipulative or creative, depending on your frame of reference, we sometimes use myths or make up stories to prevent or encourage children from doing exactly what we do or don't want them to. For example, you might tell your child that if she sits too close to the television that she will become blind.

Children are so trusting

A mom-to-be and I were chatting about the impact of our words and behavior on children and how vulnerable they are to information that is shared by parents or people that they trust. She shared a personal experience she had growing up. When she was very young, she wanted to grow her hair very long. Her mother, however, with three young children, all 18 months apart, preferred not to struggle with tangled hair and tears every day. So she convinced her daughter not to grow hers. She told her that if she were to grow her hair long, then all of the food she ate would go towards nourishing her hair and that her body, as a result, would not grow.

The image this conjured in her daughter's mind was so frightening that she never did fulfill her dream of long hair. At 12 years old, she warned a friend of the dangers of growing her hair long. Over 20 years later, this mom-to-be still remembers what a fool she felt when her friend challenged what she had been led to believe.

Reena, a 27-year-old mother of a 1-year-old, remembers when she was 3 years old and her dad lied to her. He had dropped her off in the care of a neighbor and, concerned that she would be upset by his leaving, decided to leave without saying goodbye. He told her that he was going to the bathroom and would be back. When Reena went looking for him, he wasn't there. "I was traumatized," she says.

Delaying the inevitable

If you child asks you to join her class on a school field trip and you say "maybe" when you know that you won't be able to, you may be evading the truth at that moment but delaying inevitable disappointment.

As parents, we feel guilty if we don't participate when our child asks us to. We wonder if we should change our plans to accommodate our child's wishes, even though we prefer not to.

By saying "maybe" we buy time. We may even think that tomorrow might find us in a better frame of mind to deal with the disappointment or nagging.

On the other hand, we give our child false hope by not making a firm commitment and sticking to it. We teach our child to put off for tomorrow what can be done today.

I suggest that if you are completely sure that you cannot go with your child, tell him right away. Acknowledge his disappointment, explain why you can't be there, and deal with the consequences. Don't try to make it all better by offering something in exchange, such as "I'll take you for ice cream this afternoon instead." Disappointment is a part of life and cannot always be soothed by a double mint chocolate chip ice cream (well, maybe!).

Confronting your past

As your children move into the teen years, they may ask you questions about your past. Questions such as "Have you ever smoked pot?" or "Were you a virgin when you were my age?" Typically, parents respond with no to the former and yes to the latter, regardless of the truth.

If you are not telling the truth in regards to drug use, my guess is that your reluctance to do so is because you don't want your teen to get the impression that you are condoning his or her use of illegal drugs. You also don't want to be in the position of your child turning the tables around by reminding you that "you did it, why shouldn't I?"

Mary, a 44-year-old mother of two young teens, lies when her kids ask if she smokes cigarettes. "I don't want them to smoke, but I do occasionally. I know it's very bad modeling." So she sneaks cigarettes behind their backs and tries to camouflage the smell with body spray.

However, what happens if your child overhears your childhood friend reminiscing with you about the time when you were 18 and got high at an all-night party? Or the time when you spent the night at a hotel with your boyfriend? What might your teen think then? Might he decide that you're not to be trusted at all, or is he mature enough to understand your parental desire to shroud him from your not-so-innocent past?

Depending on your child's age, level of maturity, ability to make good decisions, and how influenced he is by his peers, you may decide to answer his or her question truthfully. Find out why he or she wants to know about your past. Keep an open mind. Try to remain nonjudgmental. Keep emotional distance by pretending that you are talking to a good friend's teenager. Once you have considered all of the above, you may decide that being honest is not so bad.

If you decide to be honest about drug use, it may not be wise to go into details about the wild and crazy parties you attended or the special brownies you baked for your parents' friends. Talk about the possible impact of drug use on his wellbeing, the legal implications, and the safety measures he should take if he plans on experimenting. You may also want to talk about what you regretted about taking drugs and how you might do things differently if you could go back in time.

I'll be there in a minute

Most of us are familiar with "Mom, Dad, can you come up here now?" Our response is typically, "I'll be there in a minute."

Many of us use this as a figure of speech without actually considering how long we'll really be. After all, a minute doesn't sound too long, does it? If, however, we said, "I'll be there in 10 minutes," we know that we might have to deal with a tirade of questions such as "Why so long?" or "What are you doing, anyway?"

> In fact, over 90 percent of the parents who responded to the questionnaire admitted to telling their child that they would be there in a minute and really taking ten.

Is it any wonder then that young children develop a distorted view of what a minute feels like? Any wonder that they mimic our words or actions when we call them for dinner? Is it any wonder that older children, who can tell time, begin nagging and whining about you not being true to your word?

My friend Rozanne recently responded to her daughter with "I'll be there when I've finished changing the baby's diaper." Instead of giving her a specific time, she helped her 4-year-old daughter understand that she could not drop whatever she was doing and run to her. She also helped her realize that different tasks take different lengths of time to complete. Other options include saying, "I'll be there in 10 minutes" and maybe even showing up ahead of time or actually showing up in a minute.

Similarly, when a child asks if you'll stay close by until she falls asleep, and you say "yes" but then sneak away, you run the risk of being caught in the act and having to work your way out of the lie.

> Almost 50 percent of the parents who completed the questionnaire said that they had told their children that they would stay upstairs and then snuck down.

On those occasions I have been asked to stay upstairs, agreed to do so, and then gotten caught breaking my promise, I have sometimes returned, grudgingly. Other times I have gotten angry at my daughter or myself for agreeing to do something I'd rather not.

I realize that by lying and telling her what she wants to hear, she is calmer. When she is calmer, she falls asleep more quickly. This allows me to relinquish my post upstairs and move to another area of the house. I also realize that my daughter is not learning how to calm herself when I am not in close proximity. I plan on talking to her about why she feels unsafe when I am not upstairs and brainstorm strategies that she can implement toward confronting her fears of being alone upstairs.

Deliberate lying

Some parents lie deliberately and others without intending to. Rozanne, a 36-year-old mother of a 4-year-old and a newborn, says that she purposely lies to protect her sanity. For example, she doesn't share their plans for the day in advance of them happening. So if her daughter asks her what they are doing that afternoon, she'll say, "I don't know," even when she does. "I know if I tell her that we're going out for lunch with someone at a specific time, she will drive me absolutely insane asking 'Is it time to go yet?' Also, if people let us down, then she has a very hard time coping with the disappointment. Because I know how she is, I will often evade the truth when she asks me questions."

Even though Rozanne realizes that avoiding and evading will not ultimately help her daughter handle disappointment, she's still firm on her position. She believes that "there are plenty of other times for her to deal with disappointment. For example, she consistently goes into my room and asks if she can have my beautiful owl candle. I'm not giving in, and I tell her she cannot have it. It's sentimental and it belongs to me."

WHAT CHILDREN LEARN FROM OUR LIES

I recently admitted to my 16-year-old that I lied when I said that I had not taken something from her room to give to her sister. I tried to manipulate her mood with humor when I broke the news, as I was afraid of the explosion that might follow. I was shocked but very proud when she responded, "Well, I'm not happy that you took it without asking, but I appreciate your honesty."

Unfortunately, children learn from what we don't mean to model, too. Think of the times when you unintentionally modelled the art of lying to your children. This may have been when you lied about your child's age in order to get her into an attraction at a lower admission price or a time when your child overheard you on the phone lying to someone about why you hadn't made it to your appointment or couldn't attend a function.

Young children in particular are not able to differentiate between these lies and other bigger ones. Older children may understand that we sometimes lie to protect someone's feelings ("I have another commitment" is better than "I don't want to attend your boring party") or because we feel that we are entitled to a break on an entrance fee that seems extravagant.

No matter the age of your child, it's important to remember that they are always listening and learning from your actions and words. If you are not proud of what you have done or said, it might be wise to discuss this with your child. While there may be no legitimate explanation for lying about your child's age, for example, you could share that it is not something that you are particularly proud of and acknowledge that your actions were self-serving and a way of saving money. By offering these suggestions, I don't mean to condone this type of behavior. However, I also realize that parents are not always perfect. Most important is our awareness of how our behavior impacts our children.

10

May I Take Your Order?
Doing For Your Children What They Can Do For Themselves

⟨⟩

Michael,
I know that you will probably not even miss Dad and me when we are in Hawaii, but I wanted you to know that we will be thinking of you lots. Please take note of the following:

Plastic lunch bags for school lunches are in cupboard next to receipt file. Don't eat deli meat every day. There is cheese and peanut butter and tins of tuna in cupboard. Make sure you take a fruit with you to school every day. Bananas in dining room on round white trolley because they bring fruit flies into the kitchen. There is another large container of orange juice in fridge in basement . . . and there are chocolate milk boxes in door of basement fridge as well as cans of drink for school lunches.

Try and remember to take out your food for the next day from the freezer the night before and leave it in the fridge. Also your bagel and your muffin for the morning! All in the freezer in the kitchen. Also there is some fried rice (not much) in that freezer and you can make pasta for yourself or Kraft dinner or regular rice.

Pasta: Boil half pot of water with a pinch of salt and then add pasta (not too much, remember, it swells) and cook till soft. Watch it doesn't go over the top of the pot. Strain through big strainer and rinse with cold water.

Love,
Mom

(Excerpt from a mom's letter to her 21-year-old
university student living at home)

"MAY I TAKE your order now?" I jokingly inquire of my kids, notebook and pen in hand. They're sprawled across the couch, one at each end, a cozy velour blanket draped over them. It's 6 o'clock and I can't think what to make for supper. "I'll have mashed egg and a bagel," my youngest responds. "Kraft dinner and chicken nuggets for me," says my oldest.

SHORT ORDER COOK

I am guilty of sometimes being a short order cook instead of just serving the special of the day—guilty of bending like a willow tree to accommodate my children's finicky eating habits. Other parents have shared stories of running out just before the mall closes to buy a piece of Bristol board for an overdue project, rushing to school to deliver a forgotten lunch, or feeling like a jack-in-the-box to get an extra glass, utensil, or napkin during meal time.

Jennifer Wise, author, artist, and associate professor of theater history at the University of Victoria in British Columbia, Canada, has chosen to remain childless. Her essay "Who Wants to Be a Mommy" is part of a compilation of essays in a book entitled *Nobody's Mother: Life without Kids*. As an outsider looking in, she writes that motherhood is a "thankless and impossible task likely to drive you stark raving mad—if, that is, you're lucky enough to escape being bedridden by a postpartum depression."

She says that her worst fears about becoming a parent were confirmed as she watched mothers "on the streetcar and in the stores. They looked like serfs of an invisible master, forced in public to perform simple, everyday tasks made virtually impossible by the burden of babies, bottles, blankets, and bags. It was heartbreaking and horrifying at the same time, like something out of Beckett. Poor sweating wretches! Sure, I'd open a door or retrieve a fallen pacifier, but there was little I could do to improve their lives. I could, however, make better choices in mine. Motherhood was clearly no proper job for a woman who cherished her mental and physical wellbeing and valued her time."

Despite Wise's take on motherhood, I can honestly say that I really enjoy being a parent—most of the time. I feel that my time with my children is precious and that good moments outweigh the bad. For the most part, I feel appreciated by them. They say thank you when I drive them places, make their beds, help with homework, and give up my place on the couch so they can watch their favorite television shows.

Other times I feel taken for granted, unappreciated, and poorly treated. Apparently I am good company.

> Almost 60 percent of the parents who responded to the questionnaire said that they too felt unappreciated despite bending over backwards to accommodate their children.

Before we become parents, many of us believe that our children will always admire, appreciate, and adore us. This is mostly true for the first 6 to 8 years of a child's life, but after that, we often fall from our pedestal. Parenting is not a two-way street. For the most part, parents give and children take. Today, for example, as I sat in front of my computer writing this chapter, my 16-year-old announced that she was going to be late if she walked to school. "Can you drive me now?" she asked. I contemplated saying no. After all, only 10 minutes earlier, when I asked her to do something for me, she had denied my request. Although she regularly shows that she cares for me, I was reminded once again that I shouldn't expect an entirely reciprocal relationship. We cannot expect back as much as we give. However, we are entitled to an equal amount of respect, love, care, and consideration.

RECIPROCAL RESPECT

A good friend of mine recently shared an experience she had with her 16-year-old son. Prior to his leaving to visit a friend, she asked what time he would be returning home. Since her husband was working late, she wanted to know if she should wait to eat dinner with him. He assured her that he would be home by 6 and that they would eat together. Typically a man of his word, she was surprised that he wasn't home by the time he promised. He eventually called at 6:15 to enquire if she would mind if he stayed until 6:30.

Although my friend considers herself to be a fairly flexible mom, she's the antithesis of a pushover parent. She's not strict per se, but firm and consistent with her kids, strong in her convictions, and stresses the importance of sticking to commitments. She told me that had her son called prior to 6, even 5:45, and asked if he could stay longer, she would have agreed. However, since he did not give her the courtesy of calling to say that he would be late, thereby leaving her waiting, she told him that he could not stay and needed to come home right away. Usually obedient, he whined about her decision and rebelled by not coming home immediately but about 20 minutes later. The rest of the evening was spent with each giving the other the silent treatment.

The next morning, my friend asked her son if he was planning on talking to her about what had happened the night before. She shared how hurt she felt about being stood up and then not having him respect her wish for him to come home right away. She helped him understand why his behavior was inappropriate. She asked how it would seem if they were all invited to another family's home and they called their host after the time at which they were supposed to arrive to say that they would be late. Her son, understanding the consequences of his behavior, apologized. She felt good about the direction of their conversation and proud that she had helped to teach him a valuable lesson.

WE ARE NOT SLAVES

We also want to teach children that we are their mentors, their helpers, but not their slaves. We want to encourage them to feel capable of taking on responsibilities for themselves and others that are appropriate for their age and level of maturity. We walk a fine line between giving in to our basic parental desire to nurture and pamper versus teaching children to become self-reliant. We often don't stop to evaluate when we have crossed the line by not considering our children's capabilities. In fact, we may rob them of the opportunity to learn and grow by always doing for them what they can do for themselves.

> When asked, "Do you ever do for your child what you know he or she is capable of doing for him or herself," almost 80 percent of the parents who responded to the questionnaire said yes.

CAPABLE KIDS

I am sure that you can think of a thousand times you've been challenged by this.

For example, have you ever run after your child with food because you were afraid that if you didn't, he wouldn't eat? Ever been concerned that you are helping with toileting beyond the age at which your child should be capable of wiping her own bum? Other things that parents commented on doing for their kids beyond the age at which they were physically capable of doing for themselves included tying their shoelaces, zippering their jackets, brushing their teeth, choosing their clothing, getting them dressed, making their snacks, and peeling their apples. Many shared that they helped a little too much with homework, including coming up with ideas for school projects. One mom said that she was still washing her 15-year-old's hair and laying out clothes for her 12-year-old in the morning, making their beds, and tidying up their rooms. A 52-year-old mom with a child of 24 admitted to cooking for her daughter even after she went to university.

For some parents, doing for their children often means less conflict at home, a quicker departure out the door in the morning, or a task done according to their expectations. For others, it's about filling a need to be useful when you say, "Here, let me do that for you" long after he is capable of doing for himself.

Dr. Erik Mansager, psychologist and professor at the Adler School of Professional Psychology in Chicago, says that self-esteem in kids "comes from being allowed to do age-appropriate things for themselves."

OVER MANAGING AND OVER MONITORING

Lynn Lott, an American family therapist, parent educator, and best-selling author of books such as *Chores without Wars*, agrees. She says that "pampering kids is something that I have seen forever, but what's happening now is even more insidious than bending over backwards." She calls it "parenting from fear. Parents who are just terrified that if they don't hold their kid the minute he cries and soothe and soothe and soothe, then they are not doing a good enough job. What I see parents doing," she says, "is over managing and over monitoring their children."

Lott believes that "parents take on way too much responsibility and think that everything their kids do reflects back on them."

> In fact, 86 percent of the parents who responded to the questionnaire did feel that their children's behavior was a reflection of them.

HELICOPTER PARENTS

So rampant is this phenomenon that the phrase "helicopter parent" was coined to describe a parent who hovers over every aspect of her child's life. It is especially used to describe college student's parents who continue to monitor and manage their child's life even after he or she has left home. College administrators share stories of parents who continue to call to wake their grown children up every morning, who continue to do their laundry, cook for them, and help with homework assignments. Although they do all this with the best of intentions, some experts say that helicopter parents may unfortunately be sending their children the message that they are incapable of handling their own lives.

However, a new study that looked at the effects of "helicopter parenting" was released in November 2007 and presents a different spin. In his article "New Study gives Hovering Parents Extra Credit," Jay Matthews at the *Washington Post*, writes that data from 24 colleges and universities was gathered for the National Survey of Student involvement, and the results indicated that "despite the negative reputation of helicopter parents, those moms and dads who hover over children in college and swoop into their academic affairs appear to be doing plenty of good."

Matthews quotes the survey director, George D. Kuh, an Indiana University professor, as saying that "children of helicopter parents were more satisfied with every aspect of their college experience, gained more in such areas as writing and critical thinking, and were more likely to talk with faculty and peers about substantive topics."

GIVING IN

One of the reasons that parents bend over backwards to accommodate their children's needs is because they are afraid of being blamed by them for not having done enough. Heather, a 45-year-old mother of a 13- and 14-year-old, says that "one of the trends amongst my 13-year-old daughter's peers is to be 'signed with a [modeling] agency.' How could she be the *only one* without an agency? So we found one. Maybe I did it for me. At the very least, I will not be the 'Mom Who Didn't Support Her', and our conversations now reach beyond 'her imminent modeling career.'"

Heather is wisely able to recognize her personal motivation for giving in to her child. Many don't. Instead, we typically blame our children for being "spoiled." They are not at fault. It's normal for children to grab what they can. We need to look at ourselves and ask: Have I taught my child that if he nags long enough, I will give in?

> Just over 60 percent of the parents who answered the questionnaire said yes. When asked if their child nags long enough, he will get what he wants as a way of shutting him up.

Can your child distinguish between needs and wants? Do you always comply with what your child demands of you?

PUSHOVER PARENT

Are you a pushover parent? Embarrassed to let others see how your child treats and speaks to you?

Twenty-six percent of the parents who responded to the questionnaire felt that they were sometimes abused—hit, kicked, bitten, or punched—by their children. Almost half felt that, at times, they had lost the "power" or authority to get their children to behave in a way that they saw fit.·

So, what should you do if your child is aggressive towards you? Some parents believe that if they pinch or kick back, that their children will learn what this feels like and not do it again. However, I don't advocate this. After all, you want to model an appropriate response. I recommend that you take a firm but fair approach. Make sure that you are eye level with your child and say, "hitting hurts. If you are upset or angry, use your words. The next time you hit me, you will need to spend some time on your own." Setting clear limits about respecting one another is very important.

Children should grow up feeling acknowledged but not empowered to such an extent that they feel that they are in charge. It saddens me when I see children with very little concern for the way that they behave around adults. They are sometimes rude and disrespectful, don't know to give up their seat to an adult if there are no more available, don't curb their swearing when adults are present, and often seem to feel too great a sense of power and entitlement.

Goldie Plotkin, rabbi's wife, educator, and mother of eight, thinks that "a lot of parents are pushovers and allow their children to talk to them disrespectfully." According to the Torah, she says "children have to respect their parents. There's no commandment that says that parents have to respect their children or honor them. Our responsibility is to feed them, clothe them, nourish them, and teach them manners and respect."

She recognizes that "when a child says 'get me this or that,' a mother might think, 'I'm the mother, why should I say no?'" She says that the "child should be taught from a young age that there's a better way to talk to Mommy. In fact, the Torah says that the child should get things for Mommy. Now, if you're standing anyway and you want to get that something for your child, that's okay."

Goldie agrees that "children must be taught to give. They must, for example, help to set and clear the table." Goldie says that the reason that the Torah doesn't talk about parents always doing for their children is because "we automatically will do for our children. It's part of a parent's nature. Since it is not natural for children to want to do for parents, the code of Jewish law has set up certain rules for them. It says that children are not allowed to sit on a parent's chair and that when a parent walks into the room, the children should stand up for them. Also, children don't walk into their parent's room unless they knock on the door first and if no one is there, they don't walk in at all. The parent's bedroom is a room of sanctity, a room that is private."

It occurred to me that although my upbringing wasn't consciously based on the Torah, I too was raised to give up my seat to an adult, to respect my parents and their right to privacy, to behave differently in the company of adults than I did when with my peers. I did not feel entitled to the same privileges as the adults in my life.

With the very best of intentions, parents today believe that by giving, they are showing their children how much they are cherished and loved. As normal as it is to want to give everything we've got (and more) to our children, we may not be doing them a favor. My sentiments are echoed by the words of Dr. Erik Mansager, a Psychologist and Professor at the Adler School of Professional Psychology in Chicago, who says that "by always giving to your kids, they do not learn how to give but how to expect."

Conclusion:

Normal Defined

"A normal parent is someone who isn't afraid to get messy
in sticky situations"

—Talia, age 16

I FOUND TALIA'S statement to be thought provoking. Parenting is often messy—literally and figuratively. We change stinky diapers, wear shirts that our babies have puked on, and scrub little hands free of play dough, markers, and sticky sweets. Figuratively, a normal parent, according to my daughter, is one who isn't afraid to get involved when unpleasant situations present themselves. Some may be a little messy—for example, a confrontation with a teacher who does not appear to be fair or a meeting with the parents of a child who is bullying kids in the neighborhood.

Patti Kirk, co-owner of Parentbooks in Toronto says that defining normal can be hard. "Normal," she says "is a range. Just the same as in child development."

Not an exact science

Some children develop at a rate that is very average or typical of their same-age peers. For others, there is a deviation of months in either direction. Defining normal is not an exact science. Unlike taking one's temperature and knowing that anything above 98.6 degrees Fahrenheit is not a healthy temperature, normal behavior, thoughts and feelings cannot be as precisely defined.

A SPECTRUM OF NORMALCY

However, there are a range of feelings, thoughts, and behaviors that are on the spectrum of normalcy. These may differ depending on how and where you were raised. After reading *Am I a Normal Parent?*, you may feel that you are "normal" when it comes to certain aspects of parenting but not others. For example, you may be reassured to read that you are not the only overprotective or overwhelmed parent in the world. On the other hand, you may be surprised to learn that it is not typical for parents to share intimate details of their lives with their children and therefore, decide to change your behavior.

Lana, a 48-year-old mom, thinks that as parents we "need to question and challenge our typical practices. We need to figure out what we're doing today to prepare our children for tomorrow. We need to ask if it is in our child's best interests that we follow typical parental behavior just because everyone else is."

WHAT DO YOU SEE?

When you look in the mirror, what kind of parent do you see? Do you still want to be normal? Do you feel that your thoughts, feelings and behavior are typical of others? If not, are you okay with standing apart? Is there anything that you'd like to change? Learning to feel comfortable in your skin, no matter how different you are, is important. Feeling good about who we are helps us to parent with confidence.

Attending parenting courses and seminars helps us to grow as parents and normalizes our experiences. Attending parenting programs is in vogue.

> Almost 40 percent of the parents who completed the questionnaire said they had attended parenting courses and/or seminars.

PARENTING WITH CONFIDENCE

Michelle, a 41-year-old single parent of an 7-year-old, says that she is generally a confident person who makes parenting decisions with confidence. When she looks around at other parents, she realizes that she may be different from most. For example, she spends the majority of her nonworking hours with her child and does not believe in yelling. She prefers to remain true to herself rather than fitting in for the sake of being typical. "Normal does not define good or not," she says. "I think that I'm a great mom."

Goldie Plotkin, rabbi's wife, educator, and mother of eight children, believes that it's normal for parents to sometimes lack assurance. She says that when we, as parents, end our sentences with "okay?" our children falsely believe that we are asking their permission.

> About 45 percent of the questionnaire respondents said that they felt more confident as a parent than in their career, fewer than 15 percent felt that their confidence as a parent was lower, and about 12 percent felt that their levels for both were about the same. The remainder said that the question did not apply to them.

One mom wrote that her children were her career and another mom felt that her career and parenting were so distinct that she was not able to compare one to the other.

ZERO DOUBT

It's normal for all parents to sometimes experience self doubt. However, Goldie suggests that we aspire to "zero doubt." She explains the concept by sharing a story of a couple who are about to be married by a rabbi. She says that "the rabbi, in his blessing, says that the couple should be as happy as Adam and Eve in the Garden of Eden. You might ask, what was so great about the Garden of Eden? Well, in it, Adam and Eve had zero doubt. Adam knew he was marrying the right girl and Eve knew she was marrying the right guy. Why? Because there was no one else. When you are under the chuppah (a wedding canopy under which the ceremony is conducted), you should have no doubt. When you have no doubt, then 50 percent of our challenges are eliminated. When we parent our children with confidence and zero doubt, children sense that. Children feel that their parents really know where they're doing. That they have values. That they're not wishy-washy. When you have zero doubt, children don't challenge you as much."

NEVER FULLY CONFIDENT

However, Janet Chan, mother of two, editorial director for the Parenting Group and editor in chief of *Parenting* magazine, has an alternate view. She says that "the mom who is most comfortable with herself is the mom who can appreciate that she will never feel fully confident. You have to accept the feeling of not always being confident. The whole point of parenting is that once you get a handle on something, it will change because your child is growing so rapidly, and so are you."

CHOOSING NOT TO BE "NORMAL"

Pam, a 41-year-old parent of a 3-year-old says that she and her husband were older and more mature when they became first-time parents and as a result, may have felt less concerned about fitting in. "As a couple, we share the same values and have a great connection. We also feel blessed that we have such similar parenting styles. We came into this relationship with an understanding of parenting norms and prefer to be chameleon-like. By that I mean that we fit into things when need be, but we actually prefer to live on the outside of what is considered normal."

Renee, a 41-year-old mother of two boys, ages 6 and 4, does not think that she is a "normal" parent but prefers it that way, too.

Renee's Story

Renee compares herself to six close girlfriends whom she met over 6 years ago at a new mom's group. From the beginning, Renee felt that she was a "little more on the outer fringes. They are more mainstream than me," she says. "I was the only one who chose not to circumcise or vaccinate. When they started their babies on pablum and rice cereal and stuff like that, I started my kids on homemade mashed vegetables and fruits."

Although Renee identifies her approach as being a little "abnormal" she prefers being less typical as an alternative to not questioning anything or doing whatever "big pharmaceutical-pushing doctors," for example, recommend.

Renee shunned her own parents' way of raising kids. "I want to bring up my kids on the opposite end of the spectrum to how I was raised. My mother felt that she knew nothing and that doctors were almighty." Renee was first-born of five children. She says that her father was an alcoholic and so her mother was too busy single-handedly running a farm with no bathroom or running water to be available to her children. Renee said that her mother was never the kind of person to ask "Why?"

Renee, on the other hand, asks lots of questions before she takes action. When she was pregnant with her first child she met a woman whose child was going to a Waldorf school. In the years to come, the Waldorf way became a huge influence in Renee's approach to parenting.

At Waldorf, "we frown down upon brand names or characters on clothing and don't dress the children in black. We don't allow jewellery or nail polish for younger kids. School lunches are only brought in reusable containers and the teachers, who provide a morning snack, use a grain grinder to grind the oat they serve."

Renee recognizes that many of her neighbors may be raising their children quite differently.

She says, "we have new kids about the same ages as my sons that just moved onto the street. We rode our bikes past their house yesterday, and one of the children was carrying a toy gun painted in the colors of army paint. We watched him tackle his sister gently to the ground, but then he pulled out a pair of handcuffs and he handcuffed her. I was thinking to myself, holy geez."

Renee plans on adhering to the rules that she has already established and staying true to her belief system about parenting. Her children are in bed by 7 p.m., even during the summer months when it's still light outside. "My kids need 11 hours of sleep," she says. By sticking to this schedule, Renee and her family are sometimes unable to join evening activities with other families. Up until now, her children have not challenged them. She says that "without question, for as long as I can get away with it, I will stick with it."

Renee acknowledges that the six friends she made years ago at the baby group are not "like-minded" but her circle of friends from Waldorf is. I asked Renee how she would feel if she thought of herself as the only person in the world to parent the way she does. "If I didn't have at least a couple of people who were doing exactly the same thing as me, I would feel really insecure about it. I certainly feel the strength by being part of a community—even though it's small."

Choosing not to follow the norms as defined by others is what makes Renee happy. Many parents want to be considered "normal" by others but then may realize that normal is not always what it's cracked up to be.

PARENTS PAINT PICTURES OF "NORMAL"

Joe, a 30-year-old father of two young daughters, paints a bleak picture of a normal parent in the twenty-first century. He says that when he looks at his generation, his friends in their 30s, he sees that "no one wants to take care of their kids anymore. They'd rather drop them off at day care or get a nanny. We want to have kids, but we don't want 100 percent responsibility."

When asked whether parenting was what they had expected it to be, many said that it was more tiring, more work, and took more time than they'd imagined. Some said that it was harder and more expensive. Some wrote that although it was different from what they'd expected, it was actually better, even more fulfilling than anticipated.

One such parent was Caroline, a 44-year-old mother of three girls ages 16, 12, and 10, living in England. She wrote, "Our kids know we're always there for them and know exactly how to manipulate us to make sure they get exactly what they want! Every new experience and situation we have to face as parents causes us hours of discussion and consultation with our friends and involves letting go (not our immediate natural instinct!), and it feels like a stab in the dark. The children come to us for advice, love us for it, and value it. Then they ignore everything we advised and do what they wanted anyway. They either learn from their mistakes or we learn to realize they are much more grown up than we thought! We love our kids, that's pretty normal. We're proud of everything about them. We think they're the best kids on the planet . . . but they make us feel like we're ancient. They drive us crazy. Sometimes we feel we don't really like them. They make us feel like tearing our hair out, like we're talking to walls, and their mess makes us want to scream. All pretty normal, yes!"

MY LIST OF NORMAL

Now that my manuscript for *Am I a Normal Parent?* is complete, I have my own list of what defines us as normal. I have concluded that a normal parent is someone who experiences a host of different emotions, such as frustration, anger, and resentment along with exhilaration, pride, and satisfaction. Normal parents know to expect the unexpected. Normal parents carry snack bags "just in case" and occasionally lose track of time so that they forget to pick their child up from school or another activity. A normal parent is vulnerable to the comments and criticisms of others, walks a fine line between being protective and overprotective and worries about being considered neurotic if she leans too much to the "over" side. A normal parent doesn't always tell the truth to her kids and struggles with juggling career, kids, and everything else that life throws her way.

A normal parent often spends too much time on the computer, cell phone, and at work and feels guilty about how little quality time she spends with her children. Normal parents don't always keep their promises or consistently follow through with punishments. Normal parents don't always say what they mean and mean what they say. Normal parents worry that their child's misbehavior is a reflection of themselves. Normal parents don't always model the behavior they want to see. A normal parent often gives in to her child for a few minutes peace and does for her children what she knows they can do for themselves. A normal parent sometimes wants to run away from home, if only for a short break, and often feels unappreciated and abused.

Normal parents sometimes feels as if they have lost all power or authority at home but even then, most do not regret having become a parent.

Why? Because, according to my 8-year-old daughter's friend, Tyla, above all else, a "normal parent is someone who loves her child."

Appendix:

Where to Find the Answers to the Questionnaire

1. Have you ever asked out loud or of yourself "Am I a normal parent?" —Intro Chapter

2. Do you ever resent being asked to put a project/activity on hold to accommodate your child(ren)?—Chapter 4—No Time for Me or We

3. Do you ever threaten your child(ren) with punishment that you know you'll never follow through with?—Chapter 3—True Confessions

4. Have you ever promised to take your child out for an ice cream, for example, and then not followed through?—Chapter 3—True Confessions

5. Have you had an argument with your child, had him/her go to bed angry at you and then quietly kissed his/her head as he/she slept? —Chapter 8—Feeling Bad When You're Mad

6. When angry, have you ever had thoughts/fears of hurting your child? —Chapter 8—Feeling Bad When You're Mad

7. Do you feel that there are enough hours in the day to accomplish everything? —Chapter 4—No Time for Me or We

8. Have you ever felt the need to protect your child(ren) from knowing intimate details of your life that might hurt them emotionally (e.g., diagnosis of illness, conflict in your relationship with your partner, personal use of alcohol or drugs)? —Chapter 2—Conventional Wisdom

9. Do you feel that your child's behavior is a reflection of you? —Chapter 10—May I Take Your Order?

10. Have you ever told your child "I'll be there in a minute" but really taken 10? —Chapter 9—I'll be There in A Minute

11. Have you ever told your child that you will stay close by while he/she is sleeping and then snuck away? —Chapter 9—I'll be There in A Minute

12. Have you ever told your child, "If you don't stop hurting your brother/sister, I'm going to hit you"? —Chapter 8—Feeling Bad When You're Mad

13. Have you ever insisted that your child eat fruits and vegetables but not been responsible about eating them yourself? —Chapter 2—Conventional Wisdom

14. Do you always speak to older adults/parents in the way that you would like your child(ren) to speak/behave toward you? —Chapter 2—Conventional Wisdom

15. Would you leave a 3-year-old child alone in a car while you ran into a store for a couple of minutes? —Chapter 5—The Electronic Umbilical Cord

If not, at what age might you consider doing so? —Chapter 5—The Electronic Umbilical Cord

16. Have you ever worried that you were being "neurotic" in regard to your child's safety/wellbeing? —Chapter 5—The Electronic Umbilical Cord

17. Have you ever said something nasty to your child? Regretted it later?—Chapter 8—Feeling Bad When You're Mad

18. Do you ever feel that of all the households in the neighborhood, yours could win the "Mornings from Hell" award? — Chapter 4—No Time for Me or We

19. Ever feel that it is difficult to juggle all your responsibilities? —Chapter 4—No Time for Me or We

20. Have you ever disobeyed the law or rules in regard to your children (e.g., taken a child out a car or booster seat before the law allows)? —Chapter 2—Conventional Wisdom

21. If you're at a party with your children and your children are tired, do you leave even if you want to stay? —Chapter 2—Conventional Wisdom

22. Do you ever put your own needs ahead of your children's?—Chapter 8—Feeling Bad When You're Mad

23. If you're at a pool party with other adults and children, do you change your behavior as a result of having children present (e.g., reduce drinking, dress more conservatively, censor your conversations with other adults)?—Chapter 2—Conventional Wisdom

24. Do you ever feel that you like one of your children more than the other? —Chapter 8—I'll be There in A Minute

25. Do you ever feel that other parents are judgemental of your behavior toward your child(ren)? —Chapter 7—Being Judged

26. Do you ever feel guilty about how you prioritize your daily list of chores (e.g., laundry before lovemaking or paying bills before playing with the kids)? —Chapter 4—No Time for Me or We

27. Do you ever feel that the boundary lines between work and home have become blurred (e.g., receiving business calls at home, working on a laptop for work-related duties while on vacation with the family)? —Chapter 4—No Time for Me or We

28. Do you ever have long-winded conversations on your cell phone while in the company of your kids? —Chapter 2—Conventional Wisdom

29. Have you ever not shared a secret about your feelings or thoughts as a parent for fear of being considered not normal by others? —Chapter 7—Being Judged

30. Do you ever feel like running away from home, if only for one night? —Chapter 3—True Confessions

31. Do you ever long for life the way it was before kids? —Chapter 3—True Confessions

32. Do you ever wish that you were still a kid yourself? —Chapter 3—True Confessions

33. Do you ever feel that, despite bending over backwards to accommodate your children, you are not appreciated by them?—Chapter 10—May I Take Your Order?

34. Do you ever feel that you are being "abused" by your children? This may be in the form of swearing at you, kicking, hitting, pinching, biting etc. —Chapter 10—May I Take Your Order?

35. Do you ever feel that you have lost the "power" or authority to get your children to behave in a way that you see fit? —Chapter 10—May I Take Your Order?

36. Did you feel an immediate connection/fall in love with your child the moment he/she was born? —Chapter 3— True Confessions

37. Within the first few months of your child's life, did you feel that parenting was one of the most wonderful things that had ever happened to you? —Chapter 3—True Confessions

38. Have you ever felt that you weren't cut out to be a parent?—Chapter 3—True Confessions

39. Have you ever regretted becoming a parent? —Chapter 3— True Confessions

40. Do you ever worry about the amount of time or the quality of time that you spend with your children? —Chapter 4—No Time for Me or We

41. Do ever wonder if your rules are different than any other parents? For example, insisting that your children wash their hands as soon as they come into the house or not allowing them to have friends up to their bedrooms? — Chapter 2—Conventional Wisdom

42. Do you feel that your sex life (i.e., frequency, quality) has changed since you had children? —Chapter 4—No Time for Me or We

43. Do you ever attend parenting classes or seminars? —Conclusion: Normal Defined

44. At what age do you feel that it is appropriate for your child to:

_____ Walk to school alone—Chapter 5—The Electronic Umbilical Cord

_____ Tell you, rather than ask your permission to go out—Chapter 2—Conventional Wisdom

_____ Date—Chapter 2—Conventional Wisdom

_____ Go to a mall/movie or public place with friends—Chapter 5—The Electronic Umbilical Cord

_____ Own an iPod/cell phone—Chapter 2—Conventional Wisdom

_____ Stop sleeping in the same bed with the opposite sex parent—Chapter 2—Conventional Wisdom

_____ Stop bathing/showering with the opposite sex parent—Chapter 2—Conventional Wisdom

_____ Be left alone in the house—Chapter 5 —The Electronic Umbilical Cord

_____ Be allowed to drink alcohol at home—Chapter 2—Conventional Wisdom

45. Is your confidence as a parent higher, lower, or not applicable when compared to your confidence in your career? —Conclusion: Normal Defined

46. How influenced are you to change your behavior as a result of how you perceive others regard you as a parent? —Chapter 7—Being Judged

47. Is parenting what you had expected it to be?—Chapter 3—True Confessions

48. Do you ever give your child what he/she wants as a result of his/her nagging as a way of shutting him/her up?—Chapter 10—May I Take Your Order?

49. Do you ever give in to your child because he/she says that other parents are letting their children do what your child is requesting of you—even though you would have preferred not to have consented to that activity?—Chapter 7—Being Judged

50. Do you ever do for your child what you know he/she is capable of doing for him/herself (e.g., cutting food at table, helping with toileting)? —Chapter 10—May I Take Your Order?

Resources

www.helpmesara.com

www.canadianparents.com

www.drsusanbartell.com

www.fabermazlish.com

www.helpwevegotkids.com

www.joysofparenting.com

www.lynnlott.com

www.onlineparentclass.com

www.parentbooks.com

www.parentchildhelp.com

www.parenting.com

www.parentingtoday.ca

www.todaysparent.com

www.truemomconfessions.com

www.truedadconfessions.com

Index

Index

Index

Normal, defining, 1–4, 147, 153–155
Normalcy, spectrum of, 148–149
Norms and standards, 4–5
Novick, Dr. Ari, 6, 101

O
Over managing and over monitoring, 142–143

P
Paleg, Kim, 122
Parental confessions, online, 30–33
Parents' problems, children and their, 25–26
Peer pressure, 71–72
Personal reflection, 101–102
Positive Discipline A-Z, 12, 48
Prioritizing our time, 51
Private time for parents, 53–54
Privileges and responsibilities, 73–74
Pushover parent, 144–147

R
Rage, Rebellion, and Rudeness, 74
Reality, setting in of, 36–37
Religious convictions, role of, 92–97
Resentment, parental, 51–52
Responsibilities, teaching our children about their, 141–142
Rules, differences in household, 22–23

S
Separation anxiety, 69
Siblings Without Rivalry, 77

Sleep deprivation, role of, 34–35
Solve Your Child's Sleep Problems, 9

T
Today's Parent Magazine, 9, 37
Tradition, role of, 12–13, 83–92
True confessions, 33–40
Trusting your instincts, 77–78

U
Unwanted thoughts, 33–34

W
When Anger Hurts your Kids, 122
Who's in Charge Anyway?, 69–70
Wooding, Dr. Scott, 18, 74
Working full-time, 47–49
Working part-time, 46–47

Y
Yourselves, defining, 9–10

Z
Zero doubt, 150

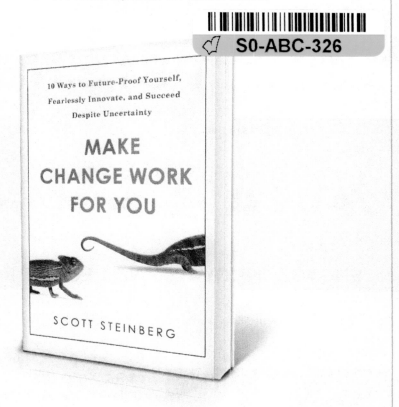

CREATE VALUE. STAY AHEAD OF THE CURVE.

SCOTT STEINBERG

KEYNOTE SPEAKER | STRATEGIC CONSULTANT
BESTSELLING AUTHOR | TECHNOLOGY FUTURIST

AS SEEN IN:

ENGAGE, INNOVATE AND BECOME INVALUABLE

ACCELERATE GROWTH AND TRANSFORMATION THROUGH STRATEGIC INNOVATION AND COMPETITIVE ADVANTAGE

#1-RANKED BUSINESS STRATEGIST, TECHNOLOGY AND TREND FORECASTER

- World-famous for 10+ years of accurately predicting business, consumer and technology trends
- Bestselling author featured in 600+ outlets from NPR to USA Today
- Google's #1-ranked technology expert – seen by 1 billion+ worldwide
- Strategic advisor to Fortune 500 businesses and brands
- Expert columnist on change and innovation for CNN, Rolling Stone and The Huffington Post
- Noted entrepreneur who's built and sold startups and divisions

SPEAKING TOPICS

- » Business
- » Leadership
- » Management
- » Marketing
- » Sales
- » Social Media
- » Communication
- » Education
- » Healthcare
- » Technology
- » Teamwork
- » Customer Service

TO BOOK SCOTT PLEASE CONTACT:

Perceptive Research LLC | info@akeynotespeaker.com | 888-507-2246
www.AKeynoteSpeaker.com

10 Ways to Future-Proof Yourself, Fearlessly Innovate, and Succeed Despite Uncertainty

MAKE
CHANGE WORK
FOR YOU

PARENTING HIGH-TECH KIDS
The Ultimate Internet, Web, and Online Safety Guide

To order copies or to request permission to reprint, contact the publisher at:
Published by READ.ME and TechSavvy Global LLC

www.AKeynoteSpeaker.com
www.TechSavvyGlobal.com

DEDICATION

For Z – a guiding light and inspiration. May the lessons contained here guide and serve you well. And for today's family, educator and youth worker: Nevermore will you be alone, or unprepared.

TABLE OF CONTENTS

TECHNOLOGY AND KIDS – GETTING PLUGGED IN

INTRODUCTION

Families have been celebrating "firsts" since time immemorial, including baby's first words, a child's first loose tooth, and little ones getting dropped off for their first day of school. But today, there are an entirely new and equally important number of major life milestones that kids and parents must be prepared to greet as well. For example: Highly memorable high-tech moments such as your tween receiving their first cell phone; registering a child to receive their first e-mail address; or even the first time that your kids create their own Facebook profile, team up to play online video games, or send siblings a text message.

Moreover, just as parents observing their baby beginning to walk can expect the process to be accompanied by ample bumps, bruises and scratches, so too must modern parents ready themselves to contend with similar high-tech hiccups. Just like riding a bike for the first time can result in the occasional scrape or even head-on collision, entry into today's Internet and online world can also be a bumpy ride, complete with its own important concerns and hazards which modern parents must be prepared to address. Now that technology's influence on the modern family dynamic has become pronounced, ongoing, and hugely influential, the time to tackle these issues is here and now. As positive an influence as technology and online connectivity can exert on today's world, as responsible parents and digital citizens, we must always remember: Children cannot be allowed to come of age in a digital world which we've left them unprepared to greet.

Vital to consider is the fact that between the rise of computers, social networks, apps, and Internet-ready mobile devices such as smartphones, tablet PCs and gaming systems, today's families are more connected than ever. Not only are educators, lawmakers and non-profits nationwide increasingly rolling out programs devoted to extolling and educating families on the virtues of technology. In the US alone, there are now more than 300 million Internet users — a large proportion of this audience including adolescents, young adults and even children barely out of diapers. According to the US Senate, 80% of kids are now spending at least one hour per week in cyberspace, starting in kindergarten and running through the 12th grade. Not only that, but another recent study reveals that children ages 5 to 16 routinely spend an average of six and a half hours in front of a screen each day. And, as Internet security software maker Trend Micro also points out, 93% of kids between 12 and 17 are now online — and that's even before you consider that consumer watchdog Common Sense Media estimates that half (!) of five to eight year-olds now currently utilize high-tech devices. Needless to say, all this high-tech activity adds up to a tremendous amount of time spent online by children of all ages in a virtual world which contains its own set of rules, behaviors and potential exposure to outside influences – activity which often occurs outside of parents' otherwise watchful eyes.

Equally important to note is that much of this online activity is quickly being embraced and welcomed by families as well – especially adults, whose own enthusiasm for technology can color the tone, nature and degree of influence it can exert on the household. In fact, according to a recent BabyCenter survey, 43% of moms say that if they left their wallet at home, they would leave it, but would in fact return to retrieve their smartphone. (The previous year, this figure was 34%.) Of the women surveyed, nearly 60% considered their smartphones their back-up brains. (Ad network Greystripe additionally says that 66% of mothers shop with and through the device – a clear wake-up call for casual observers, as well as businesses and brands, which speaks directly to modern families' changing needs, tastes and consumption habits.) Likewise, recent research from Cisco reveals that nearly three-quarters of dads are more enthused to show kids how to use tech tools than real-world equivalents, while anti-virus provider AVG points out that tots aged two to five are now better able

to run downloaded apps than tie their shoelaces. And if these numbers weren't eye-opening enough, Microsoft and AARP's "Connecting Generations" survey goes a step further, noting that 83% of all respondents, ranging in ages from 13 to 75, believe that going online is helpful to family and intergenerational communication.

As we discovered while researching this book, the deeper you dive into the rabbit hole, the further it goes. Case in point: Strikingly, today, some 40% of tablet PC users include women and children as well, with over half of all purchases made by households containing children under 18, according to Forrester Research. And that's before you even include the household impact of electronic reading devices, or eReaders, with the Pew Center suggesting that more than 50% of adult Americans own either a tablet or an eReader or both. Moreover, a whopping 80% of tablet PC owners have also made downloadable purchases from these devices such as apps, books and music, speaking to the public's growing appetite for digital media consumption. It's a figure that becomes even more telling when you ponder that seven in ten children under age 12 in tablet-owning households use these devices regularly.

The bottom line being as follows: From a practical, everyday standpoint, what all these facts and figures add up to is an entire generation, not just of children, but of extended families for whom technology has changed everything from education to interpersonal relationships and viewing habits — a nation of individuals we define as "Generation Tech," whose lives are impacted by new technologies, innovations and communications methods at virtually every turn, from childhood's earliest days on up.

Such insights may seem eye opening at first blush. But they become even more telling in light of revelations that, despite the American Academy of Pediatrics' recommendation that children under age two receive no screen time whatsoever, over 80% of kids now enjoy an online presence in some form or fashion before they're 24 months old, according to a recent report by the Pew Research and Internet Project. And, for that matter, perhaps doubly so knowing that while Emily Post's Etiquette now includes entire sections on virtual conduct and The Oxford English Dictionary's definition of friend has expanded in less than six years to include "a contact on a social networking website," the contemporary family's basic knowledge of digital citizenship and safe computing habits can many times be shamefully anemic.

The net result of these advancements is that an entire generation of parents and experts is currently struggling to bridge the gap between generations, since grown into a gaping chasm, only further serving to underscore the desperate need to provide today's family with basic high-tech life skills and training solutions. With 70% of parents clamoring for more high-tech education in schools, and four-fifths of teachers believing that more formalized digital citizenship programs are desperately needed, it's no longer an individual problem either. Suddenly, across the world, it's a problem that every society, culture and generation now shares. As such insights clearly illustrate, it's not just technology that's changed in the wireless, streaming and always-connected era. From personal and professional interactions to basic aspects of learning and behavioral development, it's the fundamental rules of family and parenting that have transformed as well.

Eye-opening as all these stats and figures may be though, keep in mind that, in the interest of community service and informed discussion, it's also vital to look beyond them and keep things in perspective too. Happily for high-tech parents and children hoping to navigate a hyperkinetic world defined by buzzing Android and Apple smartphones, bleeping video game consoles, and frazzled working moms struggling just to stand up, let alone get dinner on the table while chasing screaming toddlers around the house after a grueling 10-hour workday, connectivity can also be a huge plus. From helping to better engage kids; boost learning and retention rates; enhance intergenerational communications; and foster creativity and promote interest in real-world subjects, technology's beneficial effects on family life can be both pronounced and ample. Whether videoconferencing with distant friends or relatives, connecting online to explore educational and career-related resources, or simply discovering new ways to share information and consume news of the world and current events, the potential upsides that high-tech tools and services offer kids and adults alike are plentiful. Technology should not be feared, but rather embraced, researched and continually discussed and debated from all standpoints, so as to allow for healthier usage, and more informed decision-making, amongst all age groups. Ultimately, both the high-tech world's positives and negatives add up to one foregone conclusion, however: Technology has suddenly infiltrated every facet of family life, and even the youngest children are now being exposed to and rapidly embracing its onset.

Note that many companies will soon be offering parents ample options to soothe even screaming newborns using screens, play mats, and infant accessories that offer ways to connect with high-tech devices (portable media players, cell phones, etc.) and the Internet. Toddlers and preschoolers additionally have many new adult-like technologies and devices being created specifically to meet their needs, including tablet computers exclusively designed for preschoolers, with many action figures and dolls also now including built-in digital cameras and companion apps as a matter of course. From the toys they play with to the media they consume – including TV shows with companion second-screen experiences or that are inspired by games and apps themselves – today's digital kids won't just expect technology and Internet connectivity to be present in all facets of life going forward. They'll actually see it as the everyday norm, and it will allow them to expand their horizons in virtual ways that to them will appear second nature, but to parents may still seem like something straight out of a science-fiction movie.

Consider that familiar storybooks from the likes of Dr. Seuss and Sesame Street have also now become wildly popular "storybook apps" – and are more interactive than yesterday's bibliophile could possibly have imagined. Video games like Activision's popular Skylanders series, which allows kids to take real-life toys and play with these characters in simulated 3D universes, or a growing number of licensed virtual worlds in which popular animated characters appear online for players to interact with, are also growingly in popularity. Many humble trading cards now even contain online and digital components. Surely, we've all marveled at some of these amazing innovations that we could only have dreamed of when we were kids. Can you imagine explaining to your younger self that by the time your children were in school, you'd not only own a pocket-sized phone that makes calls virtually anytime and anywhere, but also one that can send messages, photos or videos made on the fly to friends and family in seconds; play sophisticated 3D video games; and stream movies, music and software programs down for play anytime on-demand?

Alas, as these innovations underscore, parenting kids based on solely on our own prior technological experience isn't enough anymore. Even for those of us who grew up with computers in our bedrooms, it's crucial to recall: Both technology and the Internet are increasingly impacting and influencing kids' lives from the moment that they're born, and often in new and unexpected ways. Such advancements' impact on today's household is suddenly a foregone conclusion, with big questions no longer surrounding if, but simply when – and to what profound degree – they will irrevocably redefine modern household life. As leading experts will tell you, the field's progress hasn't just reached critical mass – it's currently doing laps around the average household, and trailing smoke as it moves at Road Runner-style cartoon speeds.

"Children are going to have to learn how to use these high-tech vehicles responsibly because they're going to be a part of their everyday life," explains Laurie Nathan, deputy director of programs and partnerships for the National Center for Missing & Exploited Children. Knowing this, if they wish to relate to and comprehend kids' changing lives going forward, parents must now take action, and make a running commitment to educating both themselves and their families on technology's forward progress. Suddenly, we as a society not only need to research, debate and discuss the latest that technology has to offer on a constant, running basis. We must also take pronounced steps to carve out the time required, and embrace the more receptive mindset that's necessary, to properly equip ourselves with the vital, game-changing information that's integral to understanding and preparing kids for meeting the challenges that will inevitably come with its continued progress and deployment. Nor can we expect children to figure out how to make sense of this new digital world all on their own – as ever, only by serving as positive role models and examples can we help to guide and shape their experiences for the positive.

The mandate for modern families is simple: Under no circumstance can you afford to parent part-time where technology is concerned. As responsible adults and caregivers, we owe it to both ourselves and our children to dive into and learn as much as we can about the different ways today's kids are connecting, sharing, and consuming information, online or otherwise. Happily, successful high-tech parenting bears little difference to traditional parenting if you remember the fundamental rule – homework isn't just for children alone. "Parents need to partner with kids in a positive, protective way [to make sense of high-tech devices and interactions]," explains Judi Warren, president of Web Wise Kids, in no uncertain terms. Acknowledging the growing role that technology and the Internet play in your life, she says, is a big step, with it mandatory for today's parents – as with any aspect of parenting – to stay informed. "Kids are often the ones teaching adults about technology," she says. "It needs to be the other way around."

With this in mind, we'd like to welcome you to our all-new companion to the bestselling The Modern Parent's Guide series, and invite you to join us as we begin our journey into the exciting and ever-changing world of Internet and online safety. To start, we'll take closer look at a few of the many ways that today's kids are connecting to and using the Internet. Devices and opportunities that allow access to online tools, apps, services, websites and worlds now abound everywhere. So without further ado, let's jump right in.

PART I:

LIFE IN A CONNECTED WORLD

LIFE IN A CONNECTED WORLD

The proliferation of technology in today's world is actually quite remarkable. Already, it's difficult to imagine a life without devices such as the iPad, which was first announced by Apple in early 2010. Connectivity and high-tech usage is quickly proliferating and evolving, and it's being ingrained into children's vernacular from the youngest age.

Across the full range of connected devices, one thing remains constant: Parents must remain vigilant where the Internet and access to online content consumption and sharing are concerned. Every child will use each device uniquely, and all will invariably encounter questionable content – through ongoing education, hands-on instruction and leading by example, parents must strive to teach online safety essentials and positive computing habits.

On the bright side, the Internet is, in and of itself, simply a tabula rasa – and one, which can be used to your family's tremendous benefit. "Technology is not inherently good or bad... only the way in which we choose to use it," explains Web Wise Kids president Judi Warren. As parents, we need to empower kids to take advantage of the enormous opportunity that today's connected world provides them, while simultaneously doing our best to teach best practices as related to online behavior, information sharing and product usage.

There are now a myriad of options available for kids and families to connect online, and here's a top-level sampling of the many ways that today's world is more connected than ever before.

Desktop and Laptop PCs – It used to be noteworthy that many families had their own home computer, and something of a major event when a new PC was purchased by each household. (And still remains so for many homes, as there's nothing more exciting for children than ripping the plastic, cardboard, and Styrofoam off a shiny new system.) However, these days, thanks to declining hardware prices and booming interest in smartphones, tablet PCs and other mobile devices, the humble PC has become a growingly commoditized and often secondary way to access the Internet for many individuals. A whopping 97% of families with parents who went to college now own a computer though, and in fact the average household now contains two, according to the Kaiser Family Foundation.

To date, one of the best tips experts have offered for keeping kids safe online is to make sure that home computers are placed in common areas such as playrooms and dens, and to confine

Internet access and online-connected activities to within these shared environments. The process effectively allows you to not only monitor children's computing habits, but also favorite sites, software and services; how and when they access them; types of media consumed and in which fashion; the length of online sessions; and whom children interact with online and the nature of these interactions. But as Symantec Internet Safety Advocate Marian Merritt points out, the notion of attempting to keep computer usage confined to shared family spaces is quickly becoming antiquated.

"As media consumption goes more mobile, the idea that everyone is computing while sitting at the kitchen table is foolish," she explains. Consider one recent study from online monitoring service SocialShield. Based on its findings, while two-thirds of parents report that kids access social networks from the family computer, nearly 90% say they're also accessing them from their own computers – and smartphones, tablet PCs, iPods, school computers, or friend's houses as well.

Laptops are likewise portable by nature, and connected cell phones even more so, meaning that simply defaulting to public placement of high-tech access points is no longer always an effective deterrent to engaging in unproductive or negative computing behaviors. As such, it's important to recognize that while it's

still wise to encourage your family to keep their high-tech activities out in the open, especially when using a computer, there's more to the story today when it comes to keeping kids safe on computers. With just a few of the many potential options for connectivity offered by today's PCs including web browsing, email, instant messaging, social networks, downloadable apps and programs, location-based services, and online multimedia sharing, we'll dive into greater detail on how to protect your children on these systems in later sections.

Mobile Phones and Smartphones – Once upon a time, many kids dreamed of getting their own landline – one they didn't have to share with other family members, and where they'd worry about someone accidentally interrupting online transmissions by picking up the handset in the middle of them. Today, the decision to let your kids use a cell phone is virtually a non-option, being less a choice of if, but rather simply when you'll get one for them. Portable handsets are becoming increasingly affordable, with many cell phone carriers even providing families with mobile phones for free in exchange for fixed monthly subscription plan signups. Thankfully, basic feature phones and smartphones alike can provide invaluable peace of mind for parents, helping kids stay in touch when out of sight or in case of emergencies, helping you keep tabs on them and enjoy a sense of sustained contact even when they're away from the nest.

Near ubiquitous, some would argue that you may actually be doing kids a disservice by not providing access to these handsets, with 77% or more of kids aged 12-17 now owning a cell phone, according to Pew Internet Research. Other surveys that have examined a broader range of age groups have found similarly widespread ownership levels, indicating that at least two-thirds of kids between 8 and 18 today boast their own cellular device — no surprise, given the constant connectivity and handy access to everyday tools (e.g. maps, local business information, and weather reports) such devices provide. But it bears remembering that while many of these gadgets are simply basic cell phone models, sometimes referred to as "feature phones," a large portion of those in kids' hands are so-called "smartphones," which provide much more than convenient ways to make phone calls.

Offering Internet access and hardware performance that's growingly on-par with home computers, these portable solutions can provide similar functionality, and even display Web pages or run software programs, the same way that a desktop PC does. Mobile computers unto themselves, smartphones let kids share photos, videos and status updates online; chat and connect with one another; send multimedia or text messages directly to other handsets; purchase and download applications that let you share information such as personal likes, interests and locations; and make it possible for children to engage in playing games, communicating online and videoconferencing with their friends, growing trends that more and more kids are enjoying.

Many children actually use their smartphones as a primary way to stay connected to social media services and networks, such as Facebook, Twitter, Instagram, Pinterest, Snapchat and more. As a point of note, the ubiquity of smartphones and their increasing usage levels amongst tweens and teens has actually led to a sharp increase in kids' consumption of media. From Apple's critically-acclaimed iPhone to prominent rivals that instead utilize thepopular Android operating system, smartphones all also present opportunities for kids to purchase, download and install apps (short for applications). Bite-sized and often free or value-priced software programs that add a wealth of functionality, letting devices double as everything from TV remote controls to foreign language translators and GPS navigation systems, apps have become tremendously popular on a host of devices. But they can also present a whole host of opportunities for connecting online too, whether playing games simultaneously, tracking friends' movements on virtual maps, or just simply chatting with acquaintances in ways that can't be monitored.

App stores (online storefronts where these programs can be browsed and accessed) are now built by default into the majority of devices, and – like multimedia retail services such as Apple's well-known iTunes digital distribution portal – provide ample opportunities for impulse shopping. Numerous apps also offer subscription packages and "microtransactions," or small in-app purchases that can be made from within them (often at not so small prices, once they're added up), as part of their design. As concerning as the content children choose to consume here is the ready availability of virtual goods that kids may be tempted to buy. Whether shopping for original apps, downloading favorite TV shows, songs and movies, or even buying special in-app items that help advance gameplay in digital diversions, impulse buys – and access to them – are plentiful. There are literally millions of different apps available for download today, and that's before you count individual pieces of content like songs and videos that kids can also access on-demand. Needless to say, no one parent can hope to keep tabs on all – and that's before you even consider the potential impact on kids' shopping and spending habits.

In addition, many of the tried and true solutions that experts and parents once turned to for keeping kids safe on computers, such as traditional anti-virus and Web monitoring software, simply aren't as effective anymore on mobile devices. "With smartphones, suddenly it's all out the window," says Mike Vance, senior director of product management of RealNetworks. "These things are portable custom computers, and you can't enforce the same usage rules as you could when the device was a common appliance." Certainly, many software makers and solutions providers offer tools that aid parents with online search result filtering, Internet tracking and the blocking of access to controversial websites. But so many apps and online services offering so much functionality now come out at such a blistering pace (even before you factor in constant the ongoing feature and software updates numerous programs offer), any given number of which may provide kids with a viable workaround, that keeping children safe is now a moving target.

Parents who buy smartphones for their children should therefore be aware of what they're getting their kids into, as they're full-fledged computers, urges Vance. "Kids are way smarter than parents when it comes to knowing how to use these devices," he cautions."[Unlike in other areas and fields,] kids are the more advanced users here." As he explains, an intelligent and motivated child can take an Android phone that's been "locked down" with parental controls, download a certain app for it, wipe away monitoring features, and then reinstall an operating system and use the phone in whatever manner they choose. There are also other applications that allow kids to chat, send pictures, and even speak directly to each other or engage in video chats with no way to track this activity. What you don't know may come back to haunt you. "Just because you don't see it doesn't mean it didn't happen," Vance warns chillingly.

That said, it also bears remembering that many smartphone interactions are highly positive in nature, and that a healthy, well-adjusted child will certainly be able to utilize these handsets in a responsible manner given proper training and supervision. Worth recalling as well: Just because you've decided to purchase a phone for your kids doesn't meant that you have to start them out with a smartphone model, despite the fact that they'll surely try to convince you of the necessity of doing so. In fact, many experts recommend giving kids more basic phones such as FamilyBase or Kajeet, which can limit numbers that may be dialed, let you track tots' current location, or provide a set amount of call time each month. Whichever route you choose, realize that an ounce of prevention far outweighs a pound of cure, however. In addition to providing kids with basic training and creating a healthy environment in which they feel comfortable coming forward and discussing related concerns, you'll still

need to actively monitor children's activities in cyberspace, and work to teach kids the healthy computing habits and digital citizenship basics they need to be safe online.

Don't be fooled either: Kids with feature phones can often use the Internet just as actively as smartphone users would too. Even though these less advanced handsets may lack a keyboard and/or serious computing horsepower, and require use of the numeric keypad to assemble words or phrases, you'd be amazed just how far they can take a determined netizen. To wit, despite seeming limitations, such devices can still keep kids connected to the Internet through basic Web browsers, texting and e-mail capabilities. Consider any cellular phone a potential source of high-tech communications and connectivity.

Tablet PCs and Mobile Devices – A hyper-intuitive and ever-popular breed of consumer electronics device that marries the best aspects of PCs and portable media players with smartphones' versatile nature and connectivity, slate-like tablets use a touchscreen interface to help kids surf the web, play games, email, download software and enjoy multimedia content. Among today's hottest new forms of mobile computing, thanks to burgeoning interest in the category (largely kick-started by the success of Apple's bar-raising iPad and Amazon's wildly successful Kindle units) they're becoming an increasingly popular part of family life– and one being introduced to kids at an earlier age. Capable of running apps (a.k.a. software programs), music, videos, web browsers, eBooks and more, a recent report from comScore underscores the growing ubiquity and of tablet computers: Whereas it took seven years for 40 million Americans to purchase a smartphone, tablet PCs reached this milestone in less than two years alone.

Interestingly, the majority of parents and families trust their kids to have tablets because of the potential educational benefits. Research from iYogi Insights shows that 92% of parents approve of an iPad as a homework tool, and that on average, parents are willing to allow their kids to use these tablets for nearly two hours a day.

Whether you own an iPad or Android-based model, there are literally dozens of new tablet choices available today, with even popular eReaders increasingly starting to sport similar functionality. Knowing this, the question is quickly changing from whether or not your family owns or intends to purchase one, to rather which system(s) your household prefers. Capable of being used in similar fashion as a home PC, albeit in a portable, motion-sensing format, many experts suggest that a family's tablet usage habits should be more closely akin to how members share

their living room TV. Instead of everyone in the family purchasing their own, they suggest that these devices are great for sharing, and can be used for streaming movies, listening to music or playing games in mixed company. Ultimately, parents need to know that tablets (and even digital music and portable media players such as iPod touch units, which are starting to sport similar capabilities, albeit on a smaller scale) can be customized and used in similar fashion as home PCs. They therefore need to be aware of access and browsing habits, stay abreast of content being consumed, and configure these devices so that kids can't rack up unwanted bills, or access questionable media, apps, services or websites on their own. Happily, parental controls are built into most of these devices, and parents can use them as a basic starting line of defense against the most common issues.

eReaders – The line between eReader and tablet computer is beginning to blur. However, a true eReader is designed primarily as a device for reading eBooks (potentially like the one you're enjoying right now). Many new models tack on extra features though, such as WiFi or mobile network (a.k.a. high-speed) connectivity, and built-in support for downloadable songs, movies or applications, though. In addition to making it easy to download and read books, they can be used to surf the web, watch videos, play music and download software programs and games – all things kids love to do. Think of them as "lite" versions of tablets that offer a similar range of functionality, if often less computing power.

The continued increase in popularity of eReaders has already had a marked impact on the way people purchase and consume books. Amazon.com actually sells more digital copies than print volumes now, and many insiders say that the popularity of eBooks helped contribute to the decline of brick and mortar bookstores, such as Borders, which shuttered its doors in 2011. A study from Harris Interactive goes so far as to show that, more than 50% of U.S. adults were using an electronic reader device such to catch up their favorite classics, independent-published books and New York Times bestsellers.

Overall, most important for parents to remember is as follows. Market leaders are actively working to make eReaders more powerful and PC-like in nature, even as prices continue to fall. This means that devices labeled as humble eReaders will, going forward, as often as not often much more comprehensive computing and connectivity features. Like any connected devices, they're a small window onto a much larger online universe.

Home A/V: HDTV, 4K/8K TV, 3DTV and Smart Televisions – You may not realize it, but today's growingly powerful HDTVs, Ultra HD TVs, 3D TVs and so-called

Smart TVs (read: Internet-connected sets) can also provide kids with extensive ways to connect online. Although not all sets offer such capabilities, many can be connected to your Wi-Fi network to stream and share content on-demand, or provide access to downloadable apps offering social networking, media sharing, gaming or videoconferencing features. Photos, videos and status updates can all be exchanged and consumed through such devices, and pay-per-view, rental, or permanent purchases made as well. From YouTube to Skype, eBay and Facebook, countless services can be accessed from the living room, with numbers growing every day.

Other home audio and video devices may also offer similar features, such as Blu-ray players that include or provide online access to apps such as Netflix and Pandora for streaming movies and music, respectively. Even without fully tapping into such offerings or your TV's online capabilities directly, many cable and satellite boxes offer added access to video recording on on-demand content streaming features, putting them at kids' fingertips the second they enter the home. From digital video recorders (DVRs), which let you tape shows to on-demand movie rentals and purchases, or streaming access to adult channels, the high-tech age has ushered in a wealth of new ways for kids to consume content. It's important to be cognizant of all. With the US Bureau of Labor reporting that watching TV is the most popular leisure activity time-wise amongst families, who watch an average of 2.7 hours a day, as crucial as monitoring access to on-demand media is making sure that children consume age-appropriate content.

Video Game Consoles –Today's video game consoles such as the PlayStation 4, Xbox One, Xbox 360, PlayStation 3, Wii and Wii U all rely heavily on online elements as key features, allowing players to team up with others online; engage in text, voice or video chat; download digital music, movies, apps and games; pass virtual notes between friends; participate in massively multiplayer online virtual worlds (MMOs); and sample software demos, social networks and streaming media subscription services, among other potential uses. Popular handheld systems like the PlayStation Vita and the Nintendo 3DS also have built in online functionality that allows owners to stream and share multimedia, play online games, download apps, access social networks, and connect with one another across WiFi, high-speed wireless and broadband networks.

While owning such systems doesn't mean having to connect them to the Internet, many are meant to serve as digital entertainment hubs and online access points as much as multiplayer-friendly options and virtual storefronts – as such, a great deal of value is derived from online elements.

From downloading value-priced exclusive digital titles right from your couch to checking out the latest football game live on ESPN using voice commands, accessing online libraries of millions of songs, or competing head-to-head against other players while enjoying unfiltered and unmoderated voice chat, the connected options such systems offer are plentiful, and highly compelling. Today's home video game systems offer families the chance to do much more than just play video games. With sample uses including connecting with friends to watch movies in shared company to enjoying live streaming programming or chatting and hanging out with people who share similar interests, each provides a vast gateway to a realm of high-tech entertainment experiences.

Thankfully for parents who may feel concerned and overwhelmed by the prospect, it's worth recalling that millions worldwide enjoy positive and safe computing experiences when utilizing these devices every day. According to Doug Park, who specializes in gaming-related issues as Microsoft's online safety director, negative interactions happen far less often than casual observers might think. Keeping kids safe on video game systems is simply a matter of staying on top of three key areas, he says, those being content, conduct and contact, i.e. what games kids are consuming, how they behave when playing them, and the individuals that players interact with. In addition to monitoring all content provided through their services, which must be approved for distribution via a submissions process, manufacturers such as Sony, Nintendo and Microsoft also provide built-in parental controls within their devices. These password-protected settings can allow you to restrict content by age, rating and subject matter, as well as limit Internet access, online purchases and high-tech communications. For more on video game ratings, parental controls and what to be aware of when introducing video games to the home, we invite you to download The Modern Parent's Guide to Kids and Video Games free at www.parentsguidebooks.com.

SUMMARY

After looking at the many ways in which kids can now connect online, astute readers will note the duality of the role that parents must play in the modern high-tech world, as underscored by Lynette Owens, director of Internet safety for kids and families at Trend Micro. Owens agrees that it's our job as caregivers to do much more than simply safeguard our kids when using all these different forms of media and high-tech devices to connect online. "What we're really talking about here is not how to keep kids safe, but how to make them responsible," she says. Stressing the

importance of digital citizenship, or promoting positive online behavior, as a key part of training that must be provided by parents, teachers and kids, she touches on an important point we often make as part of our own public speaking efforts. Shepherding and stewardship are as much a parent's responsibility as safety and security — teaching kids to be caring, thoughtful and prudent are part and parcel with adequately preparing them for life in the online age.

Raising responsible kids is, at its core, one of the key pillars of Internet safety. To this extent, this book provides an extensive overview of the many types of online interaction that kids will be involved in as they grow, and a look at the many potential benefits and dangers that children may encounter. As you read through each section, note the presence of tips, perspective and research provided by an all-star panel of experts, who help weigh in on the issues present. Later chapters will also offer age-by-age suggestions on when to introduce different high-tech gadgets and technology, and provide insight into how to broach and discuss these issues with children too. It's our hope that all will provide you with a better understanding of the high-tech and online world, and help you prepare the next generation for tomorrow's connected reality in turn.

PART II:

WHAT DOES IT MEAN TO GO ONLINE?

WHAT DOES IT MEAN TO GO ONLINE?

As we parents actively adopt or introduce new technologies and work to prepare kids to "go online," it becomes clear that these two seemingly simple and innocuous words can, in actuality, have varied and powerful meanings. Just what precisely does it mean to "go online" or to have your kids connect to the Internet? Ask any two individuals the same question, and you may shocked by just how much the answers differ.

Today, connecting online means so much more than the ability to access Web pages that contain text, video and pictorial information. It means the ability for kids to videoconference with friends, family and acquaintances around the globe 24/7 nearly anytime, anywhere. It means the ability to log into social networks and share personal status updates, photos and videos, or engage in group chat sessions, from an endless array of mobile devices. It means the opportunity to send text messages, or post tweets, to others we know without a second thought in a matter of seconds, all of which may live on in perpetuity for future employers and college recruiters to see. It means playing complex 3D video games with voice chat capabilities with dozens of others in real-time even though you may be thousands miles apart, or participating in constantly evolving virtual worlds within which thousands can interact online at any given moment.

And, most of all, it means having to be constantly aware of how you're behaving, interacting, leaping in and out of the real world, and interacting with others at any given second, even as the range of options for online connectivity, and ways in which one can potentially use them, grow with each passing day.

Such unfettered access to an array of online opportunities, all of which completely differ in terms of usage and interest by device, interest and individual, is also starting at a startlingly young age. Surveys of parents with children that are under five years in age say that large percentages of their kids use the Internet. Furthermore, 82% of kids who fall into this group actually do so on a weekly basis. Amazingly, amongst these members of Generation Tech, such activity now seems as natural, or even more so, than riding a bike, having grown up as digital natives – those for whom consuming technology is second nature, and an everyday part of childhood.

From a parent's perspective, this means that in order to best relate to and understand kids' online activities, you must first understand and (whenever possible) be prepared to immerse yourselves in these activities yourself. Happily for those for whom time is tight, you needn't become an expert at every new technology, app, gadget or nuance introduced – a near-impossible task. Rather, you must simply become a generalist who's familiar with the basics of any given product, service, or trend, knows where to turn for information online, and understands the right questions to ask. The good news for parents struggling to cram 30 hours into any given day: Thousands of resources are available right at your fingertips in the form of downloadable apps, online publications and Internet forums, as well as hardware and software creators' own websites. From "how to turn off in-app purchases on the iPhone" to "configuring privacy settings on Facebook" or "where to setup parental controls on the Wii U," a simple online query via any major search engine will often turn up a wealth of answers. We offer one such resource at www.AKeynoteSpeaker.com – and steer readers to a sampling of additional resources that supplement each article. Going hands-on with new tech advancements is the best form of learning; in a pinch, however, scanning review sites, community forums, customer support databases, blogs, magazines and more can often provide answers in seconds. It seems simple, but it's worth remembering: When it comes to kids and high-tech software or devices, you're seldom the first in the world to ask any given question.

Setting a specific time aside each day or week to research these topics, or conduct hands-on testing sessions with products and services yourself, can help you be a more informed parent and smarter consumer. It can also put you in the right mindset: One that focuses on defining challenges and hunting for specific solutions, rather than agonizing over nebulous concerns. Happily, most hands-on learning that you'll engage in also often maps well across devices, apps, services, and solutions as well: While not all will share common user interfaces, many recycle common concepts, and are built on shared operating systems. As a simple example, privacy settings may not all live in the same place on specific devices or platforms – however, it's a safe bet that they're hiding somewhere in the menu system, and once you've discovered what to look for (location tracking, in-app buys, etc.) you'll know to look for these settings in other situations. Computing may not seem natural to those who didn't grow up with it: However, today's devices are built to be more user-friendly than ever. Apart from experience, a technophile's true advantage is also simply that they're curious by nature: Don't be afraid to play and tinker with the tools at hand, as even we tech experts must at times, so long as settings can easily be restored, and are clearly labeled.

Not being able to program a proverbial VCR isn't the problem – not being willing to learn how to do so is. When it comes to technology, a closed mind is the only barrier. Kids aren't such whizzes at technology because they're born geniuses, but rather because they're curious, and prone to experiment by nature. Likewise, don't beat yourself up or feel guilty because you haven't been able to devote every waking minute to learning the latest features introduced in a brand new social networking app — that's why they pay professionals to report on it, and put the answers a single online query away. Just ask the experts, who'll readily tell you that managing such issues isn't easy, even when doing so is your full-time job, given the breakneck speed at which technology evolves. "[Keeping tabs on technology] is really hard," says Symantec's Internet safety advocate Marian Merritt. "It changes constantly. Parents need to forgive themselves and understand they're not going to be perfect."

THE I-GENERATION CULTURE– AND HOW TO EMBRACE IT

"Today's youth, the I-Generation [Ed. Note – that which we refer to elsewhere as Generation Tech], live in a wonderful world of opportunity. What adults don't understand is that for these kids, there truly isn't an online and offline world anymore — modern children live in a digital universe.

I recently heard an interesting story of a young mother with a one year-old baby, who helps her baby communicate with her husband while he's at work. She helps her baby send "texts" to her dad. Of course, the text doesn't mean anything: It's just garbled letters that appear on the phone. But dad gets these messages, and he knows that his baby is writing him. So he texts back "I Love You" or a short message and the mother reads it to her baby. A powerful communication tool, the example clearly illustrates how digital contact is starting at such a young age for kids these days.

Recognizing the impact technology is having on the household, we at Web Wise Kids (WWK) are focusing on entire sphere of children's digital lives and educating them to make wise choices and be responsible citizens in a digital world. Our mission is to create responsible netizens in the high-tech age — youth we believe to be the I-Generation, whose entire world is filled with online and social media.

Many times you hear stories in the press about the misuse of this media, especially as relate to current issues like cyber bullying and sexting. We hope to empower youth, educate them about the consequences of the choices they make, and help them better understand the great new digital world they suddenly live in. It's our belief that this I-Generation needs to be equipped with the knowledge and tools to have a safe and rewarding digital experience – online, offline, or otherwise.

We need for parents and kids to understand that the entire culture of the world has changed. It is a brave new world, and we need people to educate themselves and take advantage of the resources that are out there, such as the programs that we offer to help parents get up to speed on what their kids are involved in now. As I said, it is a completely new world and parents need to be made aware of where their kids are going, what they are experiencing, and help them to be responsible citizens.

We aim to educate kids on how to have a safe and rewarding online experience. It's important to understand that this requires embracing and encouraging technology while also teaching kids how to use it safely. Kids can have great experiences with technology: We hope you'll join us in embracing the use of interactivity as a teaching tool that challenges kids to make appropriate high-tech and online decisions.

by Judi Warren, Web Wise Kids

Also worth noting: While the ability to go online shouldn't be offered as an inalienable right for kids, it's a key part of their lives that may not be practically feasible for parents to take away or block access to completely. Experts like Laurie Nathan from the National Center for Missing & Exploited Children urge parents to remember that they shouldn't simply opt to ban technology outright, because it could put their kids at a huge disadvantage. Likewise, attempting to restrict access completely as part of grounding them may be impossible, whether due to necessity (e.g. if there's a need to complete online coursework teachers have assigned) or practicality (you need your child to have a cell phone to make sure they've gotten home from school, but don't have a spare Internet-restricted model to substitute for a smartphone, whose online access you aren't able to minutely monitor). Be astute and reasonable, and craft solutions to fit each problem, allowing that in some instances, you may not always be able to track whether your rules are being respected. Ultimately, let logic reign – your child sneaking in a round of Angry Birds on the bus despite being told "no games" is far less worrisome than sending them to meet friends at a remotely-located mall without a cell phone and way to stay in contact. "Parents need to educate themselves about technology so they don't just panic and pull the plug," Nathan advises.

Mike Vance, former director of web and cloud services at T-Mobile and a champion of family safety, agrees here. "The only form of discipline many parents know is to take things away," Vance says, which in his mind isn't always effective or reasonable. "It defeats the whole point of why they got the device in the first place," he says. The message these and other experts we spoke with want to send: Before you take things away, think about the incredible opportunities your children are being afforded by be able to stay in contact and go online at-whim, and instead embrace them and come up with ways to better direct and manage their online interactions. Or, as Vance puts it, set up guardrails to guide and protect them.

But lest you feel the approach too laissez-faire, make no mistake: It's also imperative that you learn as much as you can about what kids are doing on these devices as well. "Children are obviously accessing the Internet earlier and earlier. Parents absolutely, positively need to assess their activities and take an active role in managing how and when kids are online," Nathan explains.

Over the course of the next few pages, we'll look at a small sampling of the many different ways that modern kids frequently live their lives online. As a high-level overview of the near-infinite multitude of connected possibilities at their fingertips, while we touch on and examine a few key concerns throughout this section, we likewise urge you to examine and research the common threats, problems and potential dangers outlined in the following chapter further. In addition, it's highly recommended that you look at our suggestions for age-appropriate activities, including when and how to introduce each, which we touch on later in this volume.

Web Browsing – The ability to access web pages through browsers such as Internet Explorer, Firefox, Google Chrome, Safari and other popular solutions is, to some extent, the very essence of today's online experience. Kids suddenly have access to unimaginable amounts of information with just a few taps on a touchscreen or keyboard clicks. It's hard to get an exact estimate of just how many libraries' worth of material is now available, but UK research company Netcraft estimated that there were 525 million different websites on the Internet – and that was several years back. Even if you focused on the third of those that are considered "active," spending just one second on each site would take five and half years to accomplish.

Hyperbole aside, the simple fact is that countless volumes of information exist on virtually any topic you can imagine – real, fictionalized, and for better or worse all now literally lay at your kids' fingertips. And thanks to their growing ubiquity across a range of high-tech devices from smartphones to tablets and video game systems, Web browsers are likely to be the primary way that they'll access them. With numerous solutions available based on device, personal need or age-appropriateness, choosing a browser is often simply a matter of personal preference or familiarity.

However, five of the most popular Web browsers currently are Internet Explorer, Google Chrome, Firefox, Safari and Opera, with the first three accounting for more than 90% of all online usage. Through the use of built-in parental controls, these browsers all contain tools to help make sure your kids are only accessing the pages they should be.

Not sure how to restrict access to only desired sites? As Stephen Balkam, CEO of the Family Online Safety Institute (FOSI)explains, "there really is no excuse now for parents [not to know how to] restrict their kids' Internet usage." And even if you're unsure how to go about configuring these settings, here's the good news – doing so really is as simple as punching the question into Google to find out more information, as Balkam points out. For those who use common computer operating systems, here is just a small sampling of the types of content and interactions that can be controlled:

• Web restrictions. You can restrict the websites that children can visit, make sure children only visit age-appropriate websites, indicate whether you want to allow file downloads, and setup which content you want the content filters to block and allow. You can also block or allow specific websites.

• Time limits. You can set time limits to control when children are allowed to login to the computer. Time limits prevent children from logging on during the specified hours and, if they are already logged on, they will be automatically logged off. You can set different logon hours for every day of the week.

• Games. You can control access to games, choose an age rating level, choose the types of content you want to block, and decide whether you want to allow or block unrated or specific games.

• Allow or block specific programs. You can prevent children from running programs that you don't want them to run.

While knowing how to setup and configure parental controls may have been enough for a concerned parent to be aware of in the past though, as discussed earlier, remember: The explosive growth of mobile phones and tablets shows that simply managing Web browsing and content consumption from your home computer alone is just a starting point when it comes to online safety. Remember that according to a recent report from Pew Center, more than three-quarters of teens have or have access to smartphones. These children alone are, naturally, less likely to access the Internet through traditional desktop or laptop computers.

E-mail – Through any number of free e-mail programs such as Gmail, Yahoo! Mail, Hotmail and more, kids can communicate with others by exchanging messages, which contain text and photos, as well as video and file attachments. Many e-mail providers are starting to enforce a starting age limit on e-mail accounts, but parents and determined tots can easily work around such limitations, and many families in fact start their children off by signing up for accounts around the ages of eight or nine. Although sending messages to friends on Facebook is increasing in popularity amongst children as well, the three top e-mail providers we've named combined account for more than 1 billion different accounts alone.

Giving kids their own e-mail account is one of the first steps that many parents take to provide them with online independence. But it's also key that you still maintain control of their account should the need to access to control it arise. You can do this both by linking their e-mail and related activity to your own account, but also maintaining knowledge and control of kids' passwords so you can check in on these accounts from time to time.

Aside from communications, one of the main reasons kids will want an e-mail address is that they're needed to register for many online services. However, it's not a bad thing to require kids to use their parents' e-mail accounts instead of their own, or utilize a shared account. When signing up for these services, kids should always use an account that parents control, because there are often many features provided that are designed specifically for parents to use to help manage kids' online usage.

For young children that don't have their own cell phone yet, an e-mail address and an iPod Touch with a wireless connection can act almost like "texting training wheels," providing kids with a way to communicate back and forth in quick bursts with their friends. E-mail use, however, is on the decline, as kids are using texting, IM programs and even video chat more and more as ways to communicate with their friends.

Social Networks – Whether discussing Facebook, Twitter, Instagram, Google+ or other services, the key element that defines a social network is the fact that personalized content is being created and shared between real-world users in an online space – and one specifically dedicated to facilitating these interactions.

Although the infrastructure is provided by the service (and constantly changed and updated), content contained within each network – e.g. status updates, tweets, photos, videos and article links – is primarily provided by people you have somehow chosen to be connected to, and you likewise can provide similar material to others, whether publicly or via private channels. Here's why this is important to note: Social networks need ample supporting participants, and a constant stream of contributions from active users, in order to function and thrive. This simple fact that kids are registered members of social networks isn't necessarily anything to be concerned with, however, unless they've proven to be untrustworthy when it comes to setting personal or private boundaries in the past. More important to consider are the actions that they're performing on these networks, what types of information that they're sharing and how, and to whom this data is visible.

The way kids can connect differs by social network: Some require actions (i.e. approvals) from both parties to be connected, which is one reason why many parents seem to trust Facebook – both individuals must agree to be connected in order to see each others' updates (unless privacy settings aren't correctly configured...a point we'll touch on shortly). But others like Twitter or Google+ merely require that people opt to "follow" others to gain consistent access to all the information that said party is sharing, without requiring approvals or reciprocal actions. That's why Twitter can be a useful way to keep tabs on your favorite celebrities, sports stars or other well-known individuals, but isn't necessarily the first port of all for those looking for deep, private exchanges. All material shown on the network is visible, and moves at the speed of light, making it great for exchanging information. (Not to mention parents hoping to quickly check and see who their kids are keeping tabs on: It's

nice to see that your children follow Barack Obama, although less gratifying to discover that they also follow the Kardashians.) However, if helping your child keep a low profile, or preventing strangers from observing their updates is of primary concern, you might consider other solutions.

That said, once they've connected to and begun actively using social networks, these platforms can introduce your children to people from all places, walks of life and different backgrounds. But for better or worse, social networks can also serve as an amplifier for the information that kids decide to share or consume, potentially putting this data in front of millions. Facebook spokesperson Marian Heath says that she hears from parents all the time that Facebook is a place where there kids can get in trouble. But she urges parents and teens to consider such concerns from a different angle, because such interactions needn't be negative – it's all about what you choose to share with and project to the world.

"You can build your own image," Heath explains. "Post the good things you're doing and share your interests. Have conversations online so folks can find out what's interesting to you. Ask friends about books you're reading, plays you're interested in." In other words, rather than gossip or make jokes at others' expense, post inappropriate or unflattering comments, share embarrassing images, or portray themselves in an unwelcome light, it pays for kids to instead set a positive example and use the service as it was intended. Noticeably, a clinical report from the American Academy of Pediatrics entitled "The Impact of Social Media on Children, Adolescents and Families" found that a large part of Generation Tech's social and emotional development is occurring while using social networks. The report lists a number of benefits that kids enjoy from being connected, such as better engagement with friends, family and community; enhanced learning opportunities via collaboration; connections with like-minded teens; and enhancement of creativity. As a point of note, the study further found that 22 percent of teenagers log onto their favorite social media sites more than 10 times a day.

But many parents may not realize that Facebook's terms of service actually require users to be at least 13 before registering for an account. The chief reason for this is because of the laws in place that restrict marketing to and collecting data on kids under the age of 13, found within the Children's Online Privacy Protection Act (COPPA). But still, recent estimates place the total number of children below this age already on the serviceat upwards of 7.5 million kids, and studies show that in some cases, parents are actively helping children lie in order to register. That's especially troubling as the vast majority of teens polled say that they've actively witnessed acts of meanness and cruelty firsthand on these services.

As with many things in life, though, some experts see room for personal judgment to play a role when making the call as to when to let your child register for Facebook or other social networks. "Thirteen can be an arbitrary number," says Symantec's Marian Merritt. "[Children mature and develop at different paces.] It may make sense that a 12 year-old youngest child might just want to get online to see the pictures that everyone else in the family is posting and talking about."

One your child is over 13, though, Merritt points out that they have a right to be on social networks. "However, you as a parent have a right to control their activity," she says. Interestingly, parents may also be surprised to learn that they don't have the power to take children's accounts away. Merritt says that although users can take down their own accounts, parents don't have the authority to delete kids' accounts without their teens' permission. What parents can do though, she urges, is take responsibility to educate themselves about online dangers and best practices as relate to social networks, and teach their family through active discussion and research, and leading by example.

An overwhelming number of parents claim to be very concerned about what their children are exposed to online, yet only 30% actively report visiting their child's social media profiles. Connecting and keeping tabs on what kids are up to on Facebook, Google+, Twitter, Pinterest, Instagram and other services is a great start. It's also important to note that adults and kids use Facebook very differently. While adults are very tuned into accepting friend requests from only those they know in real-life, kids are far more likely to use the service to connect with strangers. Although for many parents and adults the appeal to a service like Facebook is the sheer number of connections they have, for kids, having too many friends (in the online sense of the word) is sometimes a big turn off. We've talked to a few tweens and teens who are on Facebook because all their friends are, but that also tell us that they don't like to update their profiles often for the exact same reason — because all their friends are on it. So they're constantly searching for other services, which allow them to connect to the friends they want to in newer, fresher and more original ways.

A ways back, TRUSTe announced the results of a nationwide survey of both parents and their teens investigating their privacy habits and preferences on social networks. What the study found was that, for the most part, "the kids are alright," noting that a majority of teens use privacy controls on social networks and that most parents actively monitor their teen's privacy. But there's still room

for improvement, with more than two-thirds of teens admitting that they'd accepted a Facebook friend request from someone they didn't know, and nearly one in 10 teens admitting to accepting all friend requests that they receive.

Monitoring your teens' Facebook accounts is only part of the commitment you'll want to make to parenting on social networks, however — you'll also want to figure out how often you'll be checking in. In the TRUSTe survey, 72% of parents surveyed said that they monitor their teens' accounts, with half of these parents monitoring on a weekly basis, while 35% percent checked in daily and 10% monthly.

Not all kids are receptive to this process, however — many times, children's unspoken rules of behavior on social networks will involve how to use these sites in the manner that they choose despite the fact that they're connected to you. There are detailed instructions easily accessible via a Google search that offer kids tips on "how to friend your parents without sacrificing your privacy," which essentially provide a step-by-step guide for kids on how to setup privacy controls before accepting your friend request so that they can continue to post information without you seeing it, even if you're connected via the service. In fact, according to the same TRUSTe survey, 80% of teens have admitted to posting content to Facebook that they've hidden from certain friends and/or parents by using privacy settings. Don't be fooled: While it's important to trust your little angel, it's also crucial to do your detective work.

SHOULD ACCESS TO FACEBOOK BE A GIVEN FOR TEENS?

In February 2012, a much-shared video showed what a tech-savvy, gun-toting father could do as punishment for his child posting inappropriate and disrespectful material on Facebook. Tommy Jordan created an eight-minute YouTube video detailing his daughter's transgressions, and concluded it by literally shooting her laptop computer. After he posted the clip to Facebook, it quickly went viral and caused many parents to discuss the issue with their kids about what's appropriate to share via social networks and what's taboo.

The positive side of the incident is that it got many parents talking about the issues of teens' rights to register for Facebook, the material that they should be sharing, and also appropriate consequences for negative actions. Marian Merritt, Symantec's Internet Safety Advocate, agrees that this was a great test for parental views about how to handle teens and technology. Ultimately, she says, Jordan "lost his cool and damaged property" which is inappropriate behavior by parents under any circumstances. But his actions also provide an interesting case study, because a majority of those offering opinions on the issue via the Internet seemed to side with him — wild rampage or otherwise.

The somewhat scary thing to note about the transgression (apart from Jordan shooting the computer) is the way he found out about what his daughter posted. She had set up the post to only go to friends and not be visible to family, but she forgot to exclude the silly account the family had set up for their dog, and Jordan was able to read the posting when he logged in as his pet to make a funny comment on a different picture. High-profile stunts such as this will always be part and parcel with Internet culture, and as parents, provide pressing opportunities to bring Internet safety issues and discussions to the kitchen table. While they are not to be celebrated in any circumstance, they do provide topical reasons to bring up, address, and revisit common safety topics with your family, and how they would deal with similar instances.

-JR

Despite the fact that we as parents may only be welcomed as connections to our kids on social networks as a mere courtesy, our job remains to help them manage their online identities wisely, try and help them avoid mistakes and, hopefully, take advantage of the wonderful opportunities that social networks provide. Unfortunately, examples of what NOT to do on social networks seem all too common. Whether it's posting inappropriate videos, sharing pictures with alcohol prominently involved, or generally making distasteful updates, both schools and employers are keeping an eye on what students and employees are doing, and disciplining those who act inappropriately.

There are also some potentially grave and dangerous consequences to misuse and abuse of social networks. Consider the case of Tyler Clementi, a homosexual teen who committed suicide after his roommate posted videos of his sexual encounters on Twitter. Not only do we take a closer look into growing concerns like Cyberbullying and Identity Theft in a later chapter, but we'll also dig much deeper into the positive and negative aspects of social networks in future volumes of The Modern Parent's Guide series. Happily, as many level-headed social network users know, like any form of technology, social networks can be a perfectly safe and fun way to share ideas and form healthy relationships with others online – many of whom we'd never have otherwise had the privilege to encounter. Ultimately, triumph or failure lies entirely in how you choose to use these tools, and how skillfully and dutifully you guide your kids to make positive choices when employing them as well.

Here's a quick look at the most popular social networks:

• Facebook helps people stay connected with friends and family, and is today's most well known social network amongst all age groups. Users must both agree to become "friends" in order to view each others' updates, photos, links and more, which can be accessed from the Web, smartphones, tablets and other devices.

• Twitter is a real-time information or "micro-blogging" network in which users exchange short text messages called "Tweets" containing 140 characters or less. Anyone can access these updates through public searches, and users can subscribe to follow others' public updates, whether or not the action is reciprocated.

• Instagram is a hugely popular photo-sharing service amongst users of all ages. The service makes it simple to share life's magic moments with other users, and post images online for friends and family to see.

• Snapchat is a video messaging service in which users can send photos, videos, texts and drawings to a specified group of people. What's unique about Snapchat is that users set a time limit for how long recipients can view their snaps, after which they'll be hidden from recipients' devices, but not deleted from Snapchat's servers. What's scary is this service is often used by cyberbullies because of this very feature, and it's also used by children who do not want their parents to see what they're sending.

• Google+ connects you with other users, as does Facebook, but it also provides the option to group contacts by social circles, letting you filter the updates that friends can receive. As an example, using the service, you can share private updates only with family members, and choose to separately share more public missives with coworkers. Anyone can add you to their social circles, and it's up to you to manage who you connect with and follow.

• Pinterest is a photo-sharing site that easily lets users share and sort photos and brief captions for others to enjoy. It's exploding in popularity thanks to its highly visual nature and user-friendly interface.

• Tumblr is a "short-form" blog that allows for quick updates and photo sharing, and allows users to easily follow each other or discover other content that may be of interest.

Tips:

• If you're not already using a social networking service that your kids are,

register for it immediately. Like any other public space, children shouldn't be left unprepared or unguarded: You should have a thorough understanding of how each service works and how kids can use them. As an added benefit, this knowledge may also provide some common ground for discussions with your teens.

• Reassure kids that they don't need to be afraid to connect with you — and honor your word by treating them with respect and dignity. Remind them that you don't want to interfere with or embarrass them online; rather, that you just want to make sure they're making good choices, as in real life. And even though kids may want to "hide" things that they're posting from parents, the reality is that in today's world, once information is made available online, it's out there forever in the most visible of forums. Passively forcing kids to ask themselves "Do I want my mom to see this?" prior to posting can be hugely beneficial, saving them a world of potential hurt should something have otherwise come back to haunt them.

• It's not nice to talk about people behind their back, and many families also operate by the old saying "if you can't say anything nice, don't say anything at all" — both common maxims worth keeping in mind when operating online. Teach kids not to engage in negative banter about others, to be respectful of peers, and to not post pictures that could be seen as negative or unflattering in any light.

• Don't assume that privacy settings are automatically configured the way you'd want them to be. Take the time to configure your account and make sure updates, photos, videos and more are visible only to those you feel comfortable sharing them with. Likewise, consider using a private Twitter account to prevent unwanted messages from spambots or followers you don't know. Most social networks have extensive, easy-to-understand and searchable help sections too, so if you don't know how to do anything, never fear – help is usually just a click away.

• Although no one knows exactly what the future holds, chances are your kids may be applying to college after high school, and soon after that entering the working world. Recognize that those making life-changing decisions about your child's life are increasingly likely to examine their social media profiles in addition to any other information that your child has made public going forward. So be sure to remind kids that the things they post now can – and likely will – be used against them, even if it's five or ten years down the line.

• Not only should you know what you're getting your kids into before you authorize the setup of a social network account for them, but also establish yourself as a trusted guide, shepherding them through the sign-up process and using the opportunity to discuss privacy and sharing concerns. Doing so may also quickly provide you with a window into just how savvy children are when it comes to using the service, which could also provide an indicator that they've been using a friend or family member's account already.

• Finally, know your boundaries when it comes to following and interacting with your kids online. Refrain from posting publicly on their Facebook profile, or following their friends on the service. One good idea is to use social networks to connect to your kids' friends' parents to stay in touch. Nothing screams "OMG" like an overprotective or clueless parent posting sweet nothings to their mortified child's account in full virtual view of snickering classmates.

Voice Calls – Kids can now be reached almost anywhere thanks to mobile phones. Today's portable devices offer a host of other connected options, but still retain the standard ability for kids to call each other and chat. There are even programs like Skype that can provide devices that weren't meant to be phones with the ability to make calls through digital means as long as they have an Internet connection, speaker and microphone. On the flip side, there are also phones such as Kajeet that provide limited voice-calling options, full parental controls and even GPS tracking which can be a great introduction to the world of cellular phones for kids. Although there are many other ways for kids to stay connected, one shouldn't forget – many are still using good "old-fashioned" voice communication. According to the Pew Research Center, calling is still a central function of the cell phone for teens, and for many teens voice is their primary mode of conversing with parents. Granted, teens do make and receive far fewer phone calls on their phones than text messages, however.

According to a Pew Internet & American Life Project survey, the frequency of teens' phone conversations is actually on the decline while other electronic and Internet based forms of communication are on the rise. Only 14% of all teens say they talk daily with friends on a landline, and 26% of teens talk daily with friends on a cell phone, down from 30% and 38% in 2009. And nearly a third of teens say they never talk on a landline with friends – a fact which may come as a surprise to parents who grew up simply dreaming of having their own phone line.

Realize, though: As the "Trojan horse" that provides millions of kids with online connectivity, phones – and smartphones in particular – remain poised to offer kids the ready opportunity to make voice calls on-demand nearly anytime, anywhere. As such, wireless providers can also play an active role in providing a way for parents to monitor teens' phone usage, well beyond simply just tracking their voice calls.

T-Mobile looks at tools that provide guardrails to parents that are non-intrusive, says Mike Vance, the company's former director of web and cloud services. For example, parents can throttle the amount of data that can be used, or configure the phone's features to only be available at certain times of the day.

However, while the level of controls that parents have over these capabilities differs by provider, one of the primary control methods many parents opt for is to go the prepaid route, which means that instead of signing a one- or two-year contract for cell phone usage, service can be paid for as you go.

Interestingly enough, the Pew's surveys show that the most frequent texters are also the most frequent talkers. Texters who exchange more than 100 texts a day are much more likely than less active texters to say that they talk on their cell phone daily. More than two-thirds of heavy texters talk daily on their cell phones, compared with less than half of those who send less than 100 texts a day. In other words, if your kid's a chatterbox in everyday face-to-face scenarios, chances are they're also engaging in a lot of regular conversation – online or otherwise, whether you realize it or not.

Texting – Equipped with as little as another party's mobile phone number, kids can send messages back and forth via text or multimedia message. These missives differ from e-mails in that they're transmitted over a wireless carriers' cellular phone network as opposed to being transmitted over the Internet like e-mails. In fact, if you don't buy the right data and/or texting plan, children can quickly rack up hefty bills, since – outside of preset monthly limits associated with said plans – many phone companies will try and charge you by the message if they can.

The global average price of a text message is about $0.11, but, as alluded, many providers offer plans that allow unlimited texting for a flat rate. Again, we repeat: When signing up for cellular service, it's imperative that you make sure you have the right plan. Stories abound of parents being shocked with phone bills of $4,000 to even $20,000 or more because of not selecting the right texting packages for their family. While you may LOL at the idea some years later in life, we assure you, receiving a 20-page monthly billing statement won't seem so comical here and now.

Interestingly, the Pew Research Center has unearthed some eye-opening numbers about the prevalence and popularity of texting. A whopping 63% of all teens say they exchange text messages every day with people in their lives, which is far greater than any other form of communication amongst this demographic. Only 39% socialize via cell phone, and even when combined with the 19% who communicate with friends daily via landlines, the total still falls short of the number of teens who say that they're texting friends daily. Cheerfully for parents who fear that technology is making us more introverted, face-to-face meetings with friends still rank high on teens' social radar. But still, just 35% of those surveyed report getting to connect with friends in real-life every day. Even less have daily interactions with friends on social networks (29%), instant messages (22%) or e-mails (6%).

Moreover, the amount that teens are texting continues to rise. One in three teens sends more than 100 text messages a day, and half of teens send at least 60 texts per day. Girls, according to Pew, send and receive twice as many text messages as boys, and as teens grow, so does the amount they text, with the average amount sent by 14-17 year olds ranking at more than 100 texts per day. In addition, fully two-thirds of teen texters say that they are more likely to use their cell phones to text their friends than talk to them to them by cell phone. The key takeaway here: Texting is the dominant mode of communication for teens and the main groups of people that they're communicating with. As parents, it's imperative you learn how to text, text with your kids, and understand more about what it is they're doing and saying via this form of communication.

One of the reasons for the abundance and popularity of text messages is that they can be very brief and make use of a number of abbreviations, making them easy to compose, share and digest. This can also be a problem for a parent trying to keep tabs on kids' conversations, since all those "IDKs" or "SMHs" may look like gibberish. Be advised: It's important that you familiarize yourself with commonplace text abbreviations and their meanings. And if you come across slang terms that you don't know, a site like noslang.com can help you find out what your kids are saying by using its Internet slang translator, so you can quickly find out that "SLOS" means "someone looking over shoulder," for example.

If it all seems like gobbledygook to you, take heart: Netlingo offers an online dictionary of text abbreviations, with an extensive and searchable list of acronyms, so you can enjoy a crash course in how to speak in high-tech shorthand.

ONLINE SHORTHAND DICTIONARY: A GLOSSARY OF COMMON TERMS

Abbreviated messages have been a part of our language since the Pony Express, but they've experienced a massive resurgence with the advent of high-tech communications tools like instant messenger programs, texting, and social networks. As with previous generations who sent telegrams, users of modern technology often try to compress as much information into as little space as possible. Some solutions, like Twitter, are actually specifically designed to facilitate the exchange of short messages, while others, like phone-to-phone texting, are limited in length by necessity because transmitting each character literally costs the carrier money.

The most popular messaging services today oftentimes happen to be some of the newest, but the lingo has changed very little from the earliest days of the Internet. Following is a guide to common high-tech slang, shorthand and abbreviations that should help you translate these missives back into common English.

Here's a sample:

o ABT: About
o Addy: Address
o BBL: Be back later
o BFF: Best friends forever
o BFN/B4N: Bye for now
o BRB: Be right back
o BKA: Better known as
o BTW: By the way
o CYA: See ya
o CYE: Check your email
o FB: Facebook
o FUBAR: F***** up beyond all recognition

- o FML: F*** my life
- o FTW: For the win!
- o FYEO: For your eyes only
- o G2G: Got to go
- o GTFO: Get the f*** out
- o GTK: Good to know
- o IDK: I don't know
- o IMHO: In my humble/honest opinion
- o IMO: In my opinion
- o J/K: Just kidding
- o K: OK
- o Kewl: Cool
- o L8R: Later (as in good bye)
- o LMAO: Laughing my a** off
- o LMK: Let me know
- o LOL: Laughing out loud
- o noob: A newbie, or amateur
- o OMG: Oh my gosh
- o OTL: Out to lunch
- o Pix: Pictures
- o ROFL: Rolling on the floor laughing
- o RT: Real time
- o SMH: Shake my head
- o Srsly: Seriously?
- o STFU: Shut the f*** up
- o Thx: Thanks
- o TL;DR: Too long; didn't read
- o TTYL: Talk to you later
- o WIIFM: What's in it for me?
- o <3 :Shape of a heart - love
- o :) : Smiley face
- o :D : Big grin
- o :(: Frown
- o :P : Silly face
- o :o : Surprise or shock

(For more lists like this, make sure to check sites like NetLingo and NoSlang.com.)

Instant Messaging – Instant messenger (IM) programs allow kids to enjoy real-time chats with others by sharing text messages and animated or visual icons (typically emoticons, which convey mood or expression) instantaneously. As soon as a message is typed, it's delivered to the other party. Instant messages are typically quick back-and-forth notes, often involving short sentences and lots of abbreviations. In order to Instant Message with someone, it's typically necessary for both parties to be on each other's friends list and using the same service, but it's relatively easy in some IM programs for chats to happen between strangers and across multiple platforms.

According to a report by The Radicati Group, there were more than 2.5 billion IM accounts worldwide (and this was in 2011) – a number that will increase to 3.3 billion in 2015. Further, whether with free or paid apps, kids need only possess each others' usernames, handles or identification codes and it becomes extremely difficult to monitor their communications or even access a record of how much they're using these services.

Many of the same concerns that parents have with texting can also apply to IMs, especially when it comes to the language of abbreviations. But even worse, it's easier for strangers to try and connect with your kids via instant messaging programs. "The most common method for sexual predators to find victims," according to Stanely Holditch, a product evangelist for McAfee, "is to go to common chat rooms and lure kids into chats. And for some reason they seem to like using MSN Messenger." That's why McAfee and other security companies offer a variety of tools designed to guard against such negative interactions – be sure to seek them out where possible.

Chat Rooms and Video Chat – Believe it or not, old-fashioned chat rooms are still around, and these resources allow users to communicate quickly with many different users at the same time. There are lots of different sites available to kids that provide discussion forums focused on different topics as well. Today, chat rooms primarily serve as a group hangout, and one typically enjoyed in mixed company. Parents may wish to steer children clear of them for this reason, knowing that, as an alternative, many trusted programs allow kids to converse with familiar friends via computer without potentially exposing them to strangers' scrutiny.

One of the evolutions of the chat room now is the video chat room. Video chat is a way for kids to communicate "face-to-face" with others using webcams or other streaming media solutions to broadcast video to other parties in real time. Upsides of videoconferencing are potentially considerable, from letting doting grandparents who live out of state watch their grandkids grow to staying in touch with mom and dad when they're traveling on business trips.

A variety of videoconferencing programs can all help us stay connected, and bring the world closer together. Video chat is also being used as a tool in classrooms around the country and around the world, exposing kids to different cultures, languages and guest speakers that they otherwise might not get to experience without the aid of teleconferencing. In addition, there are networks that provide kids with the ability to easily broadcast their own streaming TV show, all thanks to the possibilities allowed by the widespread availability of webcams with streaming capability.

But just as there is great positive potential that can be recognized from video chat, it's easy to see how kids can get in trouble using it as well. On many of these services, you may find kids who are bored or curious that start broadcasting themselves via webcam only to end up being taunted, teased or propositioned by viewers. Others may choose to engage in behavior (e.g. that of a juvenile, rude or sexualized nature) that's inappropriate for public consumption – and potentially preserved on video for eternity for the world to easily share and see. Likewise, there are also programs which can match up users with webcams randomly with other webcam users for impromptu conversations. Considerable caution should be utilized when access to these tools and services are provided, and kids educated as to prospective dangers.

In addition to basic safety and digital citizenship tips, remember to teach kids who videoconference to remove all items which may contain identification or personal information from the backdrop when conversing with unknown parties. (If you allow them to chat with strangers at all, which we recommend you don't.) Likewise, they should know to unplug the camera or utilize the computer's built-in privacy shield when not in use. Under no circumstance should your webcam be aimed or activated in such a way that it displays telling information about you or your home, or that compromises household members' privacy.

Apps and Digital Downloads – App is short for "application," and potentially refers to any piece of software that you can install on your computer or mobile device, but primarily is used when referencing software programs that can easily be downloaded and run on an iPhone, iPad or any other high-tech product or mobile gadget. The numbers tell the tale, as does the signature tagline "there's an app for that" – alone, there are hundreds of thousands titles

available via Apple's App Store and Google Play, with over 1,000 new selections submitted every day. However, experts caution, "you don't need stats [to get a sense of their impact]... just go onto the App Store and look at the number of selections available for kids aged four and five years old," says McAfee's Holditch.

Apps can be free to play, or cost a small amount ranging from $.99 and up. Some also support online connectivity, location tracking, multimedia capturing or sharing, and in-app purchases. Apps are designed to be relatively inexpensive or even free to install, but developers then look to make a profit either via advertising or in-app buys.

Note that although much of the allure of these apps and digital downloads is their nominal price, providing your kids with permission to download whatever they want could quickly lead to some exorbitant bills. Stories abound of kids who have inadvertently racked up large bills by purchasing items from within their favorite programs. In fact, some parents in New York even sued Apple over the shock of receiving these charges.

To prevent hazards here, establish and enforce a family policy on downloading apps to smartphones or computers, and make sure that your kids understand it. Be certain that your kids are clear as to how and what, if anything, they can download and install, whether it costs money or not. Similarly, take steps to ensure that kids won't have access to your credit cards or account password information that would allow them to make unsupervised purchases.

Happily for parents worried about apps and children, many devices come with built-in controls that can help parents manage their usage. Adults can use each unit's parental controls toolset to change settings, control the content and features that kids can access, and also block the ability to make in-app purchases. Once set, restrictions can be password protected.

Another tip that many families use is to never associate their credit card with their online accounts. Whenever they want to purchase items, they simply use gift cards they've purchased in small denominations, or give children access to similar prepaid card solutions.

Online Gaming and Virtual Worlds –
There are plenty of online and Web browser-based games that kids can access and play for free. Some offer a collection of mini-games or adventures based on popular television or movie characters while others may provide an original, persistent world to explore as a 2D or 3D character, using a username and password system in order to save progress.

Moreover, online games aren't just for school-aged kids either. There are numerous options aimed at the preschool set and, in fact, up to 91% of tots are now video game players, says market researcher The NPD Group, noting children between two and five years of age as today's fastest-growing audience since 2009. This demographic is followed closely by girls and teens, thanks to the rise of smartphones and tablets.

On the bright side, many of the most popular online games for toddlers place a heavy emphasis on educational value, and are designed to be played by one player at a time or side-by-side if there's a multiplayer component. As kids get older, they'll become interested in playing more challenging games and connecting with others, exploring "massively multiplayer" online games in which hundreds or even thousands of other players occupy the same game world at the same time. Although there are many options for restricting and regulating chat, the appeal of these games is the ability to not only meet up and share experiences with friends, but also to play against other "human" opponents in arcade-style games, adventures and tests of skill.

Microsoft's online safety director expert Doug Park was kind enough to share some gaming tips for today's family:

- Only make friends with people you know in real life.
- Every online game has reporting tools. Be sure you're using them, because game makers don't want any inappropriate behavior to occur either. If something happens to you that you think should be reported, tell game supervisors.
- If the game offers voice chat, children and adults should only allow friends to access these features.
- Never use the same password for online games that you do for other services.
- Never give your username and password to anybody. There are times during gameplay where a friend may ask for your password, or access to your account. If this happens, report the behavior.

NOTE: We take a much deeper look into issues pertaining to kids and video games in our companion book The Modern Parent's Guide to Video Games.

Online Video and Photo Uploads – Whether from smartphones or computers, it's simpler and faster than ever to film, edit and upload a video or photo to online sites and immediately let the general public access your creation. And the amount of video content that's being uploaded and consumed every day is mind boggling. YouTube estimates that 60 hours of video are uploaded each minute and that clips receive more than three billion views a day. Many sites provide users a way to easily upload and explore user-created videos or images. Just as many applications make it easy to spread snapshots or short films on the Internet in seconds.

While videos and photos are being uploaded, and after they're live, users often have the option to decide whether to make multimedia creations public or private. However, most programs default or encourage that videos and photos be made public so that they can be searched, while many families are usually better served by keeping their materials private.

Though kids may enjoy dreaming of becoming famous by creating the next big viral video, there are also a few video basics that all families should know. For starters, once videos are uploaded, realize that your family can lose all control of who sees footage and when they view it. Video sharing sites have made it easier than ever to share and embed content on social media profiles and web sites as well, so if a video spreads like wildfire for the wrong reasons, it will be impossible to contain the damage. Additionally, many kids love posting videos of themselves doing dangerous or unwise things. And it's actually part of a college recruiter or employer's job to try and discover these missteps as part of their due diligence when considering prospective recruits and applications. So even though it may seem like harmless fun, teach your kids about potential pitfalls here, and discuss whether it's really worth it to jeopardize their future for a few dumb laughs now.

Alas, some kids really don't get it. In December of 2011, Florida police were able to capture some teen vandals who were knocking product off shelves at Target, Sears and Walmart because they had posted videos of their illegal activity online.

Digital and Streaming Music – Listening to music is one of the most frequent activities for kids online. After watching TV, downloading and listening to music is easily the second most popular leisure activity that 8 to 18 year olds engage in, according to the Kaiser Family Foundation. The average kid spends nearly two and a half hours a day listening to music, in fact, often multitasking while performing various other activities on the computer.

Whether it's searching for songs to download, chatting about tunes, engaging in group listening sessions, or using social media to share what they're listening to, kids online have the ability to access and engage with a vast array of music larger than any of us could have possibly imagined as we rifled through the cassettes at the corner record store when we were their age. Last.Fm, ReverbNation, and Bandcamp are all great ways to legally search, discover and download music. Pandora, MOG, Rdio, Slackerand Spotify all provide ways to stream music for free and share it with

friends as well, while Apple Music is poised to re-invent the way many listen to music online as well.

However, music downloads are also a way that many kids are introduced to peer-to-peer sharing, which allows file trading between computers and high-tech devices, with content frequently unregulated. Many sites also exist which encourage the illegal transfer and exchange of copyrighted material, and allow computers to share music and other content with each other free of charge. While peer-to-peer networks aren't inherently bad – like any tech tool, it's all in how users choose to utilize them – there are many reasons why your family may want to be leery of them. For example: Because content exchanges and uploads are often unsupervised, these services may be breeding grounds for malware, trojans and other harmful software, as distributing these corrupt files is as simple as renaming them after a popular song title.

In the case of one such site that was shuttered named Megaupload, the US Department of Justice targeted the leadership of the site, charging seven individuals associated with running the site with copyright infringement. The good news for families was that there were no ramifications for end users, but it only serves to underscore the fundamental problem: It's hard to know just what material is being exchanged via these services, and its potential threat level or legality. Bear in mind though, that many users safely and responsibly utilize peer-to-peer networks as well. However, it may be best to encourage children to steer clear for safety reasons.

On-Demand and Streaming Programming – Kids these days want to watch what they want when they want it – largely because virtually everything is now available on-demand. Case in point: Even if they don't tape a TV program to your digital video recorder (DVR), they can still use the television, computer, tablet PC, video game console or smartphone to purchase, rent or download it, or stream clips down via an online service like Netflix – which, for a monthly fee, provides streaming access to a vast library of content via PC, iPad, gaming console and more. Other services such as Hulu offer a number of free options for recently aired programs to be viewed with commercials, or access to an archive of shows for a monthly fee. Redbox and Amazon Prime also provide options for on-demand entertainment, with dozens more services and apps offering similar features. The moral of the story: Today's kids' world of entertainment is truly on-demand, and parents need to work harder than ever to monitor and regulate the shows, films or Web content that they watch, considering that children of all ages can access nearly anything desired with a few clicks or Internet searches.

Consider that some of these services offer parental controls, while others provide limited or no content restriction options. For safety's sake, avoid providing kids with access to your account information and passwords, and make yourself available to help them choose age-appropriate options when they're ready to watch their favorite programs.

Cloud Computing – Cloud computing refers to the practice of storing and running programs on remote servers, with results streamed back to users' desktops or video game consoles over wireless networks, rather than housed and run locally on devices. This means that, for example, if you download a song on iTunes on your home computer, and access Apple's iCloud, all your other devices linked up to your iTunes account can automatically enjoy access to the song, too. The reason this is important is the fact that kids may be able to access any sort of media that you or your family have downloaded to any device you own, even if they've never connected these gadgets directly to one other. Parents need to know about the cloud (as well as associated file, photo, video and content sharing services that that leverage it)and how to manage their data – and that kids may be able to access programs, games and content that leave little lasting footprints to track later on systems themselves.

The good news: Cloud computing isn't just cost-effective, convenient and potentially more productive for users. Some experts predict that it can play a helpful role in allowing parents who are traveling for business to remain engaged with their children's lives – even to the point that it can aid with learning and education. Not only can parents presently access grades, homework assignments and info on kids' classroom performance online – they can quickly collaborate and share documents, assignments and projects with kids as well.

Comments, Newsgroups and Online Forums – These days, nearly every piece of content encountered online offers the ability for readers to comment upon it. This can lead to extensive discussion and/or debate. There are also newsgroups and online forums that are dedicated to topics of specific interest in which the entire experience consists of the back-and-forth exchange of comments. The worry here is that it's all too easy to get caught up in arguments with strangers, and that many of these sites are linked to social network accounts, making it easy for others to see snide remarks or find out more information about you. Kids should be careful when posting comments on blogs, social networks and websites to consider how they carry themselves, whether they're being respectful of others, and what potential risks commenting exposes them to.

SUMMARY

Amazingly, despite all the ways to connect and communicate we've covered here, these selections represent just a handful of activities that connected kids can engage in online. Knowing this, it's little wonder that, from a parent's perspective, many may seem to be spending more time in the virtual world than the real one. According to the Kaiser Family Foundation, in fact, kids spend more than 7 ½ hours a day digesting some form of media, whether it's television, music, video games or other options. And they're masters at multitasking, able to effectively carry on various forms of communication and interaction via various devices simultaneously.

Clearly, while the appeal of Internet and online activity is strong, kids shouldn't be given carte blanche to do whatever they want whenever they want in cyberspace. In the next section, we'll take a closer look at the potential dangers that children may face, and provide recommendations for strategies that parents can take to mitigate them. We'll also examine appropriate times to introduce kids to various online activities and high-tech devices – another important point to consider when helping kids prepare for life in the high-tech world.

PART III:

POTENTIAL PROBLEMS, THREATS AND CONCERNS

POTENTIAL PROBLEMS, THREATS AND CONCERNS

Why do we make young children sit in car seats, or require bike riders to wear helmets? It's not that we are expecting to get in a crash or hoping that they fall off their bike, but rather that we as parents need to do everything we can to provide as much protection for kids in case something does go wrong.

"Only a small group of kids will get themselves into trouble online," notes Laurie Nathan, manager of national outreach and partnerships for the National Center for Missing & Exploited Children. "Most children are very aware of how to be appropriate online... there are just a small, select group of children who find themselves at risk." However, for the sake of these individuals, and all kids in general, it's imperative for modern parents to learn more about the potential risks which tots will face online. If you're looking for a quick crash course, sites like ConnectSafely.org, WiredSafety.org and SafeKids.org make welcome beginning points for discussing possible pitfalls surrounding social networks, instant messengers and online environments. Likewise, the NetSmartz newsletter provides a monthly update of current topics and discussion points of growing interest as relate to kids and Internet safety for parents and teachers.

The first and foremost point to remember before we dive in: As in the real world, an ounce of prevention far outweighs a pound of cure. So before we look closer at many of the specific danger areas and topics of concern when it comes to children and online safety, here are some basic rules worth remembering for kids and adults out of the gate:

• Never give out personal information such as your name, address, hometown, birthday, school, or telephone number online.

• Never upload pictures or video of yourself onto the Internet or to an online service where they can be accessed by individuals you don't personally know.

• Never tell people where you're currently located, headed soon, or are planning to visit, including when and where you're headed out for vacation.

• Don't download pictures, click on email attachments, or visit unsolicited online links from an unknown source, and be skeptical of those that arrive from friends bearing suspicious titles or arrive without
advance warning.

• Don't pass on or respond to postings that are suggestive, obscene, harassing or explicit, and use block features to prohibit further communications where possible.

- Be skeptical as to the truth of what's said online. Just because it's online doesn't mean it's true, so take everything with a grain of salt and a dose of common sense.

- Be wary of any possible real-world contact with individuals you've met online, and avoid doing so if possible. Should you choose to meet, do so in a public place, bring along a chaperone, and make sure to tell a designated contact where you are going, when you will check in with them, and reach out at regular intervals to let them know that you're OK.

- Don't forget that everyone that's online is playing a character. With grown criminals easily capable of posing as innocent grade-schoolers or sunny teens, you never who's who out there in a sea of splashy headshots or 3D cartoon avatars.

- No matter how inviting that cyberspace may seem, the same rules of conduct and etiquette that apply to interaction in any public space should also be respected in online areas.

- As with any form of screen time, every hour of online activity should be balanced with equal or greater time away from high-tech devices. Balance and moderation are key, and parents should set designated off-times when access to the Internet or mobile devices is not allowed.

- Where possible, confine use of high-tech devices to common or shared family areas so you can monitor what children are doing, whom they're doing it with, and how often these activities are occurring.

- Understand the features and capabilities of any high-tech device before putting it in kids' hands, and educate them as to potential pitfalls. Know that introducing to them to new technologies, products and services requires a running commitment on your part to remain educated and aware as to possible dangers.

- Set ground rules regarding the use of high-tech devices for your household, discuss them with children up-front, and enforce these rules.

- Before allowing kids online access, teach them digital citizenship and online safety basics, and encourage them to come forward with any questions or concerns. Create an encouraging and supportive home environment where all can feel free to air potential issues or problem areas.

These all-purpose tips apply to any situation where kids and technology are involved, and serve as a good starting point for any family looking to set some ground rules. What's important to remember above all else, remind many experts, is that parental involvement is key. "Online safety does not have a technological solution," says McAfee's Holditch. "It's a wild, hairy world for parents and teachers, so parental supervision needs to be constant and vigilant."

"Communicating effectively is probably the most important thing that parents can do to keep kids safe," says the National Center for Missing & Exploited Youth's Nathan. "And they must start young. Kids need to know that if they're uncomfortable, scared or confused, they should seek out and tell a trusted adult about these feelings. Open dialogue is vital."

Should you choose to use Internet activity tracking software, Holditch further thinks that you should be open with children, and let kids know if and when their online activities are being monitored. In fact, his company's filtering software is specifically designed to be transparent to children. Explain to your kids why you've chosen to go this route, should you choose to employ safety or user tracking software, he says, be clear with them about the situation, and value their input. "The point is that there are no secrets: Ultimately you need to have a relationship of trust if your kid is going to go online."

Kids bear a lot of responsibility, too, says Symantec Internet safety advocate Marian Merritt. She thinks that it's not fair or right to place the entire burden of protecting digital kids squarely on parents' shoulders. Certainly, she agrees, parents must provide safe computing devices, teach positive digital habits and establish family rules. But kids need to be responsible users, and understand that when parents investigate their activities, that adults are doing so to try and protect them, not because they're being mean or nosy.

It's also important for parents to remember that they're not monitoring kids' Internet usage to pry into their personal lives, but rather to safeguard against possible threats. There's a fine line that must be walked here, but ultimately, logic should rule. So while it's important to know that your child isn't being cyber-bullied, and that they're not downloading dozens of illegal software programs, you don't need to get caught up in minute details. Ask yourself: Do you really need to know whom they have a crush on or what they're doing every single micro-second of every day? Perhaps it's better to look at their overall activities and behaviors from a more broad perspective.

So what are some of the most major and concerns for parents as relate to kids and Internet safety?

While some are issues you may just be reading about for the first time, many of these concerns aren't necessarily new. Concerns like pornography, violent imagery, and solutions that teach kids how to cheat have all been youth-related concerns for decades – the difference now is simply the volume available, and ease of accessibility with which they can be accessed. Furthermore, because of the rise of smartphones, tablet PCs and Internet connectivity, these hazards are increasingly becoming accessible to kids at younger ages, and must be addressed.

As parents to members of Generation Tech, we must not only understand what it is our kids are doing online, but also be aware of potential pitfalls so that we can be ready for them, and have contingency plans in place should concerns arise. Here, we'll take a closer peek at these startling and sometimes slightly frightening issues. But as you peruse the following descriptions, remember: It's important not to let fear rule. Consider the information strictly referential in nature – and, potentially, a form of virtual safety equipment, helping you prepare your kids for that big bike or car wreck that they'll hopefully never have to experience.

Cyberbullying

Just as technology has provided a number of ways for kids to connect and create online, it's also being used by some wayward individuals to harass, embarrass and intimidate others. Welcome to the era of cyberbullying, where taunting and teasing can occur in many insidious forms online, and bullies, victims and scenarios play out in varied shades of gray. Even an act as simple as

forwarding an embarrassing or unflattering picture to someone's friends without their consent can prompt serious concerns, and the topic of cyberbullying has quickly come to full attention of school administrators, lawmakers, parents and more.

Put simply, cyberbullying is the use of high-tech devices, services and technologies to tease, degrade or put down others in a deliberate and hostile manner. It can range from seemingly very innocuous actions, such as spreading an untrue rumor about someone to friends, to potentially more serious actions such as mercilessly taunting them on social networks or online message boards. One need look no further than the tragic endings to the cases of teens Jamey Rodemeyer, Megan Meier, Tyler Clementi and Phoebe Prince to understand the very serious and real potential ramifications of cyberbullying. These tragic suicides underscore the point that online harassment cannot simply be ignored or dismissed.

But that also doesn't mean that cyberbullying is the only cause that may lead to hostile, negative or extreme behavior on children's part. Negative online activity is often a catalyst, trigger or accelerator for other underlying behavioral or psychological issues. However, it's one that parents must absolutely be aware of and monitor, and understand the potential repercussions of. Symantec's Marian Merritt cautions that cyberbullying is often used as a scapegoat in high-profile media cases in which there is a correlation, but not necessarily causation involved. For example, the tragic school shootings in Columbine were ultimately blamed on video game playing, but clearly a number of factors contributed. "It's easy to point fingers for folks that want to find a magic bullet," says Merritt.

Because of the broad range of acts that can be considered cyberbullying, estimates on its scope and lasting influence vary. But according to various sources, between a third and half of all kids online have been subjected to some sort of online harassment – eye-opening numbers. Recent research from Cyberbullying.us further shows that 20% of students experience cyberbullying in their lifetime. Merritt urges parents to take caution, but not overreact based on these statistics, though. "It's important to remember that a study that says a fifth of kids have been threatened on some level also means that 80% have not reported [facing such encounters] at all," she explains. "That's good news, but again goes back to the issue of capturing attention with fear-based motivation."

Nonetheless, you could rightly argue that 20% of students is still 20% too much. In hopes of addressing this issue, most major applications and services from companies like Facebook, Google, Yahoo! and more have taken strong stands against cyberbullying. Terms of use further prohibit the practice and can lead to guilty users being blocked, banned or removed. Facebook's Family Safety Center actually offers tips for parents, educators, law enforcement officials and teens for dealing with issues like cyberbullying. Microsoft further a vast array of resources and tips to help keep your family safe online, as does Yahoo!, which offers a number of tips about the issue. However, with limited legal and health industry care still available to victims and their families, cyberbullying remains an area of paramount concern. Like actual incidences of cyberbullying themselves, and the methods for their delivery, policy, research and scientific studies continue to evolve here, and should be actively monitored by parents.

Tips:

•   Even though most parents report that they report that they "friend" their child online in order to track social networking activity, more must be done to make sure that they don't fall prey to cyberbullies. As discussed earlier, social networks are but one place where kids are connecting. Texts, IMs and any number of apps through which kids communicate all present potential problem areas – know that what you don't see can harm you.

•   Make sure children understand the importance of being kind, respectful and open-minded to others, and know that online harassment is never okay. Even a casual deprecating joke delivered via text message can be misconstrued and extremely hurtful, so be certain that they're aware of how their actions may affect others online.

• If your children are being cyberbullied, you need to know when to involve the proper authorities. Monitor your child's behavior patterns, keep detailed notes of any suspected cyberbullying activity and don't hesitate to reach out for qualified professional help where appropriate. Happily, a growing number of healthcare practitioners, treatment centers and law enforcement bodies are actively working to address the issue of cyberbullying, and stand ready to provide aid on-call if issues arise.

• Modern schools are doing their best to educate themselves and become better-equipped to handle suspected incidents. If parents can identify that bullying is being provoked by a classmate, they can reach out to administrators for help. Kids can likewise report issues to the principal, a teacher or even a counselor. Should situations prove more serious, don't hesitate to involve your local police department.

• Bystanders are key to cyberbullying. "We encourage kids to report incidents, but there's hesitation not to be the next target of the bully," says Laurie Nathan of the National Center for Missing & Exploited Children. To promote action on children's part, she encourages using anonymous reporting systems such CyberTipline.

• An important point to keep in mind as well: Cyberstalking is an even more personal form of cyberbullying, and involves the constant and repetitive use of e-mails, messages, videos or other online communication to a recipient who does not wish to receive them. Cyberstalking can be dangerous and should be reported to law enforce¬ment, Internet service providers, and website hosting services immediately.

Being able to appropriately respond and deal with incidences of cyberbullying is extremely important, and the lessons here can easily be translated into real life. If your child experiences cyberbullying, one simple starting point may simply be to encourage them not to respond, as doing so can only provoke further actions. However, solutions are varied as actual situations and the individuals involved.

Note: Just as important as knowing what to do if your child is the victim of cyberbullying is for them to know how to react when they see others being cyberbullied. For starters, kids should know not to participate in the activity as that could only encourage further incidences of inappropriate behavior. Additionally, children should learn to be compassionate toward the victims or targets, and encouraged to reach out to them with words of empathy and support. Steven Balkam from the Family Online Safety Institute (FOSI) further recommends that it's a good idea to have a ready response should the cyberbully try to bring harassment into real life. His organization suggests teaching your children to say something like "My mom was working on the computer last night, maybe she saw it," if anybody asks whether they witnessed the cyberbullying act.

Of primary concern here is to focus on the positive as you talk to your kids about cyberbullying. As Microsoft Research's Danah Boyd and Alice Marwick recently wrote in The New York Times, kids aren't necessarily equipped to view themselves as victims. The aim when addressing cyberbullying should be to work within teenagers' cultural framework, and not portray them as oppressed. Encourage empathy and focus on positive concepts like healthy relationships and digital citizenship rather than the negatively charged concept of bullying. The key is to help young people feel independently strong, confident, and capable without first requiring them to see themselves as either an oppressed person or an oppressor.

Monitoring software, such as that discussed earlier, can also provide parents with warning signs about cyberbullying, such as a marked change in browsing habits. You must first establish a baseline for what's considered normal in terms of computing habits, and then monitor for big changes or warning signs. Examples of solutions here include MobileSpy, MobileMonitor and NetNanny. Programs like McAfee Mobile Security also have the ability to lock devices and wipe content remotely. Losing smartphones is a common way that kids first become bullied. So installing one of these programs may also offer a level of protection that helps prevent kids from being susceptible to cyberbullying should their phone fall into the wrong hands.

Cybercrime

Cybercrime is a broad catch-all term that seeks to encompass nearly every illegal activity in which the Internet or technology is involved. Whether you use it to refer to the practice of sending spam e-mails to perpetuate online fraud or using a computer to engage in sexual predation, both included crimes and penalties can be severe. It's also a subject that all parents should be aware of for pressing reasons: Online protection firm Norton has conducted several global studies on the subject and determined that 2/3 of adults globally have already been a victim of one form of cybercrime or another.

Troublingly, a report from Pandalabs shows that the problem is growing exponentially. According to the report, "five years ago there were only 92,000 strains of malware [read: malicious software] catalogued throughout the company's 15-year history. This figure rose to 14 million by 2008 and 60 million by 2010." And malware is just one type of cybercrime, before you even consider the countless stories reported in past decades of sexual predators luring underage kids into inappropriate relationships. These are the types of issues that can send chills up parents' spines, and only serve to reinforce the point that there indeed people out there who are preying often on others over technology tools and services – potentially in growing numbers.

However, while the situation may seem scary, it's also slightly heartening to know that often it's simply a few bad seeds perpetuating these crimes – most Internet users are good apples. But it's still imperative to keep your guard up to protect against a growing range of threats and criminals. Consider that most cybercrimes come from one of three sources, according to Symantec's Marian Merritt: Bad people you don't know, good people you do know who make a mistake, and mistakes that you make. Learning how to prepare and protect yourself from all three trouble areas will help keep you and your family safer.

It's also worth noting, according to Lynette Owens, the director of Internet safety for kids and families at Trend Micro, that cybercriminals aren't necessarily targeting kids per se, but rather just going where kids and other potential targets go. This means turning to text messages, social networks and video sites – anywhere troublemakers think that they can persuade folks to click or provide info, cybercriminals are popping up. And it just so happens that kids not only happen to use these popular online destinations and services – they're also very susceptible to potential scams.

The US Department of Justice breaks cybercrime down into the following areas:

• Hacking/Computer Intrusion
• Password Trafficking
• Child Pornography or Exploitation
• Internet Fraud and Spam
• Internet Harassment
• Internet Bomb Threats
• Trafficking in explosive or Incendiary Devices or Firearms Over the Internet

That's obviously a broad list, but one that the government and law enforcement officials take very seriously. As a parent, it's also one whose dangers you should take to heart too.

Tips:

• Just as you would keep your kids out of bad neighborhoods where crimes occur and gangs are, you should also keep your kids out of places on the

Internet where others may do them harm.

• Be alert and be on the defensive about any and all online interactions with others. If you think you've come across someone using the Internet for illegal online activities, report the incident to the appropriate authorities. Internet-related crime, like any other form of crime, should be referred to law enforcement and investigative authorities at the local, state, federal, or international levels, depending on the scope of the crime. Note that citizens who are aware of federal crimes should report them to local offices of federal law enforcement.

• Bookmark key threat reporting sites and stay abreast of the latest scams from sites like the Internet Crime Complaint Center (www.ic3.gov).

• Don't respond to e-mails asking for personal information such as bank accounts, place of birth or other info.

• Review bank and credit card statements to make sure there aren't any strange charges from online sites.

• Be leery of any solicitations from parties that are located outside of your home territory.

The Cybercrime section of the Department of Justice's website offers several great tips on where to report different forms of cybercrime. While you obviously don't need to make the police aware of every piece of spam e-mail you get, the site does provide resources to turn to when faced with more serious crimes such as hacking and even bomb threats. Similarly, Cybertipline is a congressionally-mandated service where you can report crimes ranging from possession and the manufacture and distribution of child pornography to embedding words or images into a website to deliberately mislead a minor into viewing them.

Here are three more tips from Norton Online Safety for preventing Cybercrime:

• Use caution when taking advantage of Wi-Fi hotspots – Wireless hotspots are a great resource and may feel like a lifesaver in some instances, but don't use them to make online purchases or check your bank account. Make sure you're using a secure network for tasks involving the transmission of personal or monetary information.

• Use complex and unique passwords for each site or service – Use a combination of uppercase and lowercase letters, symbols and numbers and make your passwords as random as possible, rather than basing them on commonly-used dictionary words. [Ed. Note: We dig much deeper into safe password planning and online safety tips in the next section.]

- Stay educated about trends in online security and cybercrime – Reading books such as the one you're holding show that you're actively working to stay on top of the latest issues facing your family online. It's a good habit to get in, and one increasingly easily managed thanks to a wealth of online resources readily available to concerned parents via desktop, app and mobile device.

Online Predators

As you might expect, as many wonderful people inhabit this world, the sad truth is that there are some extremely troubled and disturbed individuals within it as well. One need only watch an episode of NBC's "To Catch a Predator" to see how many of these will jump at the chance to translate an online relationship into a sexual one, even if it is with a minor.

For concerned adults, it may be only small solace to learn that the problem of online predators may be slightly overblown. Consider that The National Center for Missing and Exploited Children conducted a recent study showing that one in seven children will be solicited sexually online – a large number, but still largely the minority. However, in either case, it's worth nothing that most of those inappropriate contacts come from peers, rather than strangers. "In the last decade, we've seen a lot of fear-based messaging that scared the heck out of parents," says

Steven Balkam, chief executive offer of the Family Online Safety Institute. "But only 1% of sexual crimes were being committed by Internet-based relationships, while 80% were committed through family members."

But as with other online concerns, this doesn't mean parents shouldn't let their guard down. Just as we teach kids about "stranger danger" from an early age, so too must we make sure that healthy fear of suspicious parties and interactions translates to the Internet world. When kids start out online, they need to learn that it's seldom okay to communicate in any way with someone they don't know. And, as they get older and begin to expand their circles of interaction through various forms of online communication, such as web forums, comments or email, that while they may begin to feel like they know someone from interactions online, all that they really recognize is a username. The fact is that unless you've met someone in real life, they're still a stranger (and even then may remain so until you've gotten to know them better). And, more importantly, kids should never attempt to set up any sort of real-life meeting without first involving grown-ups in the scenario.

According to the FBI website, here are warning signs which may indicate your child is at risk from a sexual predator.

o   Your child spends large amounts of time online, especially at night.

o   You find pornography on your child's computer.

o   Your child receives phone calls from men you don't know or is making calls, sometimes long distance, to numbers you don't recognize.

o   Your child receives mail, gifts, or packages from someone you don't know.

o   Your child turns the computer monitor off or quickly changes the screen on the monitor when you come into the room.

o   Your child becomes withdrawn from the family.

o   Your child is using an online account belonging to someone else.

Through The National Center for Missing and Exploited Children, there's an easy way to report any sort of child exploitation. Congress has mandated the following reporting categories, which can all be easily reported at www.cybertipline.com.

• Possession, Manufacture, and Distribution of Child Pornography
• Online Enticement of Children for Sexual Acts
• Child Prostitution
• Sex Tourism Involving Children
• Extrafamilial Child Sexual Molestation
• Unsolicited Obscene Material Sent to a Child
• Misleading Domain Names
• Misleading Words or Digital Images on the Internet

If any of the following situations occur, contact your local or state law enforcement agency, the FBI, and the National Center for Missing and Exploited Children:

o   Your child or anyone in the household has received child pornography.

o   Your child has been sexually solicited by someone who knows that your child is under 18 years of age.

o   Your child has received sexually explicit images from someone that knows your child is under the age of 18.

Reporting predators to all these agencies is important since local law enforcement may not have jurisdiction over the matter.

Tips:

• Make sure your kids understand these rules:

1.   Never arrange a face-to-face meeting with someone they've met online without appropriate planning and supervision.

2.   Never upload (post) pictures of themselves onto the Internet or an online service to people they do not personally know.

3.   Never give out identifying information such as their name, home address, school name, or telephone number.

4.   Never download pictures from an unknown source, as there is a chance that there could be sexually explicit images.

5.   Never respond to messages or online postings that are suggestive, obscene, belligerent, or harassing.

6. Be aware that whatever children are told online may not be true.

• If you think that your child has been in touch with an online predator, talk openly about your suspicions. Make sure that kids are aware of the dangers that these individuals present. Know the danger signs of an online predator, and tell kids to immediately find a parent and make them aware if they think that someone is soliciting them online.

• Be an investigator, and review the sites that your child is visiting. This could be as simple as checking your browser history, but savvy kids may easily be able to cover their tracks there. Learn how to monitor cookies and your computer's cache – sources of info that are harder for your kids to delete.

• Control your phone. Check phone records and make sure you can justify any calls your family is making or receiving. Consider activating an anonymous call blocker feature, available from most phone companies.

• Consider periodically checking your child's e-mail account to make sure there are no suspicious e-mails. Should you opt to go this route, tell your kids that you'll be performing these random checks – but remember, the reason you're checking isn't because you're spying on them, it's to keep them safe, so don't get bogged down in the details of their personal lives.

• Don't be afraid to talk and ask questions of your child's friends, schoolmates and teachers, and find out about how accessible chat rooms and other breeding grounds for predators are at the library. It's the weakest link theory, and you need to make sure you're being vigilant about your child's access, even when it's not under your control.

• Take advantage of parental controls, both in your browser and in the games your kids may be playing online. By restricting and monitoring Internet use to sites with parental controls and games with safe or limited chat, you can eliminate the chance of inappropriate conduct. As we mentioned before, there's really no good reason for kids to be connecting with random strangers through IMs, chats or video calls, so parents should restrict and prohibit those activities.

• We said it before and we'll say it again – there's really no real reason for kids to be engaging strangers in chat rooms or video chat rooms, unless you feel that this behavior is warranted, i.e. if it's taking place within safe confines or under your supervision. Prohibit this activity, within reason, and teach your kids about the dangers of it and you'll cut off the way that the majority of online predators reach their prey.

Spam

Unwanted e-mail is known as spam, and these days there is a lot of it. Experts estimate that around 90% of all e-mail is spam, with some placing the number even higher. Research conducted by theRadicati Groupestimates the number of emails sent per day to be close to 300 billion. If 90% of these multitudes of messages are indeed spam and viruses, this means that more than 3 million spam e-mails are sent EVERY SECOND of the day.

The goal of spammers is to get their unsolicited messages in front of as many people as possible, increasing the chances that some of them will click on links contained within and expose personal information, make impulse buys, or fall for whatever scam the sender is pushing. And just as companies are constantly working hard every day to control and stem the flow of spam, so too are spammers constantly working hard to create new ways to circumvent any spam filters or other restrictions.

Happily, many e-mail programs such as Yahoo! and Gmail do a solid job of filtering out a lot of junk e-mail automatically. Several corporate giants are also increasingly uniting to fight spam and phishing. The idea is that the e-mail providers will work with major companies on the technical back-end to make sure that any e-mail that says it's from them really is from authenticated sources.

However, with the rise of technology, there's more to spam these days than just junk e-mail, as spammers are now creating fake websites, using harmful QR codes to direct users to sites that install malware, or spreading password-swiping links via social networks claiming that you "liked" a story that you really didn't.

Social engineering, or con-artistry, is a huge part of the spammer's world, says Lynette Owens from Trend Micro. She alerted us to the recent spike in "Likejacking" where an eye-catching notice shows up in a news stream, such as a story from the BBC saying that Lady Gaga is dead. Since this is the type of news that kids might be interested in reading, and because they see that their friends "liked" the story, they'll click it to be taken to a page that is semi-official looking and contains a news story. But the simple act of clicking on this fraudulent post triggers negative consequences, and the action of your liking the story allows it to spread to your own news stream, which could lead your friends to click on it, continuing the vicious cycle.

Tips:

• When you first set up an e-mail account for your child, protect it and use it selectively. Although companies promise not to give out e-mail addresses to third parties, it's amazing to see the amount of spam an e-mail address can generate once spammers know it's active.

• Luckily, most major e-mail programs offer a great level of basic spam protection. As we discuss in greater detail later in this book, when your kids are ready for an e-mail account, you can avoid hassles here by using a reputable online mail program for your kids, which should be able to catch most of the unwanted e-mail. As an added bonus, helping your kids set up a Gmail, Hotmail or Yahoo! account will also help you take the first steps toward staying in control of their passwords, too.

• Be aware also that spam exists outside of e-mail channels as well. Whether via text messages, social network direct messages, links posted on Twitter or likejacked stories shared on Facebook, children need to be on guard when using any sort of Internet-based communication.

• Resist the urge to attempt to "unsubscribe" to spam. Replying to messages will often do nothing more than confirm that your e-mail address works for the sender, leading to more spam being sent. Instead, teach your kids to use the "Report" or "Mark as Spam" button from their e-mail program to deal with unwanted messages.

• Remember that kids should be leery of any e-mail or other communication received from someone they don't know. If they don't know what a note is, what material it contains or who it's from, teach them not to click on it.

• As they grow older, teach your kids some of the basics on how to identify spam, potential scams and offers that appear too good to be true.

• Check the To: and From: fields in an e-mail if you think it might be spam. If there are many other addresses on the To: line, it's likely spam. Additionally, hard to remember or nonsensical e-mail addresses, e.g. those containing random strings of letters and numbers, are also likely spam.

• Hover over links with your cursor to make sure that their destination leads to where it claims to. And just because these URLs match doesn't mean to click on them – it's safest to skip doing so until you can verify it's a legitimate site. If you have questions, instead of clicking the link, input the URL into Google and see what comes up.

• E-mails that promise big prizes or require "urgent" action are usually also spam.

• If friends' e-mail addresses are suddenly sending you spam, make sure to contact your friend via a different method and let them know that their account has been compromised. Often, simply changing the password puts an end to the unwanted e-mailing.

• To help the Federal Trade Commission control spam, forward it to spam@uce.gov.

• Don't post your e-mail address in its full, normal form as text on a publicly accessible Web page. Instead, consider using alternate descriptions a real human could easily interpret such as "jane[at] doe DOT com."

Malware: Viruses, Worms, Trojans and Spyware

Although most people use the power of computers for positive reasons, there are those that seek to wreak havoc throughout all corners of the Internet. Through viruses, worms, trojans and spyware – malicious software that can have harmful effects on your device, private personal information or computing habits – some misguided programmers attempt to cause problems for unsuspecting users.

A virus is a program or software code that's loaded onto your computer without knowledge or permission, and causes harmful effects. Viruses are spread through human actions, whether it's opening a program with malicious code contained within or clicking on a link you shouldn't.

A worm is also a piece of malicious code, albeit one that has the ability to replicate on its own without any human actions. If a worm starts spreading, it may automatically e-mail itself out to everyone in your address book, for example.

A Trojan horse is a piece of software that a user might think is harmless and/or useful but really contains a virus or a worm. The idea being that unsuspecting end-users are tricked into clicking on or executing a file because they think they're activating a real program, but in actuality the program causes harmful effects, e.g. the deletion of files or wiping clean of an entire hard drive.

Spyware is software that is installed on your computer and tracks your activities, keystrokes and more. Hackers can then use this information to log into your e-mail accounts, access bank records and pull up personal information – anything you've done while your computer is infected with Spyware can essentially be replicated by remote users.

While many of these forms of malware are introduced via e-mails or unsafe websites and downloads, online safety provider McAfee cites online music, movie and download sites as a major source of potential threat exposure for kids today as well. Their impact is considerable as well: Consumer Reports recently reported that malware cost consumers $2.3 billion through the repairing or replacing infected computers and devices. Some experts even see malware as the biggest threat for families online today. Not just because of such programs' tricky and growingly ubiquitous nature, but also because as more kids get access to smartphones, they're also gaining access to more and more potentially dangerous ways to infect their device or compromise online accounts.

So why would somebody go to the trouble of causing other high-tech users harm? There are a multitude of reasons why these nefarious hoodlums spread their malicious code far and wide. Some do it simply for the thrill and notoriety. Others do it to try and make money off unsuspecting dupes. And some groups band together to perform targeted acts of mayhem and disruption in order to make a larger point or to retaliate against individuals, corporations or initiatives that conflict with their principles. No matter the reasons for these attacks, it's often innocent families who suffer where viruses, worms, trojans and spyware involved. When it comes to malware, you can never be too paranoid: Remember – only you can prevent your family from becoming collateral damage.

10 Anti-Virus and Spyware Programs to Install

- AVG
- Avira
- Bit Defender
- ESET
- Kaspersky
- McAfee
- Norton
- Panda
- Trend Micro

Tips:

- Help keep your children and your computers safe by installing Internet security software on your family's computers and making sure it's updated with the latest protection files. Offerings from ESET, McAfee, Symantec, Trend Micro, Lookout, Panda, Kaspersky and more are all reliable and trustworthy options, but make sure you don't install more than one at a time, otherwise it may cause problems for your computer or mobile device.

- If you think you've been infected by a virus, malware or piece of spyware in the past, use anti-virus or malware tools to help search for and wipe your system clean of the infection.

- Use a firewall (safeguard against unwanted intrusion) to protect your home network: While most spyware comes from sources you've clicked on or sites you've visited, there still are some hackers who can access your network and place it remotely on computers. Installing and using a firewall provides a helpful defense against allowing others to have access to your system, files and personal information.

• Tell your children never to turn off a device's virus scanner or firewall, even if they think it might speed up a program or game that they're enjoying.

• Teach your kids not to try and blindly guess website URLs for companies, services or products that they're looking to visit and type these guesses straight into your browser. This can lead to typos or errors that could potentially take you to harmful, misleading or inappropriate sites (often spelled just one character different, and designed to capitalize on these common user gaffes). Instead, type the name of what you're looking for into a reputable search engine, and click the link that's provided in the search results that will take you to the site you're looking for. Many virus scanners offer check marks or warning signs on search results pages to let you know if featured sites are verified as safe or known to be potential threat sources.

• Instill a healthy dose of skepticism in your family and assume that every attachment or e-mail you get is potentially a virus, worm or spyware. Instead of assuming that everything is okay, assume that everything is NOT okay and take steps to convince yourself that what you are about to open is real and is not a threat. Unless you can be absolutely certain, you're best to leave it alone. If it came from a known acquaintance but you're still not sure, contact them via phone or talk to them in person about it. Treat websites the same as well. If a search engine is directing you to a link, convince yourself that you're positive it will be free from anything that could potentially harm your computer.

• Adjust browser settings to ensure maximum security by limiting which data you've entered is remembered by the program and websites visited, and how much information overall that websites are able to access.

• Only download programs from websites you trust.

• Read all security warnings, license agreements, and privacy statements associated with any software you download.

• Make sure when you set up different accounts on your computer that everyone is using a standard account instead of an administrator account. This helps protect your computer by preventing users from making changes that affect everyone who uses the computer, such as deleting files that are required for the computer to work.

• Don't open an e-mail attachment unless you were expecting it.

• Download and install software only from trusted sources. Close windows containing pop-up ads or unexpected warnings by closing the entire window by clicking on the X in the corner, not by clicking a selection within the window that says "Agree" or "OK."

• Make sure your Web browser's pop-up blocker is active and working.

Protecting Mobile Devices Against Malware and Phishing

Children use their phones for a variety of tasks these days. From downloading gaming apps and clicking on links contained within texts and emails to surfing the Web and social media sites, there are a variety of ways phones can become compromised. Here are a few quick tips for parents from Lookout Mobile Security in order to keep children, and themselves, safe from phishing attacks (cons facilitated via fraudulent emails or websites which pretend to be those provided by trusted sources) and malware on your mobile device:

General Tips:

• Set a password. A password is a basic first line of defense so that only you can access important data on your phone. Have your child set a password and make sure you know it.

• Download software updates for your phone. It is important to stay up-to-date with operating system software on your phone and current versions of apps because these updates can include patches that remedy security flaws that can put your information at risk.

• Download a security app. Just like you would for your PC, you should download security software designed to stop malware, spyware and malicious apps. With the right app, you can also locate a lost or stolen phone, or even shut it down, wipe data off it or sound an alarm. Make sure that both your phone and your child's phone have security apps installed.

• Use discretion when downloading apps. One of the most exciting things to do with a new smartphone is explore all the great applications that you can download onto it. Kids are especially eager to download the latest entertainment, social networking and gaming apps. Encourage them to be careful, however, making sure to only download apps from trusted sites, check the app's rating, and read supporting reviews to make sure the app is widely used and respected.

How to Be a Smarter Mobile User

As part of research itconducted on mobile threats, Lookout identified some specific instances where people should use extra caution when downloading apps or clicking links on their phone, including the following scenarios:

• Visiting third party app stores. Lookout found that malware writers often test malware in alternative app markets before trying to place it in Google or Apple'sapp stores. When discovered, malware is usually pulled more quickly from these primary distributors than it is from lesser-known or heavily-regulated markets. The likelihood of you encountering malware on an alternative app store increases dramatically.

• Downloading gaming and utility applications. Be careful to check reviews on these apps before you download. These types of apps are most likely to have malware hidden inside of them — and these are just the types of apps that kids love!

• Clicking on a shortened URL (e.g. bit.ly link) in an SMS message or on a social networking site. Users are three times more likely to click on a phishing link on their mobile device than they are on their PC. Because malware writers are expected to increase web-based distribution, it's important to start using extra caution when clicking on links on mobile phones.

• An app asks you to click "OK." Don't simply skim on autopilot through the prompts an app shows you in order to perform a certain function or deliver a service. Sometimes these apps are a

form of greyware, which hide in fine print that they will charge you via premium rate text messages.

• Clicking on in-app advertisements. Not all advertisements are bad. In fact, most are okay. But some are examples of malvertising and could direct you to a malicious website, prompt you to download malware, or violate your privacy. When clicking on ads, you need to make sure that the ad directs to where you expect to be directed.

Using Facebook & Twitter Safely

Lookout is also increasingly seeing phishing attacks come through social network sites. Here's what to keep watch for, and know in order to protect yourself on two of the leading services.

Twitter: Many of us have seen messages or tweets come from friends that tempt us to click on links. Case in point – the following example: Receiving a message that says something along the lines of "So I guess there's a bad blog going around about you, seen it?" If you click on such a link, you are taken to a page that looks almost identical to the Twitter homepage. However, the URL of this webpage is twittler.com instead of twitter.com, which on a mobile device is even harder to distinguish because the text is so small. If you mistake this fake page for the actual login screen and enter your login information, the people behind the phishing scam now have access to your account and can continue sending the scam to all of your Twitter contacts.

Facebook: Lookout also witnessed malware writers going social by using a drive-by-download technique to spread malware on Facebook. The process begins when a person receives a "Friend Request" from an unknown person. Curious to learn more about this alleged "Friend," the person may visit this person's Facebook profile. Here they will see a website URL listed in the "About Me" section of the page, and if they click the link, an application will begin downloading to their phone. If the malware is installed on a device, it can send unauthorized third-party premium rate phone services.

It's always a good idea to exercise caution when clicking on links and videos within social media sites (especially when coming from unknown sources or "friends"). In addition to using good judgment, follow these quick steps for added protection:

• If you see a scam on Facebook, don't click on it, but report it instead. You can help stop malware early on by reporting suspicious activity as soon as you see it.

• Be alert for unusual behaviors on your phone, which could indicate that your phone is infected. These behaviors may include unusual text messages, strange charges to your phone bill, and suddenly decreased battery life.

• Install a mobile security app to protect against malware — some will literally scan every link you click while surfing the web, checking email, or texting.

SOURCE: Lookout Mobile Security

Phishing and Scamware

Phishing refers to fake e-mails or websites which are put together to try and entice users to click on harmful links or respond with personal information because they are misled into believing they must visit the website or provide the required info. Recently on Twitter, for example, there's been one phishing scam going around that encourages folks to click on a link to see "the bad things that someone wrote about you." Phishing requests also might take the form of an official looking e-mail from a bank or an airline. These scams often feed into readers' fears and curiosities to get them to click links, which they'd otherwise know better to avoid.

Scamware is a specific type of malware that's designed to trick the user into thinking they are doing something positive when in reality they're doing the opposite. Often, these issues take the forms of pop-up ads from obscure sites that kids may stumble upon via search engines or accidental keystrokes. In some instances, for example, ads are designed to look like a "Virus Alert" coming from the computer's anti-virus software, but clicking the "Scan" or "Fix" button actually installs and activates malicious code on your computer.

Many of today's phishing scams have gotten extremely sophisticated, using official looking letterhead and websites, and providing neatly spoofed e-mail addresses. Again, we recommend that parents and kids assume that every e-mail they receive is potentially dangerous, and look for telltale signs of fraudulent activity before assuming it's safe to accept.

For reference, the FBI keeps a website of the latest e-scams it has taken note of. This resource may come in handy for those wishing to research or reference potential threats.

Tips:

• If your family has accidentally installed scamware, it may be hard to remove. But there is help available from companies like Norton, which has a free tool available called Norton Power Eraser that will help remove these items, which can also be utilized via thumb drive if you're having trouble accessing the Internet from your own computer because it is so infected.

• You can hover over hotlinks with your cursor in emails to see if the destination site they lead to is really the same as what's listed in the text. If it's not, don't click it.

• A simple online search of some key terms contained in an e-mail you suspect of being a scam could also help verify whether it's a fake or not. Sites such as snopes.com and scambusters.org keep track of scams, and can help debunk these types of e-mail as well.

• Be leery of shortened URLs. While these bit.ly/WHATEVER links (or similarly-formatted links) help abbreviate potentially lengthy website links, they can also disguise potentially dangerous destinations. Sites like www.urlunshortener.com can be used to see the destination address of an abbreviated link without clicking on it.

• Tell kids it's never okay for them to install any piece of software without a grown-up's presence and permission. If a window pops up on your device, even if they think they know what it is from, teach them that they must get a grown-up to help them remove it.

• Use a pop-up blocker to prevent pop-ups from happening. Typically, these solutions stop the vast majority of threats, but do be advised —due to a constantly changing and evolving array of threats, there are still some that can slip through.

- Activate parental settings on your Web browser to prevent access to harmful sites. Also consider using a browser designed for kids.

Privacy and Identity Theft

Perhaps the most valuable piece of currency on the Internet today is personal information. Just as in real life, it needs to be zealously guarded and protected from falling into the wrong hands. Scammers can use nefariously-obtained personal info to open credit card accounts, purchase expensive items and commit other illegal activities that can harm your credit, personal standing and reputation. And although such crimes using provide just a momentarily gratifying experience for the criminal, they can lead to years and years of grief and confusion for the identity theft victim.

According to the most recent data available from the FTC, less than 1% of identity theft victims were under 19 years old. But many experts think that this statistic is inaccurate, as many families don't discover identity theft until their children are around 18 and beginning to enter the workforce or college and attempt to access their own credit for the first time. A 2011 survey from ID Analytics estimated 140,000 instances of identity fraud are committed against minors each year. And FTC identity protection

specialist Steve Toporoff recently told an NBC investigator that "recent studies suggest child identity theft is more prevalent than even identity theft against adults."

To help protect your family, make sure your kids understand what private information is. An easy way to do this is to let them know that anything that can be used to identify them in real life should be considered confidential. Whether it's your name, phone number, address or even the school which your children attend, this information should be safeguarded and only given out when absolutely necessary, and with a grown-up's permission.

It's also important to realize that there are generational differences at play here, and things that may seem obvious to you not to share aren't necessarily so for your kids. In a recent survey by Pew Internet Research about the future impact of the Internet, two-thirds of experts thought the Millennial generation will lead society into a new world of personal disclosure and information-sharing using new media. So while Baby Boomers may be more apt to keep their info guarded, these experts said that such so-called "digital natives," whom we refer to as Generation Tech, will continue to share more and more personal information as part of their daily online lives as they grow older.

Nonetheless, the experts from the survey do agree that a "trial-and-error period is unfolding and will continue over the next decade, as people adjust to new realities about how social networks perform and as new boundaries are set about the personal information that is appropriate to share."

Tips:

• Lifelock, Identity Guard or Trusted ID and other protection services may be worth the investment for your family if identity theft is an issue you are particularly worried about. For often as little as $10 a month, these services will keep an eye on your personal information and, in some cases, even monitor your credit reports for you.

• At least once a year, it's good to check up on credit reports for you and all members of your family. This can be done by visiting www.annualcreditreport.com. According to the Federal Trade Commisssion, this is the only site authorized to provide you with the free credit report you're entitled to by law. If you find something wrong, you'll not only want to contact the credit companies directly, but also the proper authorities. All this information can found at www.ftc.gov.

• Teach your kids to practice safe computing habits and password guarding, just as you guard your ATM code when using an ATM machine.

• The FBI also recently warned families against a surprising side-effect of posting images online: The potential accessing of geolocation tags embedded in the image to show exactly where on earth the picture was taken. This could be dangerous because you could be unwittingly letting others know where you live and work via photos you are posting online. We recommend disabling all "Location Services" on your family's smartphones, which can easily be done on the Settings menu of most devices.

• Credit service Equifax recently launched a family plan that keeps tabs on the identities of two adults and up to four children, but it comes with a potentially steep monthly price tag. For the price, parents can get an e-mail or text message whenever someone tries to use any of their family's IDs.

• Although this advice may seem obvious, be certain to protect your child's social security number. Don't be afraid to question if entering it is really necessary on any form, or giving it out in response to a query is required. And if it is, make sure you're comfortable knowing that the place you're turning it over to, be it a school or a doctor's office, will adequately protect it.

• If your child starts getting junk mail or credit card applications, that may be a sign that someone is using their identity. Contact the credit bureaus and check to see if they have a report.

- It's important to distinguish that you're only checking to see if a report exists when you contact credit companies. Unless you've been a victim of identity theft, they shouldn't have one, and ordering one could cause the credit bureaus to open one in your name, which is unnecessary.

- Think twice before sharing your child's name online or in public. Whether it's on your Facebook and Twitter page or on stickers you place on your car, it's possible that the wrong person can see this information and use this information to steal their identity.

- The first step if you think you are a victim of identity theft is to place a fraud alert with one of the credit companies. Once you contact them, verify that they will contact the other two credit bureaus about the fraud alert as well. You can contact any of the three:

Equifax – 1-800-525-6285
Experian – 1-888-397-3742
TransUnion – 1-800-680-7289

- In addition to taking steps to close any fraudulent accounts you find about, you'll also need to file an Identity Theft Report and a Police Report to begin the process of straightening the identity theft out. For starters, you can download and fill out the FTC Affidavit. Once you've done that, you can then take that form to your local police department and use it to fill out a police report.

- After that, you can call the credit companies and request an extended fraud alert, which will stay in effect for seven years.

- For more specific tips on what to do if you or your family fall victims to identity theft, make sure to check out this helpful guide from the FTC which contains checklists and step-by-step instructions for what to do if you've been a victim of identity theft.

- The FTC also offers a comprehensive site discussing many aspects of identity theft, including tips for how to avoid it at http://www.ftc.gov/bcp/edu/microsites/idtheft/.

Sexting

Along with improvements in communications, the rise of cell phones has also unwittingly ushered in a great rise in sexting, the transmission of sexually explicit pictures or messages via cellphones, e-mail or social networking sites – especially via text or instant message.

Reports of exactly how widespread the "sexting epidemic" is are still a source of debate, though.

A survey from CosmoGirl and the National Campaign to Prevent Teen and Unplanned Pregnancy unveiled some shocking numbers about the sharing of images that, while many experts feel are inaccurate and sensationalized, nonetheless opened many parents' and researchers' eyes to the topic of teens transmitting sexual images to one another.

According to the controversial survey, 20% of teens overall and 11% of young teen girls between 13 and 16 report that they have sent or posted nude or semi-nude pictures or video of themselves. And 39% of teens reported sending or posting sexually suggestive messages, with 48% saying they have received such messages.

Symantec's Internet Safety Advocate Marian Merritt says that these findings really came out of nowhere, and points out that this study was self-reported and that many experts have since questioned its methodology." Fewer than 1% of kids are crafting dangerous images," she insists. Anne Collier from ConnectSafely.org also paints a similarly less shocking picture, in a recent presentation about the new rules of online safety. According to Collier, only 1% of teens surveyed had appeared in sexually explicit pictures, and only 7% had received photos. "It's a small phenomenon, but kids still need to be educated about it," says Merritt.

According to a January 2012 study in the American Academy of Pediatrics Journal, 9.6% of youth who use the Internet reported appearing in, creating or receiving sexually suggestive images, numbers which are more consistent with Collier's and Merritt's observations. But since you can't rewrite history and retrieve any sexually compromising transmissions once they've been sent, the very real threat of persistent damage to your own personal image is an important danger of sexting. However, it's not the only one. Since minors are involved, chances are there are some very serious crimes being committed as part of the process as well, as we noted earlier that the transmission of pornographic images of children is an extremely grave offense.

Because of the severity of child pornography laws, some experts actually recommend that parents don't get authorities involved if they discover sexting, because of the potential negative legal ramifications to otherwise unsuspecting adolescents. Safety advocates like Wired Moms' Parry Aftab are hopeful that the laws will change to prevent the "sex offender" label from being placed on teens who may not deserve such a harsh label. "When we look at sexting, typically, we look at the criminal laws that are making our teens and preteens registered sex offenders for stupid actions," she explains in a recent blog post. "They can legally have sex with someone, but if anyone records it on video or in a still image, both can be charged with child pornography crimes under federal and most state laws."

There are laws currently being proposed in states like New York to remove the association between child pornography and consensual sexting. However, that doesn't make it any better of an idea for kids to get involved in the activity – nor does it make the ramifications any less serious.

Even though many states have reduced charges to misdemeanor, "any parent who has to deal with the juvenile court system is still going to think it's a big deal," says Laurie Nathan, manager of national outreach and partnerships for The National Center for Missing & Exploited Children.

Tips:

• Include the discussion of sexting as part of any normal and routine talks about the birds and the bees that you have with your kids. Just as they must protect their bodies, they must also protect images of their body as well.

• Kids need to know that they shouldn't allow people to take pictures of or place them in situations that could leave them vulnerable for such images to be shared.

• Treat the written word as just as powerful as the spoken word when it comes to talking about sex, and explain that any use or talk of that language may be considered inappropriate in any given context.

• Trend Micro runs a yearly video contest for kids called "What's Your Story" that invites teens to create videos warning against the dangers of sexting and other unsafe online activities. Sit down with your kids and view some of the past winners and submissions to help drive home the dangers and importance of these online issues.

• Other services such as PhoneBeagle, TextGuard and MobileMediaGuard are available that analyze pictures and text messages to look for sexting. But no software solution can completely safeguard against the practice – it's still up to parents to step in and teach digital citizenship rules and safe computing habits

• Consider checking your kids' devices and reviewing their communications periodically, and let them know that a condition of them having these devices will be providing you with full access to them from time to time to make sure nothing inappropriate is happening.

• Teach your kids to never assume that anything they send electronically is going to be private. In fact, as a rule of thumb, it's best to assume the exact opposite. Once children send an image or thought out into cyberspace, they have potentially lost all control of it. Important to teach your children: Before sending or receiving communications, it's vital to consider whether they'd want their parents, teachers, coaches or even future bosses to see these transmissions. If there's even the slightest chance not, or of such communications being misinterpreted, it's best to err on the side of caution and abstain from doing so.

• Realize that personal intentions associated with sending sexually-charged material to others may be misconstrued, and may prove of little relevance when consequences and punishments are actually handed down. While some adolescents may think that they are just being silly or joking, others – especially adults – won't perceive these actions as any laughing matter.

Pornography and Questionable Sites

With more than 500 million websites out there, it's no surprise that there are quite a few dedicated to dubious, questionable and even hateful agendas. And even with parental controls and browser filters, it's almost inevitable that the curious child will either deliberately or inadvertently stumble upon something that your family will find upsetting.

Just one example: A survey from Netsmartz.org showed that approximately one-third (34%) of children ages 10 to 17 were exposed to unwanted sexual material on the Internet in a one-year period of time. Sadly, in some cases, encountering questionable or negative material is as simple as incorrectly inputting a Web address by one letter, which can accidentally send kids surfing off to a website that's inappropriate for their viewing.

But if you should stumble across evidence that your child has been viewing negative or controversial material, and that these sites were accessed deliberately, you need to be prepared to handle the situation. Knowing that such scenarios often can and will occur, start by establishing and enforcing ground rules for appropriate content, and make sure all members of the household are aware of and agree to them. All should also know the punishments involved for violating these rules, and circumstances under which they'll be revoked. Again, being proactive pays, including teaching kids what is and isn't acceptable to view online, and why they shouldn't believe everything that they view or read.

Even educating them to keep in mind a simple litmus test such as asking themselves "would I be comfortable showing and explaining this to my grandmother" may be enough to help kids understand what's appropriate and what's not from an early age.

We provide the following list of controversial content types which potentially await even the unsuspecting Internet surfer not to frighten or sensationalize, but rather to inform parents of just a few of the potential hazards that children may encounter:

Pornography: Wherever a form of media exists, so too does pornography. However, some experts argue that threats are overrated. To give just one perspective, a September 2011 Forbes article interviewed OgiOgas, a neuroscientist who compiled data on the subject for his book "A Billion Wicked Thoughts." According to his research, in 2010, out of the million most trafficked websites in the world, 42,337 were sex-related sites, or only about 4%. Ogas also points out that while companies like Cybersitter proclaim that they block 2.5 million adult sites, he thinks those numbers are exaggerated. But at the same time, he also found that 13% of all Web searches were for erotic content — and any child who knows where to look can gain access to pornography via computer or mobile device in a matter of seconds. In short, it's not a topic parents can easily afford to dismiss.

Child Pornography: A ways back, the Internet Watch Foundation found more than 13,000 sites that contained illegal child pornography. Often, featured victims are 10 years old or younger and nearly two-thirds involve rape and sexual torture — frightening stats, indeed.

Hate Groups and Racism: According to Canada's Media Awareness Network, there are directories that list more than 170 pages of hate content that include websites, blogs, games, and more, including racist-friendly web-hosting services. The Simon Wiesenthal Center's Digital Terrorism and Hate Project tracks more than 14,000 potentially hateful websites, blogs, social networking pages and video channels in total.

Eating Disorders: Though potentially not as widespread as racist or pornographic sites, sites that go by the names "pro-ana,""pro-mia" and "thinspo" glamorize and promote health issues such as anorexia and bulimia. The first study examining the extent of the problem in 2010 found 180 different sites glorifying these eating disorders.

Historical Revisionism: These sites contest the mainstream view of historical events that actually happened. Whether it's promoting notions that our government was behind the 9/11 attacks, or that the Holocaust never happened, these sites attempt to use alternate facts, videos and interactive graphics to lay out their case.

Tips:

• Make sure that your family has a policy about checking Web browser history and not deleting it in place that everyone understands. It's important for you to be able to check this history to keep an eye out for questionable online activity, or encounters with content that may contain viruses, spyware or other malware. It's vital that you have a firm understanding of how to check your browser's history and cookies. The

Netsmartz website offers instructions on how to do so and other ways to protect your family. If you do find that your browser history is empty, it means that privacy settings are on, or your child is deleting it manually, which, in the latter case, is a good reason to engage them to ask why this activity is occurring. Note that in addition to manually checking browsing history, you can also use monitoring programs such as ESET, Webroot, Lookout, Web Watcher or Net Nanny to proactively restrict access to certain websites.

• There are also browser programs that examine websites to create a pre-approved "whitelist" of sites that an expert has deemed acceptable for young web users. Programs like MyKidsBrowser and Maxthon are designed with kids in mind, and restrict access to only safe sites.

• For mobile phones, MOBICIP filters Web browsing based on a setting of either high school, middle school or elementary school level. It categorizes all websites in a database to make sure they're appropriate.

• Make sure you're taking advantage of your computer's free parental controls and protection options.

• Make sure your kids know what to do when they accidentally come across a questionable site: Close the browser window and let a grown-up know. Realize that mistakes, unexpected encounters and poor choices of judgment can and will occur, and use them as teachable moments.

Wireless Networks

The ubiquity of wireless networks makes connecting to the Internet incredibly convenient, but you still must be mindful of how your devices are connected. Most families have a wireless network connection courtesy of their cable or phone provider, but other than during initial setup and installation, they rarely think about it unless there's an interruption in service. Wireless networks must be configured and managed properly, though, otherwise they can be intruded upon by others who will welcome the opportunity to either utilize your connection for illegal purposes or steal your personal information.

Although barely imaginable 15 years ago, wireless networks are now the primary way many are connected to the Internet. If you think about how they work — packets of information transmitted over the airwaves and quickly resorted into comprehensible information by your computer — you can see the potential dangers. For starters, encryption is key. Encryption makes these flying packets of information unreadable except by the devices for which they're intended. Most home routers are equipped with a 10 digit security key, which is often printed on the device, or may be the phone number associated with the account.

But these days, smartphones easily show that wireless networks are suddenly everywhere. Whenever you turn WiFi access on, phones automatically seek out any networks in range. Yet it's important you only connect to wireless networks you trust. Whether it's your home or work network, or even a "hotspot" located in a public place such as an airport terminal or the local coffee shop, make sure you're connecting to what you think you're connecting to. If you do go online in a public place, you must also alter your browsing habits and not visit sites that require personal, confidential or sensitive information to be entered, as they may be easily viewable by others who are watching these networks and attempting to gather just this type of info.

Note that these days, 4G LTE smartphones can even be used to act as a portable wireless hotspot for other devices, enabling high-speed access for nearby gadgets.

Tips:

• Most wireless routers have a default security setting when first installed. After ensuring that their router is password-protected, the next step many users take is giving their network an ominous or scary name to deter others from trying to connect. Some of the funnier examples we've seen are "Air Virus," "Hackers Haven" or even "Connect Here for Identity Theft."

• Since wireless networks are a gateway to the Internet, some parents have also been known to give their wireless router a curfew of its own. By disconnecting or powering down the Internet connection every night, it's one way to ensure that kids won't be spending time online when they should be sleeping or doing their homework.

• Most computers and anti-virus systems employ a line of defense against potential Internet problems called a "firewall," which is a virtual barrier that's placed between your computer and the Internet. Firewalls are mainly used to protect your computer's private information by regulating how and when data can pass through. Windows computers even have a built-in firewall that Microsoft likens to "locking the front door of your house" that is automatically activated by default. The company suggests you fine-tune your connection, tweaking the way your computer allows incoming connections, especially if you will be connecting it in public places.

• Even if your wireless connection has a firewall, you'll still want to make sure you to use other protection methods. In addition to your router's firewall, you'll also want to make sure your computer's firewall is up to date as well as make sure you're keeping your operating system and your anti-virus protection up to date. Threats can evolve quickly, and you want to make sure your computer and network are equipped to handle any emerging dangers.

Software Piracy

With access to so much content suddenly available for kids online and on-demand, sometimes it can be tough to understand the different between legal download sites and sites that are providing pirated (a.k.a. illegally copied and distributed) material.

Pirated content can range from video games and comic books to movies, music, books and more, which are being made available for free or a deeply discounted price because they are being provided without the creator or copyright owner's consent. That doesn't mean that the surviving Beastie Boys have to approve everyone that wants to download Check Your Head off of iTunes. But it does mean that artists who create works are entitled to royalties or other benefits whenever someone purchases, downloads or uses their creations. Although there are lots of legal ways for children to get their hands on media and other types of content, the Internet makes it really easy to enjoy these materials without paying for them. We won't list out specific sites that

facilitate distribution here (nor could anyone hope to catalogue all), but will mention that high-profile sites such as MegaUpload.com were targeted by the Department of Justice for providing free "peer-to-peer" file sharing.

While many experts are noting a reduction in P2P downloads with the continued popularity of sites like Netflix, Steam, and iTunes, others are seeing the segment — which allows direct file transfer between devices over the Internet — continue to boom. In a recent interview with Wired.com, a Sandvine spokesperson said that "from 2009 to 2010, real-time entertainment grew to represent 42.7% (up from 29.5%) of total Internet traffic in the evening, while in that same time, P2P file sharing also grew, from 15.1% to 19.2%."

Tips:

• By using a monitoring program such as Web Watcher Kids, parents can easily monitor downloads to track what's coming in. Any music and movie downloads should likely raise a flag for your family, especially if they're being enjoyed without your consent.

• Although enforcement may be hard to execute, educate your children about the repercussions of illegally sharing and downloading content — the sharing of copyrighted material without permission is against the law, and a serious offense that, as of press time, can carry punishments of up to five years in jail and fines of $250,000.

- Note that your ISP may contact you if they notice large data transfers happening on your account, such as those potentially associated with illegal activity. Not only could your Internet provider potentially throttle your bandwidth as a result, they may begin charging you more for data transfer.

- It can be tough to understand why kids "getting a good deal" on entertainment is a bad thing, but we must teach our kids that piracy is no different than stealing. The US Patent and Trademark Office equates the issue of software piracy with the traditional image of pirates in an effort to educate kids on the downsides of the issue, explaining that piracy is wrong "because a lot of people who put a lot of hard work into making the DVD or computer game will not be paid."

- Also important to note: Many times pirated software comes from untrustworthy sources. A recent study found that a quarter of websites that offered counterfeit or pirated software also attempted to install spyware or Trojans.

Cheating and Plagiarism

It would certainly be ironic if we were to botch this citation, so we are choosing our words very carefully here when we say that, according to Plagiarism.org, an online site ostensibly designed "to help people all over the world prevent plagiarism and restore integrity to written work," that many potential cases of plagiarism can be prevented by simply citing sources.

Regardless of where you stand on copying, regardless of references, the fact is that the Internet makes plagiarism easy for children and college students. Think about how simple it is to go to Wikipedia or another popular reference website, look up a subject and then copy and paste the material. Not surprisingly, swiping others' research, words or original material and reusing it has become a widespread problem in schools, and one that can carry some serious consequences. At the very least, many teachers will automatically give students Fs on the assignment if they find out that pupils have copied or stolen someone else's work.

Moreover, when Bay Area students at Leland High School were recently caught cheating on finals by using a password to steal copies of the test before it was given out, one student told the San Jose Mercury News that "it's pretty much normal that kids are cheating on tests." Numbers alone tell the tale, with the statistics on cheating today somewhat shocking. A Rutgers Business School survey reported that two-thirds of high school students admit to cheating in some form.

Considering the growing ubiquity of smartphones, it's not a tough leap to make to see that kids are using the Internet to cheat, both in school and at home with increasing frequency as well. More than two-thirds of college students admit to using online sources when cheating. In fact, in a recent study of high-tech cheating conducted by Common Sense Media, 38% of kids aged 13-17 said they'd copied text from the Internet and passed it off as their own, and more than a third admitted to using their cell phones to cheat.

According to NoCheating.org, nine out of ten middle-schoolers admit to copying each other's homework, and two-thirds say they've cheated on exams. Fully one-fifth of boys and one quarter of girls report that cheating started for them in first grade, showing that this behavior begins at an early age. Needless to say, it's easy to do the math here – and from a parent's perspective, it's hard to be pleased with how the numbers add up when it comes to the chances that their kids may be using the Internet to cheat.

Tips:

• While tools and resources such as TurnItIn, iThenticate or CheckForPlagiarism.net can help catch plagiarizers, there's no 100% foolproof way to prevent the act of plagiarism. But you can help prevent it by actively speaking with your kids, teaching them not to do so, and explaining why stealing others' work is wrong. Have the conversation with kids, and let them know you're aware of the issue – the fact you're potentially watching over their shoulder won't be a magic cure-all for the problem, but it will provide added deterrent.

• There's a great guide for discussing plagiarism with your children at KidsHealth.org called "What is Plagiarism?" In addition to providing an anti-plagiarism checklist, the site offers a clear definition and examples of plagiarism that are designed to be understood even by elementary school children.

• Some families allow children a brief window during which the computer and Internet may be used at the start of a homework assignment, and then require either that the computer be turned off or the Internet connection disabled for the rest of the assignment. Not only can that prevent cutting and pasting or accessing answers online, but it can also prevent other distractions. However, it's worth noting that precluding access to online research or reference material may have potentially detrimental effects on children's ability to complete assignments as well – let logic rule here.

• Common Sense Media suggests that kids need to learn that they must always credit a source when referencing it, and recommends talking to teachers and principals to ensure that kids understand the proper techniques for source citation. However, children should also understand just how much material is appropriate to cite – simply noting a source does not give them the right to copy content wholesale, let alone in bulk.

• Encourage your kids to double check their work for any citations or quotes contained within, and be sure to attribute them to proper sources. Also make a point of personally going back and examining the source material referenced to make sure it's not been simply copied outright.

Online Shopping and In-App Spending

Did you know that customers spend tens of billions of dollars online just during the holiday season alone? That's because it's easier than ever to click and buy real-life items online, thanks to major search engines integrated shopping info into their results, apps which enable remote purchasing, and exploding interest in Internet retailers like iTunes, eBay, Zappos and Amazon. If you're willing to wait a couple days to receive purchases, you can often get these items delivered to you for free and end up paying much less what you would have paid at a local retail outlet. And although this seems like a very adult thing to do, kids will often have no problem making purchases just as grown-ups do, as many sites store your credit card information online or allow the use of easily-purchased gift cards. Hence the need to make sure that kids know if, when and how it's appropriate to buy items online, and your family's household rules and limits when it comes to Internet shopping.

Whether actually purchasing material goods for delivery to your doorstep or buying virtual items via Facebook, online games, or smartphone apps, online shopping can lead to big bills – all of which must be paid in real-world currency. Worries are doubly present with many sites today offering convenient ordering options for adults that let them save credit card information, mailing addresses and contact information to their accounts, allowing for speedier one-click purchases. Should you fail to log out of these accounts, it's entirely possible that kids could access sites and make purchases on their own. Similarly, when using smartphones or other devices tied to credit cards and monthly billing accounts, younger kids may not realize they're spending real money when making in-app or online transactions, and older kids may still not fully grasp just how much such purchases are costing.

With more children being provided access to smartphones and portable media players at increasingly younger ages, kids are growingly confronted with instances where they must understand the value of a dollar, and consequences of their actions. As former T-Mobile director of web and cloud services Mike Vance points out, kids as old as 12 may still think that if someone is texting them, that they must know them, and thus it's okay to click on links or take action on information contained within them. Unfortunately, given the growing prevalence of spam and advertising, all may come at considerable material cost.

Additionally, online currencies are becoming increasingly common in video games, virtual worlds, and applications. But actual real-world monetary value isn't always apparent at a glance, even for adults – a growing worry with social casino games and free-to-play titles for smartphones, tablet PCs, computers and Web browsers funded by "microtransactions" (bite-sized in-app purchases) increasing in popularity. Even payment systems that social networks use should be extensively researched and reviewed before using them. Many are perfectly safe to use – however, many don't always make it apparent at a glance for adults, let alone children, just how much you're spending at any given time in terms of actual cash.

Tips:

• Make sure kids don't have access to your bank or credit card accounts. Just as you wouldn't let them have this information in real life, don't allow them access (unintentionally or otherwise) to sensitive accounts and passwords online.

• Always log off devices and out of accounts when finished using them. Although it's convenient to keep your Amazon Prime account signed in if you're a frequent shopper, it's possible that another member of the household with access to the device could make unwanted purchases using your account.

• Avoid storing credit card and contact information in online accounts, and opt out from saving or remembering these details once entered – they should only be inputted on a case-by-case basis. Similarly, use gift cards or prepaid cards to make purchases whenever possible, and/or giving them to children should you wish to allow them to make online buys of their own.

• Many devices offer parental controls and settings that let you block in-app purchases. Consider activating these features to prevent microtransactions from occurring, which represent another potential way that kids can rack up surprisingly big bills.

• One great way for parents to help keep tabs on teens' spending is to use a prepaid card. Parents can digitally load the card up with cash, and elect to provide recurring deposits, i.e. gifts delivered in the form of a weekly or monthly allowance

- Prepaid card options from major credit card companies such as Mastercard, Visa, Discover and American Express can also provide helpful options for families. However, depending on your selection, certain solutions may not offer extensive options for monitoring and controlling spending, and/or may have additional fees associated with usage.

Betting and Online Gambling

As many parents are aware, the Internet makes it unexpectedly easy to gamble and make wagers using real-world or virtual currency, whether on sporting events or games like poker, blackjack or roulette.

A recent survey by the Federal Trade Commission found that minors can easily access gambling websites, which operate on servers based outside of the US and therefore out of the jurisdiction of state and federal regulations. Furthermore, many services have inadequate or hard-to-find warnings about underage gambling, and several offer little to no warning at all. The most popular types of gambling that kids are engaging in today are card games, like Texas hold 'em poker, and sports betting.

As a result of government action, many popular online gambling destinations are now restricted from US users. They also now point users to companion sites which offer tips for responsible gambling and deny access to users who say they are under 18. Still, the threat clearly remains. Online betting and gambling methods today come in myriad forms, ranging from online poker, blackjack or other casino games to services which let you place bets on real-life occurrences, such as sporting events or even Hollywood awards ceremonies. Although most sites will restrict access to those under 18, gaining access is often as simple as entering a false birth date.

Important to consider: Not only can gambling lead to a loss of actual money and possessions, but it can also – in extreme cases – lead kids down a path towards other illegal activities such as burglary or fraud in order to cover gambling debts, or gain funds with which to gamble more. Online gambling, as with real-world gambling, can also be highly addictive.

Tips:

- In order to gamble online, kids need access to an account with each service and money to burn. Make sure they don't have such access, and you can prevent them from getting started. This includes barring access to credit cards – sometimes card numbers are all kids need to get started.

- The FTC also warns that gambling is illegal for minors, so sites will go to great lengths to verify the identity of any gambler that they are paying out. If they find out the winner was underage, they won't send the money. So make sure that your kids understand: They literally have everything to lose and nothing to gain.

• The Massachusetts Council on Compulsive Gambling offers these warning signs and tips for addressing teenage gambling:

o   Increased interest in lottery tickets or poker items. Seeing these items around the house is a potential sign that kids are dabbling in gambling. Take steps early to talk to them about the dangers and, if necessary, tips for responsible gambling, such as never wagering more than you can afford to lose.
o   Organizing sports pools around big events such as the NCAA Tournament or NFL football games.
o   Take note if your kids are taking a heightened interest in sporting events, especially ones that aren't competitively close. Kids may be rooting against the spread or for other things that don't necessarily affect the outcome of the actual game.
o   Show and explain to kids the downside of gambling. Wagering sites exist for a specific reason — because the house always has an edge. One need look no further than the gaudy decadence of Las Vegas to see that gambling can pay off big… albeit mostly for the ones taking the bets.

• If you think someone in your family has a gambling problem, be advised — sites such as the National Council on Problem Gambling and Gamblers Anonymous can help.

Trolls, Griefers and Bad Influences

Online, the term troll refers to someone who posts provocative claims and statements designed to generate a hostile or angry response. These can take the form of comments on a social network, blog or Internet message board; news stories posted on a website; or incendiary remarks or postings made anywhere there are online conversations occurring.

Griefers are similar to trolls, being users or players of multiplayer or online video games who, instead of trying to win, are taking part in the action specifically to take advantage of or harass others. Often the reason that these users do so is simply to get a rise out of people.

Ultimately, negative online behaviors promoted by these individuals can range from annoying to disruptive and stressful, and kids' may find themselves playing right into trolls' and griefers' hands if they respond to their antics.

In many cases, trolls and griefers are harmless. However, it's possible that their harassment could mark the start of a cyberbullying or cyberstalking incident, should issues persist.

Tips:

• Just as with cyberbullies, it's important for kids to understand not to feed the beast. Don't respond or "stoop to" trolls' or griefers' level, as it will only give them more ammunition and fuel for the fire. When confronted with such negative behavior, it's best to take the high road and ignore it all together.

• If you experience trolling or griefing within the boundaries of an online community, game or forum, report guilty parties to the site or service's administrators or moderators. Oftentimes, such channels are heavily policed to ensure a positive experience for all users.

• If you witness repeated acts of unacceptable behavior, be sure to document the problem in case it's necessary to provide supporting facts to administrators or authorities should incidents escalate in severity.

• In addition to looking the other way, it's also frequently simple to eliminate trolls or griefers from your life by ignoring or banning them using online privacy settings. Social networks such as Twitter give users the option to ignore certain users, and it's surprisingly simple to "de-friend" someone on Facebook who is causing problems. Other sites and services may offer similar tools that let you block commentary or communications from unwanted parties.

• Be forewarned: Some online users with a large following will sometimes publicly call out other users in the hopes that their fans or followers will deluge the victim with commentary or outreach. Akin to posting someone's information publicly and encouraging others to harass them, it not only encourages negative behavior – it can also carry serious consequences.

Internet and Online Addiction

Statistics compiled by Anne Collier of ConnectSafely.org show that 95% of 12-17 year olds are now online. But for some kids, there is a real danger of becoming too involved in online activities, or even living too much of their lives in the virtual world instead of real one. Whether it's constantly texting, staying glued to computer games for hours on end, or wasting entire days on social networks, it's easy to understand why developing children could easily become too wrapped up in online activities.

In rare cases, true symptoms of addiction can also develop, such as neglecting family, friends and even sleep in order to spend more time online. Kids who fall into this trap may even require direct help from their parents, peers, and qualified professionals to regain control of a healthy, balanced life. While a change of environment and routine can sometimes be enough to break kids out of an addictive mindset, the reality is that it's hard to prohibit kids from using technology on a regular basis, since it's such an integral part of daily life. As such, parents must take care and caution to promote responsible computing habits and online behaviors, and monitor children's usage of high-tech devices and services, as well as surrounding behaviors.

Worth keeping in mind: Millions of kids and adults use the Internet safely and responsibly every day, meaning there's no need to get up in arms about the mere fact that children can and do go online. Rather, where concern should be focused is on the how, when, and the manner in which they choose to do so – moderation is key, with high-tech activity just another item to consider when maintaining a healthy digital diet. The Internet and connected devices can be a hugely powerful force for good in children's lives. Ultimately, maintaining a healthy balance in the home all comes down to the way in which we as individuals choose to use these resources, and the support systems in place to help us understand and address potential dangers.

Tips:

According to Hilarie Cash, executive director of the ReSTART Center for Internet Addiction near Seattle, the following are signs of potential Internet addiction. If your child exhibits three or more of the below indicators it suggests abuse, she says, and five or more suggests possible addiction:

- Spending increasing amounts of time on the Internet
- Failed attempts to control behavior
- Heightened euphoria while on the Internet
- Craving more time on the Internet, restless when not there
- Neglecting family and friends
- Lying to others about online usage
- The Internet begins to interfere with on the job and school performance
- Feeling guilty or ashamed of behavior
- Changes in sleep patterns
- Weight changes, backaches, headaches, carpal tunnel
- Withdrawal from other activities

If you think that your child is engaging in addictive behavior, you need research more about what they are doing, and document instances of questionable activity or interactions. In short, you must work to understand the cause of the addictive behavior so you can better address and work towards possible resolutions.

Don't immediately ban the activity in question though, because doing so may not have desired effect, and lead to greater household conflict, say experts. Instead, become more engaged with the problem in order to gain a better understanding of why the behavior is so addictive for your child.

Families should also not be afraid to seek out qualified professional help should children exhibit the warning signs of addiction detailed above. A list of resources is available at sites like www.netaddiction.com. You can also take an online quiz at www.netaddiction.com to see if you or your child may be exhibiting warning signs. Doing so may help better tune you and your kids into the issues and warning signs to watch out for.

Health and Obesity

The most recent National Health and Nutrition Survey found that obesity rates among youth have dramatically increased in the last 25 years, and many experts are pointing to time spent on the Internet and playing games as potential reasons. What's more, there are other health issues that technology use is potentially contributing to as well. A recent study published by researchers from Harvard found that tablet PC users who situate these devices in their lap are putting extra strain on their necks, a condition some have termed "iPad neck." Such issues accompany other tech-inspired maladies such as "iPhone thumb" or more traditional problems such as carpal tunnel syndrome, which can potentially be brought on by extended time at the keyboard.

One of the emerging causes of multiple problems in kids that has been identified by pediatricians and sleep clinics is the fatigue brought on by teens sending messages to friends in the middle of the night. Some children have been shown to stay up until the early morning hours sending text messages before waking up early for school, failing to get enough rest before departing. After an afternoon nap, these individuals are then ready to stay up late again texting until the wee hours. But such an unhealthy routine causes them to not only be tired and less mentally sharp, but also has an impact on the sleep cycle that causes weaknesses in their immune system which can lead to greater chance of becoming sick. According to the American Academy of Pediatrics, there is also a new phenomenon called "Facebook Depression," prompted by the intense connections teens are making in the online world.

According to the AAP, social networks provide an easy way for teens to experience early developmental stages of separating from parents and finding peer acceptance. But doing so also opens them to marked emotional responses to negative encounters experienced online as well, such as when they're de-friended, or feel that they're not getting enough likes or comments for online activities.

That's not to say that the simple act of going online or participating in communications or leisure activities over the Internet will have a negative impact on your child or household. In fact, it can often have the opposite effect, allowing children greater access to information, individuals and experiences which they'd never encounter otherwise. But it's important not to simply dismiss health concerns outright either: Many valid issues bear further research and discussion, and may potentially intrude on your child's day to day life. All bear considering, albeit in reasonable and open-minded fashion.

Tips:

• As when addressing issues concerning addiction, experts agree that banning or prohibiting technology outright is not the answer, as doing so may deprive children of many positive benefits. However, parents can, and should be, a shield against negative online influences. When managing technology, it may help to adhere to similar principles as martial arts advocates have long counseled, with a better approach being not to forcibly stop, but rather redirect the force of an opponents' attack. Translation: Instead of trying to build walls against the outside world, which can be easily skirted (or may crack under pressure), it's often better to provide healthy detours and a roadmap to more positive routes via informed insight and suggestion.

• Also important is to monitor and regulate your family's use of high-tech devices and participation in surrounding activities. Where possible, you should make sure all devices and Internet connections are placed in common areas of the house to allow for effective observation and regulation. Such solutions can obviously be more difficult to with regard to handheld devices. But for mobile gadgets, you can consider setting an electronic curfew or boundaries for your family, with no further use of electronics allowed at or after certain times of day, and during specific occasions.

• Consider creating a common docking station for all devices in your bedroom, where all high-tech gadgets and accessories must be parked for the night before bedtime.

• The American Academy of Pediatrics says to watch for the following signs of depression associated with Internet use, and to contact your pediatrician should your child experience them: Sadness, anxiety, pessimism, difficulty concentrating, a drop in grades, insomnia, loss of appetite and irritability.

• As a general rule, many parents require kids to experience one hour or more of outside time for every one hour of video game or screen time. We encourage you to experiment here and implement rules that are a good fit for your family.

• As alluded before, make sure to set aside device-free times that the entire family can spend together as well. Parenting experts such as Richard Rende, PhD, associate research professor in the department of psychiatry and human behavior at Brown University, suggest that the use of technology in and of itself isn't necessarily what's dangerous for kids as an impediment to healthy development. Instead, problems can arise if all the use of technology and connecting is done at the expense of other proven developmentally healthy and necessary activities.

SUMMARY

Make no mistake: Thanks to the widespread availability of technology and online connections, troubling material and influences can and will find their way into children's hands. Rather than bury one's head in the sand and hope for the best, parents instead need to adopt a proactive approach, educating children as to potential dangers and solutions for dealing with problematic scenarios. By acting as a trusted guide and mentor who can provide insight into these issues, and offering a meaningful sense of perspective and healthy suggestions regarding appropriate alternatives or responses to harmful content and habits, you won't just steer kids towards a more positive outcome. You'll also provide children with a more comfortable and open forum in which to be truthful and forthcoming with their concerns. This will ultimately empower them to make better, more informed decisions and channel energy towards healthier pursuits.

Vital to keep in mind as well: While many of the aforementioned concerns are both alarming and dangerous, experts like Symantec's Merritt remind us that we shouldn't fear technology outright. "Parents have been shocked [into overreacting and paranoia] by overblown threats," she says, counseling that many of the stories we hear about the high-tech world are negatively slanted for a specific reason: "Law enforcement lives in the world of bad people, and so they're hyper-focused on noting what bad people do." As she points out, the vast majority of online and digital interactions are harmless, as are the individuals your children are apt to meet through virtual channels. Nonetheless, as she reiterates, just as you shouldn't approach the topic of technology from a position of paranoia, nor should you approach it from that of blissful naïvete.

"We spend so much time focusing on the scary stuff that it's easy to forget why we want kids to spend time on the Internet," agress McAfee safety evangelist Stanley Holditch. "Ultimately, it's an equalizer," he says. "A child with online access has a chance for advancement. We do what we do [on the online security side] not to prevent or limit access, but rather to make parents feel empowered."

So now that we've looked at many of the hot-button issues and concerns surrounding kids and high-tech usage, let's focus on tips from the experts on how to best incorporate the Internet as a positive part of your family's lives.

PART IV

EXPERT HINTS
AND TIPS

EXPERT HINTS AND TIPS

While many dangers and concerns are present in cyberspace, the Internet can also be a perfectly safe, fun and uplifting place for kids and adults alike. Used wisely, it offers many upsides including enhanced learning, sharing, communications, social involvement, and exposure to multicultural influences.

"Sometimes we don't give kids enough credit for being as smart as they are," points out Facebook spokesperson Marian Heath. Her outreach efforts focus on the fact that the vast majority of kids and families are finding the company's social network to be a useful and positive influence on their lives. However, globally, kids spend 1.6 hours a day online on average. As this figure continues to increase annually, so too do the chances of having a negative experience on the Internet. The more children are connected, the greater the need for parents to prepare their kids to meet the challenges connectivity presents becomes. Just as we teach toddlers to look both ways before crossing the street, so too must caregivers provide fundamental instruction in the basics of safety and interpersonal communication. But with 70% of parents believing that schools should do more to educate children about online safety, and four-fifths of teachers agreeing that more in-school programs of its type are needed,

at-home advice alone may not be adequate preparation enough.

Still, safe computing starts with the family. To begin with, we adults need to sharpen our online skills, and practice safe computing habits. Teach kids digital citizenship and netiquette skills (and practice them yourself) and you'll not only increase chances that they'll tread a safe and enriching path through the virtual world —you may also pick up a few fresh pointers yourself. Outside resources including nonprofits and various national or community organizations can also help in supplemental efforts, providing tools to help both caregivers and educators offer more advanced instruction. Their goal is to "train the trainers," providing tools and directions for teachers and role models to use in programs designed to help educate kids regarding proper technology usage. "The biggest threat on the Internet today is parents that are not involved in their children's use of technology," says parenting expert Judi Warren. "But it takes a unified effort to keep kids safe on the Internet."

"Such endeavors have to start with parents because the process has to start early on," she says, noting that kids as young as two years old now commonly use smartphones and other technological devices. But rather than lay the responsibility for raising digital kids strictly at the family's feet, we as a society all have to step up to the plate as well, Warren adds. "It also has to be a part of ongoing education," she insists. "Schools absolutely, positively have to teach kids to make smarter choices."

According to Warren, when kids are little, parents need to start engaging and laying plans for making technology a healthy part of their life. As she points out, it's not like high-tech progress or innovation will ever go away, and in fact is quickly becoming an intrinsic part of childhood and growing up today. Or, to put it succinctly, "introducing kids to technology is now just as important as teaching them how to ride a bike."

The bottom line: High-tech parenting is little different than traditional parenting. As ever, you have to be an involved, engaged and educated part of your children's lives. On the bright side, by paying attention to high-tech topics of interest to children, your family may also enjoy added benefits as well. Enabling more informed and constructive dialogue, genuine curiosity on a parent's part not only shows tots that you take an active interest in activities that are important to them. It also helps open lines of conversation between generations and encourages families to spend more time together – plus provides a chance to see how kids utilize items in context and offers neutral topics for discussion which otherwise

close-lipped sprouts can open up around.

Active involvement additionally provides an opportunity to bond over shared subjects of interest. You won't always agree with the options available, or appreciate "helpful" suggestions made by kids' playground buddies or older siblings. But it's important to foster a supportive household environment wherein children feel free to discuss anything questionable or disturbing that they encounter online – a means of encouraging them to come forward with and address, rather than cover up, potential problem areas. Knowing this, it's imperative you establish a common ground of trust surrounding your family's use and enjoyment of consumer electronics and high-tech services. Use these experiences as data points around which to shape your frame of reference, share your thoughts and concerns, and open a direct conduit of dialogue to children about all things technology-related.

Mary Heston, social media manager for Wired Moms, an online coalition dedicated to Internet safety, stresses that, above all else, despite all the high-tech dangers children may face, parents and educators do not need to panic about the prospects of kids going online. Instead, we need to remember that technology is always going to be a part of our children's lives and that we should embrace it. It's our job as parents to work with kids to make informed and positive choices when using these technologies and the Internet – and that means equipping yourself with a solid educational background around which to build research and discussion.

Stephen Balkam, chief executive officer of the Family Online Safety Institute (FOSI.org) encourages fostering a "culture of responsibility" when it comes to educating kids about Internet safety, in which multiple aspects of society all contribute their part to keeping kids safe. It starts at the top, with the government creating laws and providing a safe framework for families, while law enforcement does its part to actively monitor and catch the bad guys, says Balkam.

Likewise, businesses operating in the high-tech industry must provide tools and education to consumers who will use their products to connect with or use the Internet, he adds. However, the ones on the frontlines of the battle are ultimately parents, teachers and kids themselves. While teachers and community leaders can stay abreast of the latest developments and help guide students toward best practices, it's ultimately up to adults and children themselves to establish house rules, maintaining running discussion and make wise choices on the Web.

"For parents trying to raise kids and give them the technology to be successful, yet also protect them from harm, there's a sense that no one's there to tell folks what steps to take," says Symantec's Marian Merritt. Therefore you owe it to yourself, and your children, to keep a curious and open mind. It's the least we ask of today's youth – so why not ourselves? After all, trying to ignore the steady, inexorable advance of progress is like attempting to use a pail and shovel to turn back the ocean's tide.

Here are the steps we recommend that modern parents take as they prepare their family to greet a life spent online.

- Educate Yourself
- Be a Good Role Model
- Set Ground Rules
- Encourage Open Dialogue
- Take Advantage of Existing Tools
- Invest in Added Resources
- Create an Effective Password Policy

Educate Yourself

Fear of the unknown often leads well-meaning and concerned adults to outlaw, block or ignore new developments in hopes that the perceived problem will simply go away. But guess what? The Internet isn't going anywhere. Parents, like kids, are better served by willingly immersing themselves in new tools and technologies. This allows them to become better equipped to make sound decisions, gives them a more fact-based frame of reference, and provides greater insights thanks to the benefit of firsthand experience.

Not only do firsthand studies help you better understand where potential upsides and downsides, or misuses of the technology in question lie – they also provide a sense of perspective as to how kids' actually utilize the platform or product in question, and give a more accurate picture of age-appropriateness based on children's individual development levels. Likewise, in the case of questionable content, such efforts can also help you steer sprouts' interests towards healthier and more suitable choices.

But homework isn't just for kids – you've got to make a running commitment to education as well. Only by actively taking an interest in and researching new developments, features and upgrades can you hope to keep abreast of the dozens of new services, apps, games, gadgets and online destinations that launch weekly – all of which offer myriad options for connecting, communicating and interacting or sharing information.

Obviously, you're never going to be able to mirror and monitor every aspect of your child's online activity, but you should at least be familiar with all the services, tools and technologies that they use. Additionally, take advantage of privacy settings and parental controls. You may be surprised to find that there many utilities exist that can help you

better manage kids' screen time and high-tech interactions' with minimal time and effort.

Similarly, if you purchase new technology items, read associated safety information and utilize it. "All too often we hear that parents buy items and hand them to their kids [without doing further research, which could have easily prevented issues]," says Laurie Nathan of The National Center for Missing and Exploited Children. For example, handheld gaming systems such as the Nintendo 3DS and PlayStation Vita can access the Internet, yet many parents don't realize this.

Happily, more resources than ever are available at one's fingertips to research new hardware, software and multimedia developments, from manufacturer websites to professional third-party reviews, video demonstrations and complementary hands-on trials. And even if your mobile device or cable provider doesn't make the use of parental controls and privacy settings simple or clear, the truth is that if you do visit a manufacturer's website, or search online, there's usually considerable information available geared towards parents. Frequently, answers to common queries are just one Google search away – after all, odds are you're not the only one asking these questions.

If you're not doing so already, you might consider following a few key Internet safety experts on social media services as well. Doing so can keep you updated on the latest developments and hot-button issues that pertain to technology and families.

Internet Safety Experts to Follow on Twitter

@AKeynoteSpeaker – Hints, tips and advice for digital parents by high-tech parenting expert Scott Steinberg, creator of The Modern Parent's Guide series.

@AnneCollier – Co-Founder of ConnectSafely.org, who also sends out updates on family safety that she posts on Net Family News.
@CommonSenseNews – Twitter account for content watchdogs Common Sense Media, providing tips and newsletters geared toward contemporary parents.

@ConnectSafely – A leading non-profit that's at the forefront of online safety issues.

@LarryMagid – Co-founder of ConnectSafely.org, distinguished journalist and family online safety champion.

@LynetteTOwens – Director of Trend Micro's Internet Safety for Family & Kids Initiative

@MarianMerritt – Leading educator and advocate for family Internet safety issues.

@Mashable – Offers news about technology and social networks, and a great way to keep abreast of constantly changing high-tech landscape.

@Pogue – Celebrated technology journalist for The New York Times.

@StephenBalkam – Head of leading non-profit organization the Family Online Safety Institute.

@Techmama – Offers a mom's perspective on technology issues.

Be a Good Role Model

Only 5% of what children learn is from direct instruction: The other 95% comes from behaviors that are modeled for them, according to Pam Leo from the Natural Child Project. While these numbers may seem too tough to quantify, the point is that kids learn more from what you do than what you say. So if you want your kids to practice safe online habits and make smart decisions, you've got to practice what you preach. Don't be surprised when your kids bury their head in their smartphone and spend all evening reading text messages if you yourself do the same thing every six seconds.

Part of being a responsible technology user not only involves educating kids regarding potential dangers and ways to make high-tech a more organic part of everyday life. It also involves knowing when to disconnect your devices and make connecting with your family a priority instead. So set good examples regarding both when and how you use technology. Granted, can still enjoy your own online connected time for work or play as well. But by building it into your family's schedule and routine in a healthy way, you're ensuring that everyone knows and is clear about not only proper rules of netiquette, but also household rules as well.

For those who truly want to make online safety a family affair, many experts also recommend focusing on the latest trend in online safety: Digital citizenship.

Microsoft offers an interactive toolkit that can help you teach it. The site offers free brochures, fact sheets and information about a number of topics, and equates the process of teaching kids digital safety with teaching them how to swim. Using it, children can start with the basics and gradually progress to learning more advanced high-tech skills.

Another great resource for families is promised by the Family Online Safety Institute. Recently, the organization announced an initiative to create an interactive online program called Good Digital Parenting which focuses on the positive aspects of connecting online. The effort is aimed at helping teach and empower kids, teens, parents and teachers to become responsible digital citizens, and hopes to offer children achievements and awards for doing positive things like volunteering online or helping others. The

organization is hoping these "gamified" program aspects and built-in tools for public sharing help start a ripple effect of awareness, and spark further interest and conversation.

"All too often, online safety discussions focus on the dangers of technology," said Stephen Balkam, CEO of FOSI. He hopes this program will "transform the discussion and create resources to inform, inspire and empower kids to make the right choices online." The idea behind the initiative is essentially to leverage existing social media platforms that young people and their parents already use, such as Facebook and Twitter, to help spread an uplifting message. To sign up for updates, parents can visit: https://www.fosi.org/good-digital-parenting/. Teachers can also get involved, as FOSI provides them with videos and web-based activities to use to inspire their students.

PREPARING KIDS FOR THE DIGITAL WORLD

As parents, we need to go beyond simply keeping kids safe with regards to technology. We even need to go beyond making sure that they're responsible when using it. Our goal is ultimately to help them be great at using it — and while it takes time, it's not impossible. When children are younger, high-tech discussions are certainly centered on safety. But very quickly, these conversations should become discussions about responsibility and then later, about capability. Here are some basic concepts to help guide you as you prepare kids for life in a digital world:

1. Be in the driver's seat. Start as early as possible to set expectations and rules with your kids about safe, responsible technology use. This means understanding the technology you are going to let them use. There's no need to be an expert on every new technology or innovation that's introduced... but you should be familiar enough with them so that you understand how best to guide kids who'd like to utilize these solutions and have basic online safety knowledge at your fingertips whenever you need it. Once you start the conversation, keep lines of communication open. Children should be able to come to you with any concern. You don't need to know all the answers, but you should know where to turn for them should they be required.

2. Show them how. Be a good role model in your own use of technology. You might expect children to put their phones away at dinner, but do you yourself spend time checking emails or texting during family meals? If so, it will be harder to enforce rules that you yourself don't follow. Also, find ways to go hands-on with technology alongside your kids so you can show them how to best use it, or perhaps even the basics of any new technology that enters your home for the first time together – a great bonding experience.

3. See schools as your partner. Schools will introduce technology to your kids in the classroom. They will even teach your kids about its appropriate use. But don't expect them to bear the entire burden of teaching them online safety and responsibility. See schools as your ally, not your substitute. Kids are connecting at home, at school, and increasingly in the places in-between thanks to mobile devices. So ultimately, we – both schools and parents – are all responsible when it comes to teaching them safe, responsible, and successful computing habits, and reinforcing these skills so they can effectively utilize technology on their own, without adult supervision.

By Lynette T. Owens, Director Internet Safety for Kids & Families, Trend Micro

Set Ground Rules

Each family has their own set of rules regarding chores, bedtimes, curfews and other common household concerns. It's equally important that you also have a set of high-tech house rules regarding when and how consumer electronics devices and technologies can be used, and hours and occasions (e.g. dinner or shared family time) during which access to these gadgets or innovations is prohibited.

The American Academy of Pediatrics recommends that you limit a child's use of TV, movies, video and computer games to no more than one or two hours a day –

and abstain from allowing children under two access to screen time entirely. We think it's a good idea to consider setting broad limits in general for any device that has a screen, period.

Kids need to understand that time spent in front of high-tech toys shouldn't be provided as an inalienable right, but rather earned as privilege. Many families start with a daily allowance of screen time, such as one hour per day, and add or subtract time as a reward or punishment for good or bad behavior, superior performance at school or getting chores done around the house. Of course, while this system works well for younger kids and with shared household devices, when children begin using their own mobile solutions such as smartphones or iPads, whose usage is harder to monitor, you'll want to tweak rules accordingly.

As an added rule of thumb, it's also best to keep screens and screen usage out of kids' rooms whenever possible. We recommend confining computers, gaming systems and other connected devices to common areas of the house. Doing so not only allows you to keep abreast of online interactivity, usage patterns, and who kids are interacting with, as well as how. It also lets you be present when devices are used, monitor playtime and keep kids from secretly sneaking online to play World of Warcraft at 3AM on a school night. Obviously, the ability to restrict devices to common areas is not always possible, especially as relates to mobile and handheld consumer electronics. But you should push for use in shared spaces whenever possible.

Another important ground rule your family should consider implementing, as suggested earlier, are setting aside times of day that will be free of devices for everyone in the family. Whether it's at the dinner table or during a weekly Friday night movie, asking everyone to get set aside their high-tech gizmos (except those actively being shared by the whole family) will ensure more engaging and rewarding family time.

Likewise, speak with your children and establish rules concerning what types of information are acceptable to post and share with friends and which pieces of data aren't. Make it clear that personal and family business should remain private and that it is inappropriate to gossip or post vague updates about people in your life that are frustrating you. Along similar lines, it should be crystal clear who your child can communicate with and who they can't. Kids need to be able to know what to do when they receive unsolicited communication from strangers, such as reporting these outreach attempts as spam and blocking the user.

You'll also want to create other everyday rules for wise high-tech use, e.g. in the case of young children, setting a rule that only grownups can enter personal information into a website, including addresses and phone numbers. Eventually your kids will learn what is safe to input and what is not, but when just starting out, it's best to provide some basic guardrails. Important too is to specify the exact days, times and circumstances when it's alright for your kids to be on the computer, browsing the Web on your tablet PC or using their smartphones. Do homework and chores have to be done first? Are high-tech leisure-time activities appropriate to engage in on school nights? Should screens be shut down a minimum of an hour before bed? Establish guidelines ahead of time, and make sure everyone in the household understands them, so that there are no questions as to what is allowed in your home.

Setting an electronic curfew in your house may also help curtail late-night use and improve your family's overall health by promoting restful sleep. One tip when enforcing these deadlines is to create a common area of the house where all devices must be stored and charged, and requiring family members to drop off and store their devices there before bedtime each time.

Ultimately, setting and enforcing rules is important to establishing a sense of routine, as is being consistent with observing them and placing clear guidelines on both the punishments doled out for infractions and circumstances under which they can be cured. Be sure to start early, advises The National Center for Missing and Exploited Youth's Laurie Nathan. Establish expectations from an

early age, such as what sites kids can visit, how long they can stay logged on for, and who it's OK for children to talk to. She recommends the NetSmartz.org home page as an excellent starting place for sparking general online safety discussions.

Encourage Open Dialogue

Whether it's in the real world or online, you owe it to your kids to be actively engaged, readily available and always able to discuss issues of concern with them.

In addition, according to a recent study by the AARP and Microsoft, there is a huge disconnect between teens knowing that they can approach their parents, and knowing when to as well. Nearly half of parents (49%) say that their teens know to come to them to discuss anything uncomfortable they see online. However, only 29% of teens say that they would approach their parents about these topics, pointing to an issue of pressing concern, and underscoring the desperate need to bridge this generation gap.

Engaging with your kids by enjoying technology in shared company, playing games together or connecting with them on social networks may help span the distance. Not only will it provide you with greater knowledge of children, technology, and how each interacts. Active involvement in high-tech activities can also lead to enhanced connection and communication for families who suddenly find themselves with more to talk about, and in a more productive fashion, based on shared common ground.

Experts also suggest using the time spent in the car driving your kids to other real-world activities as a chance to connect through conversation about high-tech interests. Take whatever opportunities you can to engage your children about their hobbies and activities, and find topics (e.g. high-tech devices and services) that you can comfortably discuss in passing conversation without making them feel like they're being interrogated.

Take Advantage of Existing Tools

Whether it's via a Web browser like Firefox or Internet Explorer, or even built-in options within operating systems like those Apple, Google and Microsoft provide, most major consumer devices and platforms offer integrated parental controls that can regulate or prohibit access to online connectivity and content. The iPhone and iPad, as well as video game consoles like the PlayStation 4, Wii U and Xbox One are just a handful of today's most popular consumer electronics that offer such tools right at your fingertips. "Cell phones, video game systems, tablet PCs... pretty much everything comes with parental controls out of the box now," says parenting expert Judi Warren.

Also handy: Many software programs and forms of media further come with attached age ratings and warning descriptors, and/or provide integrated options to block Internet access, limit socializing to approved friends lists only, automatically scrub salty language, or confine interactivity to kid-friendly activities. All offer a basic line of defense, helping you prohibit online spending, block inappropriate material and keep an eye on how and when kids are enjoying online access. Take the time to set up and utilize these parental controls. They're a great, free form of frontline protection against many of the dangers and concerns outlined earlier.

Parents may be surprised at the sheer amount of things that they can control, in fact. For example, certain cell phone providers offer tools that can prevent phones from connecting between any preset times a parent chooses. As an example, adults can disable handsets during school hours to make sure kids aren't accessing the network when they should be focusing on their studies.

Others also offer a system of "family allowances" set up through the principal cell phone account holder, who can set rules for all phones tied to their plan. Parents can shift these allowances of time as necessary, but also add lists of approved numbers that can connect even if other allowances are met. And there's also the ability to block numbers of individuals that parents don't want contacting their kids. As onetime T-Mobile spokesman Mike Vance reminds us about the company's family safety philosophy, "the guardrails are there, and it's up to parents to step in and manage the rest."

Invest in Added Resources

We extensively covered several recommended anti-virus options earlier, and it is imperative you keep them installed and up to date on your computer. However, there are also programs available that can help you monitor your family's online use like Web Watcher, Net Nanny and CyberSitter for computers, and Mobicip for mobile devices, which gives you the ability to keep an eye on what's happening on your smartphone even when you're not around.

Wise parents will note that phones are, in fact, among today's fastest-growing threat areas, and may someday eclipse even computers as the leading battleground upon which wars against malware and spam will be fought. Knowing this, you'll want to keep them guarded. Thankfully, many tools are available to help provide security and peace of mind here, including free apps that allow parents to keep an eye on kids' smartphone activities.

"Parents know that they need to be involved in their kids' digital lives, and most actually set and discuss house rules for computer use and Internet browsing," says Marian Merritt, Norton Internet Safety Advocate. "But to make those rules work, you also need to extend them to your child's mobile phone where so much Web browsing takes place." Luckily, a growing number of mobile phones come pre-equipped with solutions by manufacturers like Lookout, courtesy of cell phone providers. Companies like ESET, McAfee, Kaspersky, Trend Micro and more also make family control a priority, and offer software packages that can help.

Taking advantage of the GPS technology contained in smartphones is also a great way that parents can keep tabs on their kids. As an example, Location Labs offers a suite of digital parenting tools at LocationLabs.com that provides parents with the ability to locate nearly any phone in real time without installing any software on the phone being tracked. But in addition to tracking children's movement, parents can also setup alerts to update them whenever their child arrives at a preset destination, such as school or a relative's house. Boundaries can additionally be created to notify parents when a child leaves a designated area, and locations can be saved to review later.

Many third-party solutions are available to the concerned parent in the form of specialized hardware, software, apps and online services. All are part of a growing range of options that you now have at your fingertips to call upon on-demand, should the need arise.

Create an Effective Password Policy

As the key to the proverbial kingdom with regards to protecting your family's custom safety restrictions and personal information online, the importance of passwords can't be overstated. The damage done should they fall in the wrong hands can take weeks or even years to potentially repair.

Each household should have a clear password policy in place, and should institute individualized passcodes to protect all safety settings, personal accounts and parental controls configurations. In addition to guarding any and all of their own data, parents would do well to claim their right to omniscience when it comes to children's passwords as well. Many parents we've spoken with ensure that they know every password that's used in their house, including those tied to children's online and social network accounts, without exception.

Admittedly, others think such actions may be a bit too drastic and also violate the basic foundation of trust one hopes to build with their children. But perhaps the answer lies somewhere in-between: While you absolutely should be aware of kids' passwords when they first dabble in the online world, you may wish to treat this practice like training wheels, and relax or remove it from your household policies as children get older and become more responsible technology users. Should you request access to children's passcodes though, be sure to remind them that the reason you need this information isn't to spy on them or tarnish their online image – rather, to simply monitor and keep them safe. One tip for families who don't choose to freely share passwords is to set up a regular time with children to access kids' accounts so you can monitor privacy filters and change settings.

With so many different accounts, though, it can be tough to remember passwords for them all. Experts are split on the best way to keep password logs. Although some experts say real-world versions are unreliable, it often makes more sense to keep such lists as separate from the computer as possible. The downside here is that if you misplace or lose this list you could be giving someone easy access to all of your online accounts, so if you do decide to do this, keep it safe and secret. Likewise, should you choose to store a master list somewhere on your computer – which we do not advise – it should be encrypted and password-protected itself. Ultimately, one thing everyone can agree on though is that you must take simple steps to make your passwords impossible for hackers to guess.

As far as creating effective passwords go, here are some basic tips, courtesy of our friends at eBay, who recommend as follows:

• Don't use personal information that others can easily obtain or guess (example: your name, phone number, or birth date).

- The longer and more complex your password is, the harder it will be to guess.

- Create a password that's secure, but still easy for you to remember. To help you remember your password, consider using a phrase or song title as your password. For example, "Somewhere Over the Rainbow" can become "Sw0tR8nBo."

- After creating your password, protect it. Don't share your password with others.

- Don't use the same password for your other online accounts, such as email, bank, and social networking accounts.

Common Sense Media points out that it can actually be fun to develop really good passwords, especially if you're converting phrases that are hard to guess for others, but easy for your family to remember, into a mixture of letters and numbers. In the end, a good password should be at least 8 characters in length; involve a variety of numerals, letters and/or punctuation marks; and not be a word found in your average, everyday dictionary. Many computer programs that hackers use can easily be configured to search for common terms in a variety of forms, including textual (e.g. "ModernParents") and numeric (i.e. "M0dernP4rents").

Remembering to log out of active accounts when finished using them is just as important as not sharing your password, too — especially on public computers or networks. If your son or daughter leaves their Facebook account open on a computer and someone else accesses their profile, the results can range from a harmless spoofed status update to a serious breach of privacy and even potential identity theft.

PART V:

KIDS AND ONLINE ACTIVITY BY AGE GROUP

KIDS AND ONLINE ACTIVITY BY AGE GROUP

According to estimates from the U.S. Senate, 35 million U.S. children from kindergarten through grade 12 have Internet access, and 80% are online at least one hour per week. It's no longer a question of "if" Internet-ready technologies should be introduced into their lives, but rather "when," with kids growingly being exposed to high-tech solutions at increasingly younger ages.

What's more, there's no doubt that ever greater numbers of kids will come to crave access to technology and the Internet. As we've seen several times over, the iPad, iPhone and other mobile devices often rank among kids aged 6 to 12's most-wanted gift items, just narrowly outranking other consumer electronics such as computers and handheld gaming systems. With more tots aged two to five able to play video games or download apps than ride a bike or tie their shoelaces nowadays as well, knowing when to start your kids on different types of technologies and devices is one of the most important questions today's digital parent must ask.

Although it seems obvious to many parents that different content is appropriate for different ages when they think about the types of movies or music they allow kids to consume, many adults struggle with figuring out when and how to introduce their kids to various online activities and high-tech devices. Not that the answer is obvious – essentially, experts say, kids climb a continuum of media consumption, slowly graduating to different types of devices and content over time.

Such journeys usually start with watching videos or gaming on a smartphone or tablet PC, which graduates to full-fledged computer usage over a period of several years. These activities then give way to enjoying on-demand entertainment, Web browsing and communicating with others, which eventually leads to the introduction of kids receiving their own iPods, cell phones and other mobile devices. Suddenly, the whole world is at kids' fingertips –including the ability to connect to who and what they want to, whenever they want to.

Worth considering as well: Despite the fact that Facebook's terms of service require users to be 13 years old to join the service, kids are still gaining access to this and other social networks at earlier ages. Consumer Reports recently estimated that 7.5 million children under 13 utilize Facebook, and that number has surely grown since initially reported. In addition, a report released by Microsoft noted that 7 in 10 parents of underage Facebook users were the ones who helped their kids setup these accounts. This means that parents actively misrepresented their kids' ages when children registered in order for Facebook to approve the account — a willful breach of protocol.

Such examples simply serve to underscore an issue which parents around the country and the globe are presently struggling with: Knowing when it's OK to introduce children of varying ages to new technologies and devices. Ask yourself: When do you feel it is appropriate to start your kids on social networks? What about giving them their own cell phones, or allowing them to use computers unsupervised? Similarly, amongst today's parents, it often seems that smartphone and tablet use is made available to children as early as age one or two. But is this really kosher? The answers aren't necessarily cut and dried.

In hopes of helping perplexed parents, here, we'll provide some rough guidelines regarding the types of technology that are appropriate for consumption by kids at four different developmental stages: Preschool, Early Elementary, Tween and Teen. Note that all are simply proposed starting points for discussion and debate — only you reserve the right to deserve what's truly appropriate for your home.

Preschool (Ages 4 and Below)

Even though the American Academy of Pediatrics recommends zero exposure to devices with screens for kids younger than two, the reality is that many members of Generation Tech will use a computer or high-tech device before their second year, especially if they have older siblings. Many parents even allow one and two year-olds to play games, watch videos and enjoy educational apps on their smartphones or tablet computers. In fact, we've all probably laughed at one point or another when we hear stories of young kids touching a TV screen or the screen on their digital camera in hopes of controlling it as they do other gesture-controlled devices. Although we don't recommend specifically purchasing any tech devices for (or providing ownership of them to) kids this young, chances are they'll use computers, tablet PCs, smartphones and even video game systems owned by the family nonetheless — and that's not necessarily a bad thing.

However, it's equally valid to consider that strong concerns may surround the usage of technology at such a young age, and its impact on overall health, attention span, and developing or impressionable minds. McAfee's Stanley Holditch wonders what can happen to kids confronted with access to the Internet's wealth of content without the proper sense of perspective to process and understand certain issues. He cites commonly-portrayed gender roles as just one potential source of confusion, and potential conflict.

Noted family researcher and Parents magazine columnist Richard Rende, associate research professor at Brown University, agrees. Alas, he says, when it comes to hard scientific data outlining such issues, there's just not enough research available on the subject yet because technology is moving so rapidly. Unfortunately, Rende explains, many extrapolations regarding technology's supposed impact on kids are being made based on a medium for which there are decades of research – specifically, television viewing. However, due to TV's passive and relatively limited contextual nature, such comparisons may not be applicable.

In the end, what Rende does recommend is that parents maintain a level of basic human interactivity when promoting technology use. Reading a storybook on the iPad with a child sitting on your lap can be similar to reading a book in the same way, he says. But you must continue to interact and stimulate your child's intellect and imagination, and not rely on the device to do so alone.

Video Games: At this age, we recommend considering limiting high-tech interactions and activities to storybooks, lightweight forms of entertainment, and (preferably) educational games and software – happily, many options available to this age group combine elements of all. Websites such as FamilyFriendlyVideoGames.com,

GamerPops.com and Common Sense Media can also help provide recommendations for apps and games by age group. Also, at this developmental stage, parents should be very familiar with the games and activities that they are letting their kids play, and at the very least playing alongside them for the first time.

Note that there are also a plethora of downloadable games and educational apps available for kids which can be grabbed on-demand. You can visit sites like Famigo, Moms with Apps or Common Sense Media for recommendations.

Internet and Web Access: Computer use for the pre-school set is a bit trickier subject to tackle, given the fact that using a keyboard is difficult since many kids can't read at this age, and aren't yet coordinated enough to use a mouse. But although the fine motor skills required for successful mouse control probably won't develop until sometime around children's 4th birthday, there are plenty of online games and activities that tots can control by simply pressing any button on the keyboard. Examples include the Sesame Street Online games, and various entertainment options provided by sites like NickJr .com, Family.Disney.com, andPBSKids.org. Each site also contains great information for parents about age appropriateness and skills learned by participation in featured activities.

E-mail: Pre-K sprouts are obviously not ready for e-mail quite yet. Nonetheless, we'll note here that many parents enjoyed the recent Google ad campaign which featured a Google Dad who set up an e-mail account to e-mail a picture a day of his young daughter when she was born. So while kids won't enjoy access to their own e-mail address at this point, it's not too early to begin introducing them to some of the concepts surrounding it, and how it works. Our own toddlers are already aware when grandparents send them a virtual note, for example, which we read aloud.

Cell Phones and Mobile Devices: While you may let your toddler fiddle with your smartphone or tablet in order to gain a few brief moments of precious peace and quiet while out in public or at home, it's worth noting that there are also tech toys designed specifically for the toddler set. From tablets to eReaders and gaming devices, numerous kid-friendly technology options are available. While many of these devices have garnered many parenting and educational awards, be aware that, like video game consoles, many require you to buy a specific type of cartridge, disc or app that's designed only for the system to be able to play. Likewise, not all parents may be comfortable introducing technology at such a young age – let personal judgment rule here.

Social Networks: Thankfully, you still have a few years before your kids get their first social network accounts. But many parents choose to make their children's photos and even names available to the public online – recent estimates say that 80% of kids will enjoy an online presence by the time they're two years old. However, we have to question whether this is wise, especially given the growing threats presented by oversharing of personal information and identity theft. Consider that everything you put online can potentially be seen by anyone – and lives on in perpetuity. So even though you're dying to post that cute picture of your child feeding a goat or riding a miniature train, you may want to think twice about sharing that information.

Tips:

• It's imperative that you make sure to activate parental controls and other restrictions on any device your kids are using before handing these devices over. For smartphones and tablets which run apps, make sure you disable the ability to make in-app purchases. You can find details on how to do this on Apple devices at http://support.apple.com/kb/ht4213.

• It's a good idea to start your quest to begin limiting screen time at this young age. Allowing a half-hour a day of screen time (potentially considered separate from TV watching), works for many of the modern parents we've spoken to.

- The need to set a good example as a parent with regards to technology starts as this young age, too. Make sure you don't get caught up focusing on your smartphone instead of your kids, or allow the usage of high-tech devices to interrupt family events.

- When shopping for apps or video games, check associated ratings. For video games, the Entertainment Software Rating Board (ESRB) provides game summaries and details on retail packaging and apps offered via the Google Play storefront (which also come with International Age Rating Coalition (IARC) ratings), while Apple has its own certification system and age recommendation for each app available via its App Store on the product's download page.

- Play along and engage with your kids about technology. They'll love telling you about what they're doing and treasure the time you are able to play together. Sure, it may not feel the same as bonding over tickle fights or classic cartoons. But it's also fun to see your kids' imagination run wild after playing games like Angry Birds.

- If possible, translate the high-tech games and activities kids enjoy doing over into real life. If they favor an alphabet tracing app, consider preparing some actual physical worksheets or stencils they can play with at the kitchen table that highlight the same skills. If

they're playing Angry Birds (or watching you do so), set up your own set of building blocks for them to knock over in the house, and learn about physics in the process. Have fun with the technology, but make it an adjunct to real life pursuits, and don't let it become a substitute for actual play.

Early Elementary (Ages 5 to 7)

By the time that kids finish kindergarten, chances are that they will have been exposed to many of the most common technological devices, all of which offer myriad ways to connect online. As they progress through grade school, they'll inevitably graduate to more advanced devices, and before you know it, you'll soon be dealing not only with how this technology works, but also how to best control, monitor and safeguard the activities they're using it for.

One of the biggest personal advancements for kids around this age is mastering the ability to read... and not just because of the joy they'll experience by exploring the wonderful world of books. Reading actually opens vast new frontiers of information for sprouts, who'll suddenly find themselves able to operate and program a DVR, follow on-screen instructions in video games, and surf the Web. The ability to read introduces entirely new ways for kids to interact with and use the Internet, even if they're still too young to have their own e-mail address.

From a parent's perspective, it's also important to ensure that you've got control of your cable or satellite service at this point, as kids this age will certainly become adept at using the remote. Make sure you've blocked adult and other materials. Some service providers even require users to setup parental controls the first time they use their service, choosing which material and content to block and which to allow before viewing programs. It won't come as a surprise when more providers start employing similar requirements in increasing numbers as a default installation option, and such actions will certainly help encourage more parents to use these built-in safety features.

Video Games: It is at this age that many parents will first consider introducing a video game console to their home. We recommend disabling any online features such systems offer to kids this young. By this point, kids should also posses the coordination needed to handle today's video game controllers, including gesture-tracking systems in which your body acts as the controller.

Many families struggle when deciding which gaming system to buy their family. But many good answers present themselves: Nintendo's Wii and Wii U, Microsoft's Xbox One and Sony's PlayStation 4 all provide welcome options for families, with many child-friendly titles. Kids this age will also enjoy playing handheld games, whether it's on your smartphone or via systems like the PlayStation Vita or the Nintendo 3DS – however, be aware that such systems may offer online access, downloadable apps, social networking abilities and/or location-tracking features. Be certain to set online, privacy and parental controls before handing them over.

Internet and Web Access: Whether at home or via the school computer lab, by this age, kids will enjoy widespread access to computers and the Internet. This is a great developmental stage at which to sharpen and develop smart computing habits, including learning to type and communicate. In terms of actual high-tech activity, there is likely to still be a heavy focus amongst kids on games and educational material at this point in time. That said, stick to websites and services that you know are reputable, or come highly recommended by real-life friends and family. With so many great choices out there, there's no reason for kids to end up on random sites that may contain inappropriate content or malware. Looking for symbols such as certification from organizations like KidSAFE will ensure that sites are compliant with the latest privacy-protection policies for minors.

E-mail: Many kids this age are considered still too young to have their own e-mail address – you might well consider prohibiting access until they're older.

Cell Phones and Mobile Devices: At this stage of life, kids still don't need their own cell phones, as they'll be largely chaperoned during real-life and virtual activities. However, it's likely that at this age they'll also be asking for even more time with the family's tablet computer or apps on mom and dad's smartphone. Be cautious with the content which you allow them to consume, and cognizant of online connectivity or in-app purchase features contained within apps, software, sites and services that children are allowed access to.

Social Networks: During the early elementary years, kids will start to become more aware of social networks like Facebook and Twitter simply because they'll hear parents, family, teachers, TV personalities and others talk about them. It's OK to show children posts or photos from family or friends that are age-appropriate as well – but don't get sucked into using these networks obsessively while they're around. It sets a bad example, and potentially exposes kids to seeing inappropriate content and issues for which they're developmentally and intellectually unprepared to greet.

Tips:

• At this stage in life, you might consider increasing screen time limits, and adding or subtracting time as a reward for good behavior, or punishment for bad behavior. Apps like Screen Time provide easy ways to start with a baseline number and manage from there. Kids can also "bank" their screen time in an effort to earn other real-life rewards, like a trip to the amusement part or other special activity.

• Enforce device-free times. In addition to a technology blackout at dinner, consider a family movie or game night in which everyone promises to give their full attention without being distracted by their phones or other forms of technology.

• Sit down with your kids while they play games online. It's a great way to connect and learn about how they're using these digital diversions, and provides you with great chances for discussion concerning a number of related topics. Parents who play games with their kids report a higher sense of connection, and studies have shown that girls especially benefit from this parental bonding time.

• Remember the importance of password protection and privacy. Establish your family's password policy and practices while kids are just beginning to get up to speed with technology.

Tweens – Elementary and Middle School (Ages 8 to 12)

As your kids enter their socially awkward middle-school years, they're not only growing into respectable members of society, they're also officially entering the digital domain. At this stage, they'll begin securing their own e-mail accounts; instant messaging and chatting; and, potentially, taking possession of their very own mobile devices (including smartphones, iPads, portable media players and more).

The tween years are a critical time for parents, as they must leverage the groundwork they've been laying since their kids were in preschool to ensure that their offspring have enough savvy and common sense to capably establish their first online footprints. Stressing the importance of online safety and privacy will also be doubly important, as children begin to connect and communicate with the entire world for the first time.

Note that kids this age will also discuss and inherit ideas from their friends, siblings, schoolmates and others that they come into contact with about which websites to visit, games to play, devices to buy, and high-tech services to sign up for. Even if you are confident that all your preparation and hard work towards protecting your kids from the unseemly side of the Internet is working, be aware – these outside influences will nonetheless ensure that kids are going to come across material and influences that you'd rather they didn't.

The subject of which technology devices and services to offer children of this age can also be a tricky one, as children's communications, online safety, and digital citizenship skills first begin to develop. We're certainly familiar with families who have purchased tablet PCs, eReaders, and smartphones for children of this age. However, parents who do elect to provide access to such items at this age need to be aware and cognizant of both the devices' features and potential online interactions their children will be exposed to. Should you opt to provide access at this point, at bare minimum, take steps to configure parental controls and privacy settings before handing gadgets or online accounts over to children. Likewise, make a running commitment to educating yourself about high-tech devices, apps, programs and innovations, and maintaining sustained awareness of not only the features and capabilities all offer, but also how your children are using them.

In addition to safeguarding standard high-tech items, also be certain that parental controls are set on your TV, smartphone, and other subscription services in order to restrict content and the ability to purchase and view content on-demand. Make sure you keep all passcodes a secret from your kids, or they can easily bypass every safeguard you've set up. In the case of paid services, check your bills for a log of all activities and programs consumed... many services offer a full recap of everything that's been accessed or purchased in the previous month.

Most of all, remember that as parents, if you decide to give phones, tablets or even social network accounts or e-mail addresses to kids at this age, you'll also need to provide guardrails and guidelines.

Video Games: It's around this age that kids who play video games will start to want to go online via multiplayer services. Many offer the ability to link your child's account to an adult's so you can manage what your children can and can't do, as well as whom they interact with.

Microsoft online safety director Doug Park counsels parents to use your child's real age when setting up online accounts on your console: It may seem obvious, but doing so will help ensure that age-appropriate safeguards are put in place or used to their fullest. "A lot of parents don't understand that when they create an account, they're setting up the entire experience," Park says.

Virtual worlds will also be a popular draw with young adults. Many provide gaming options that allow kids to play for free, but also contain "premium" content that can only be accessed by paying for them on-demand or by signing up to contribute a monthly fee.

However, online connectivity and shopping and access to age-appropriate material are just a handful of many concerns parents of contemporary gamers will face. For a more in-depth look at managing and promoting healthy interactions around gaming, and picking the right software titles, see our companion book The Modern Parent's Guide to Kids and Video Games.

Internet and Web Access: Middle school aged children are going to need Internet access, whether as a part of everyday schoolwork, after-school activities or homework projects. In fact, many schools now offer websites that act as online portals specifically designed to supplement coursework with additional downloadable materials, and serve as communities where children, adults and teachers can interact, share insights and retrieve grades or attendance records on-demand.

However, kids are going to come across inappropriate material once they're set free online. Bearing this in mind, the key to successful parenting of older children as relates to technology isn't just being engaged in children's lives and putting proper safeguards in place — it's also teaching them to know how to identify questionable content, and what to do when they come across it. Children must also be encouraged to come forward with questions or concerns, and provided open forums for dialogue and strong support systems that can address these issues.

Don't simply let kids' lives, or Internet activities, speed by in a blur as you set your awareness to cruise control. Instead, check in regularly with your kids about how, where and in what ways they use the Internet. Ask them what sites they like to visit, services they use, apps and programs they prefer, and to what extent and in which ways they're choosing to interact with these resources. Be specific when seeking out pieces of information, e.g. where they turn to exchange messages with friends online. But also be thoughtful, and consider the bigger picture: How children use the Internet, and alongside whom, is every bit as important as the specific program or service which facilitates these interactions – as is the way such exchanges make them feel, react or see topics from different perspectives. Start asking questions, and you may be surprised by just how grown up many children's online universe are – and in just how many ways they're learning to process information about and interpret the world around them.

E-mail: Many families allow their kids to sign up for e-mail accounts around the age of nine. However, services themselves often restrict usage to older children, i.e. Google, who requires kids to be 13 to register for their own Gmail account. Although (as with any similar service) there are reports that some families were able to request and receive accounts for younger children, the launch of Google+ and heightened public concerns surrounding children's privacy have caused Google to exercise growing care when enforcing age limits.

One option for children seeking a first email address, or concerned parents, is to set up a Zoobuh.com account, which costs $1 per month. This service allows you to preview your children's e-mail before they receive it.

"If you are going to let a child under 13 years of age have an e-mail account, you should absolutely connect it to your own account," says Symantec's Merritt. She recommends actively overseeing their online activities here, and setting up so-called "whitelists" and "blacklists" that restrict who they can and can't e-mail, respectively. The monitoring of children's accounts also acts as a strong deterrent to kids that may prevent them from sending or receiving inappropriate materials. Should another child consider forwarding unwanted or undesirable material, your child's warning that you check their account may prompt second thoughts from sprouts who'd rather avoid aggravating a concerned adult. Again, keep in mind that any monitoring activities you conduct should be treated like training wheels and that once kids have matured and grown in experience

Cell Phones and Mobile Devices:
Although many wait until children reach their teenage years to provide access to cellular phones, 13 is rapidly becoming a common age at which some kids receive their first handset. Parry Aftab from Wired Moms suggests that parents keep several tips in mind when providing young adults with their first phone. For starters, she reminds parents that you don't have to buy smartphones loaded with connectivity features – basic "feature phones" that lack downloadable apps, streaming multimedia access, and high-end Web browsers are often a safer alternative. A common mistake, experts agree, is when parents opt to buy kids full-fledged smartphones (e.g. the iPhone) and provide them with unlimited online access before they're prepared for or even need to use these devices or surrounding capabilities. Buying a basic phone with fewer gee-whiz technical features and strong parental controls, and setting and enforcing limits about its usage, is often the wiser choice.

Aftab also offers a strong reminder about the effect that mobile devices can have on children's academic performance, cautioning parents that cell phones don't belong in the classroom, unless teachers' specify a pressing educational need for them to be present. These devices aren't just distracting, Aftab points out – they're also often used to pass notes, cheat on tests, or otherwise distract from children's studies. Also worth pointing out, she suggests, is that even when supplied to children, these devices are provided strictly as privileges, and that parents should ultimately remain in control of them and revoke usage rights if either family or school rules aren't followed.

In addition, kids this age will quickly embrace instant messaging and chat functions, whether through online services, dedicated desktop software programs, or via mobile devices. Make sure they're only connecting to and conversing with people they know, educate them as to the potential dangers of meeting strangers online, and don't be shy about researching and tracking these interactions if you feel there's a potential problem.

Of potential interest to today's parent – studies show that most kids receive their first mobile handset between the ages of 12 and 13. But before many kids make the leap to having their own phone, more possess their own digital music (MP3) or portable media player, handheld video game system or mobile device that can connect to the Internet and be used for texting, e-mails and song downloads, such as an iPod. However, adults may not always realize just how much power they're placing at children's fingertips.

"When many parents give 10 year-olds an iPod, they're not realizing that they're giving them a pocket computer," says FOSI's Stephen Balkam. So don't just fully research and understand the features and capabilities of any high-tech device before putting it in kids' hands. Be sure you are also closely watching the apps they download, services they subscribe to, and programs they use, and consider setting up built-in controls or installing third-party software to filter the content children consume. Also, be aware that if such options are offered, kids will likely be syncing connected devices to wireless networks, giving them full access to the Internet as well.

Social Networks: Although kids technically can't join social networks until they're 13 years old, they're by now going to be heavily exposed to popular mainstream sites and services such as Twitter, Instagram, Facebook, Google+ and Pinterest. Even if they can't ostensibly register for an account while still a tween, know that many workarounds exist as well, as children can easily utilize another family member's Facebook profile or search for Twitter users and tweets without even needing to be logged into the service. Take caution, care, and appropriate steps to educate children about social networks, content contained within, and potential issues and influences they may be exposed to through them. At the very least, it will help lay the groundwork for future discussions, which will soon become unavoidable as kids get older

and usage amongst their friends becomes more ubiquitous.

Tips:

• At this age, you still should enforce a transparent password policy with your kids. Make it clear that you need to know their account information for any activity or program they're using that requires a user login. Keep detailed notes on this information, and set rules that if you discover that any inappropriate activities or actions have taken place, these can be grounds for immediate restriction or loss of privileges. Just as you as a parent shouldn't be doing anything online that you wouldn't be comfortable showing your family, there shouldn't be anything that your kids are doing online that requires being kept secret as well.

• Teach kids what they need to know to spot something fishy, whether a piece of questionable content or unscrupulous individual. Ensure they're equipped by this age with a basic awareness of predators, criminals, shady characters, online scams, and potential sources of erroneous facts and misinformation. Cultivate a healthy sense of skepticism without instilling a sense of fear or powerlessness, and let kids know that they have a place to turn when questions or concerns arise.

• Each family should also, by this stage, have a discussion about buying new apps, music or digital downloads, what types of content is acceptable to consume, and how it may be enjoyed — then set a household policy that all members agree to abide by. Be sure to consistently apply and enforce it as well.

• Treat texting like calls when kids are first starting out with cell phones. Restrict its usage, then relax the reins slightly, relenting more as kids learn to become more responsible users. But always be careful about the plan you select, and certain to regulate and enforce policies about appropriate access times, uses and messaging limits.

• While placing your family's main computer in a common area may help deter some of kids' more ill-advised explorations, it's important that you check up on their activities if they've been left alone with the PC. Don't forget to check your browser's history and find out which sites they've been accessing. Likewise, you may also wish to do so regularly with mobile devices, to see what your kids have been up to recently — and whom they've been up to it with.

• Discussions should continue at this age regarding online safety, netiquette, and digital citizenship, and progress into more complex topics or trains of thought, e.g. some of the consequences that may arise from the online bullying of other children. Now is also a vital time to revisit the subject of what is and isn't OK to share online, especially given the ready availability and permanence of information uploaded to the Internet. As many smartphones offer built-in digital cameras, you should also be teaching kids the importance of protecting both their own and others' images, and not distributing photos or videos of third parties without their consent.

• Know your cell phone plan inside and out, and make a point of reviewing bills and statements on a regular basis. There's no reason for you to be surprised by exorbitant charges or unusual activity at this point.

Teens (Ages 13 to 17)

Like it or not, the teen years are the time when your kids will find themselves knee-deep in the process of permanently setting out on their own online, and forging a virtual identity, even though a few years yet remain before they're ready to forge their own identity in real-life. And just as a parent's duties do not end the day a child leaves the nest, so too must they continue even after you set your child free on the Internet.

For today's kids, the 13th birthday marks a major high-tech milestone, as this is the age not only at which many children receive their first cellular phone — it also signals that they're old enough to sign up for Facebook. Kids may also begin getting their own laptops or computers to use for schoolwork, and be faced by online or connected classwork and assignments. In fact, 93% of American teens aged 13 to 17 use the Internet, according to the Pew Internet and American Life Project, and 66% of children get their first cell phone before they're 14. That's a lot of online access and computing power to place in kids' hands, reinforcing the need for parents to play a pivotal role in shaping positive interactions around technology.

To this extent, parents should still maintain widespread access to kids' devices, and know how to (with a little detective work, if necessary) track just what teens have been up to on these gadgets. By now, it will hopefully be a long-running and well-established family policy that kids have willingly abided by. But by the same token, parents must also be watchful for signs of concern or duplicity, and vigilant as to potential dangers or issues that may be arise as a result of teens' growing online interests and experimentations. If you've made a running commitment to educating and enlightening them about technology's upsides and challenges, reinforced healthy computing habits and behaviors, and instilled a sense of self-awareness and savvy, you've hopefully by now raised a responsible and productive digital citizen. Nonetheless, while trusting in our children is imperative, it's also important to maintain a healthy sense of skepticism, and remain alert to potential issues – like all of us, even the brightest and best apples can and will make mistakes sometimes.

As long as we're reasonable with our concerns, and remain respectful of our children's growing sense of smarts and independence, it's possible to strike a healthy balance here, and provide a safety net that's there to gently catch them, prop them back up, and provide a reassuring pat of support when – more likely than not – they eventually fall.

Video Games: According to a recent study from the American Academy of Pediatrics, the majority (61%) of teens played video games for less than 7 hours a week – however, 39% reported playing more than that, with roughly one in ten saying that they play games for 20 hours a week or more. Like older tweens, teens who do play games will also by now be well-acquainted with titles whose emphasis is placed on controversial subjects, mature gameplay, and head-to-head multiplayer connectivity via online services.

The ESRB even maintains a T for Teen rating for games that are a bit more sophisticated and deal with more serious themes than those appropriate for younger audiences, but still falls short of titles rated M for Mature, which are reserved for ages 17 and up. T-rated selections can include the likes of wrestling simulations, first-person shooters, selections containing salty language and cartoon violence, or other outings you may take odds with. Talk to your kids about the types of games that you feel are acceptable for them to play, both at home and at their friends' houses, and create and enforce house rules concerning them. Companion volume The Modern Parent's Guide to Kids and Video Games provides a detailed look at the issues parents of teen gamers face today, and how to address them.

Internet and Web Access: In addition to other forms of online connectivity that children will have previously embraced, the use of video chat is rising amongst teenagers, according to recent studies by Ericsson – a point parents should be aware of, given users' ability to film and share footage of themselves privately or publicly in real-time. While most teens will use popular free services such as Skype for brief, informal, and largely innocent chats, others may use popular videoconferencing programs for more lascivious purposes, or forget that the camera's on and speak out of turn or make disparaging remarks despite the fact they're being filmed.

Vital to ponder as well when thinking about teens and issues surrounding online connectivity: The majority of Web access is not happening via traditional computers. Somewhat frighteningly, given how difficult its usage can be to monitor, the mobile Internet, whether accessed from smartphones or tablet PCs, is suddenly the primary way that kids are now connecting online. Lest you worry, however, the vast majority of interactions are perfectly safe and upright. According to the Pew Internet and American Life Project, here's what teens are doing online:

- 62% get news about current events and politics online.
- 48% have made online purchases like books, clothing or music, up from 31% who did so in 2000.
- 31% of online teens receive health, dieting or physical fitness information from the Internet.
- 17% report that they use the Internet to gather information about health topics that are hard to discuss with others such as drug use and sexual matters.

E-mail: While 13 year-old children can now officially sign up for e-mail accounts, recent research is finding that kids are using this form of communication with growing infrequency. According to a recent comScore report, use of e-mail dropped 31% amongst 12 to 17 year-olds, following a decline of 59% the year prior. And college-age individuals using e-mail less and less as well. "While the significant decline among teens represents a continuation of a similar trend observed last year, that 18 to 24 year-olds are now moving away from webmail suggests that a larger and more permanent shift in e-mail usage may be occurring," says the report. The fact is, with kids connecting via smartphones and tablets significantly more than through PCs, the need for e-mail is declining drastically as many are switching over to texting or instant messaging as a primary communications tool instead.

Social Networks: Now that teenagers can finally, legitimately register for Facebook, it's important to realize: Research is finding that they use the social network in very different ways than adults, and in fact would give use of the service up before jettisoning other forms of communication. A recent study by Ericsson provides further insights, as when asked what form of communication they would miss most if it was taken away, the clear majority of teen respondents replied "face to face." Less than half answered with texting, putting it in a distant second place. And Facebook was only the fourth most-popular answer after mobile phones — hardly a star turn for social networks. While the study found that kids enjoyed meeting in real life (or IRL as they know it), because of body language and nonverbal cues, however, it's worth keeping in mind when pondering the cultural shift... Teens also reported that voice phone calls are full of "awkward pauses" and see them largely as a communications tool for adults.

Cell Phones and Mobile Devices: According to the Pew Internet and American Life Project, 75% of teens now have a cell phone. Even younger adolescents are getting in on the act, with 58% of 12 year-olds now owning a handset as well. Intriguingly, teenagers are likely to have many, if not all, peers from their school contained within their Facebook friends list, and because of this, they prefer services like texting when they want to have one-on-one conversations with friends.

Anne Collier of ConnectSafely.org further reports that 87% of teens text, and send more than 50 texts a day, which equates to at least 1500 such messages a month. One third of teens send more than 100 texts a day, or at least 3000 every 30 days. In fact, the average teen exchanges more than 7 texts per waking hour — talk about sore thumbs. So be advised: With texting quickly becoming the primary means of communication amongst this audience, simply monitoring cell phone bills or situating computers in common areas may not be nearly enough to prevent unwanted communications from occurring.

Tips:

• Even though your kids are becoming more independent by this stage, it's important to still monitor and be aware of their online activities. Continue to enforce a transparent password policy, review the sites and services that they visit, and make sure that they know you are actively doing so. Be open and honest with them about issues that concern you, and let them know that you're always willing to discuss any thoughts they have about their own concerns as well.

- Google your kids' names regularly to see if any negative or unwanted mentions show up. Make sure to do the same for any usernames they utilize as well. Consider doing so with them as well from time to time, and also don't be afraid to Google your own name in shared company (don't worry, your children have probably done it already). Explain everything that's out there, positive and negative, and use personal anecdotes to help them learn from some of the mistakes you may have made yourself and avoid doing the same.

- Be aware of kids' activities on social networks. While it's easy to connect with accounts you know about, be vigilant and mindful of the potential for kids to create alternate accounts in order to communicate and conduct clandestine activity away from your watchful eyes.

- It's a good idea to purchase apps, Facebook credits and online purchases with gift cards instead of using your own credit card so as to safeguard sensitive personal information. In the event of identity theft, you'll be potentially shielded from exorbitant charges and loss of data. Likewise, preset spending caps or limits can also help minimize unwanted expenses. As kids get older, they may start working their first job, and begin enjoying access to their own discretionary funds as well, which they may wish to use to buy video games, apps, music, movies and more. Monitor their spending habits to watch for irresponsible behavior, and offer to help turn cash into gift cards as a way to regulate the amount that they're able to spend online. It's a smart choice to make kids aware that you must authorize any downloads, especially purchases, as well. When it comes to online shopping, let kids know that you have the final say and that you'll be watching.

- As your teen grows up and heads off to college, it can be tough to let go. But hopefully the sense of responsibility and care you've instilled as they've grown up will carry over to safe computing habits and behaviors, and smart decision making, as they operate online outside the periphery of your watchful eyes. Realistically, once they've left the nest, it's hard to maintain control – so before kids head off to college, it's vital to make sure that you've done everything you can to set them up for success. Maintaining a commitment to lifelong learning isn't just the cornerstone of online safety and digital citizenship: It's also the best lesson you can teach your children, and hopefully one they'll pass along someday to their own digital kids.

PART VI:

DISCUSSION GUIDE AND RESOURCES

DISCUSSION GUIDE AND RESOURCES

There's no doubt that any discussion surrounding Internet and online safety is a broad one and, even after covering so much ground, we've only begun to scratch the potential surface here. As we wrap up this volume, we'd like to leave you and your loved ones with a starting point for future discussion that can help you uncover and explore the issues and ideas which matter most to your family.

"As parents, it's important not just to talk about safety, but also teach kids about a broad range of concerns," says Lynette Owens, director of Internet safety for kids and families at Trend Micro. Moreover, she suggests, it's also vital to apply real-life thought to online activities and interactions. So think about the frameworks kids are using when they access, enjoy, and engage with technology and consumer electronics, Owens suggests. Consider what devices to allow and when it's appropriate for children to use them. And don't let discussion begin or end solely with a look at actual high-tech gadgets or innovations — use those as a foundation from which to also spark dialogue about healthy computing habits and being responsible digital citizens.

In fact, Trend Micro has created a dedicated guide for having what it calls "The Talk" — a discussion with kids about online safety, netiquette, and responsible behavior that's every bit as crucial as any chat about the birds and bees. As the company points out in the volume, "you don't need to be a technology genius to talk about things, people, and behaviors that are dangerous, but you do need to have a basic understanding of threat types and terminology." Below, we've compiled a few further discussion points based on many of the concerns we've highlighted and recommendations we've made that may prove a helpful starting point when conducting your own conversations.

IMPORTANT QUESTIONS TO ASK YOUR FAMILY

- What devices are we using to access the Internet?
- How and in what ways are we using this online access?
- What types of activities, sites and interactions do we like to engage with online?
- What websites and services do we frequent often and why?
- What are our house rules with regards to the use of high-tech devices and Internet connectivity?
- What punishments will be meted out should they be violated?
- What times are designated to be free of high-tech devices?
- What is our family's password policy?

- Have we implemented parental controls and privacy restrictions?
- Will we be monitoring children's online access? How so?
- What should we do if we encounter questionable and/or inappropriate content or behavior online?
- Do we understand the capabilities of all high-tech devices present in our home?
- Do we know where to turn if we have questions about any technology service or product, or need the help of a qualified professional?
- Is screen time an inherent right or earned privilege? How much will be allowed daily?
- What areas of the home are designated for high-tech use?
- What are our rules for appropriate high-tech usage?
- Are we aware of the basic safety rules that must be observed when using technology?
- Do we know what it means to be responsible digital citizens?
- Have we as a family made a running commitment to educate ourselves about new technology trends, topics, products and services?
- Do we all feel comfortable turning to each other for help if we have any questions?

The National Center for Missing and Exploited Youth's Laurie Nathan says that's above all else, it's imperative that parents begin engaging kids in such conversations from a young age. Not only is it easy to have these conversations with younger children, but it also helps establish routine dialogue about these matters as a normal and regular part of household life. Parents should also engage children's teachers and ask what it is that kids are doing and talking about at school, as teachers often bring a very unique perspective on kids' development, and the types of concepts and subjects that currently interest them.

Cheerfully, there are also a number of great resources available online for families interested in continuing the discussion and formalizing online safety agreements. Case in point: NetSmartz's website has a great set of pledges for both online and real-life situations, tailored for different age groups. For parents, FOSI also offers a Family Safe Contract, a set of cyber do's and don'ts for parents and kids alike, featuring a number of ground rules, such as the need to be honest with each other and parents agreeing not to overreact. Common Sense Media likewise offers Rules of the Road for Kids, which provide helpful insights like assuming everyone is watching your every action, and the importance of always applying the golden rule. Its website also provides great tips for parents, such as getting involved and striking a proper balance in terms of real-world and high-tech use. ConnectSafely.org additionally makes a number of tips on topics ranging from cyberbullying and sexting to password creation and video games available for ready access.

Marian Merritt of Norton additionally suggests a number of great conversational questions in her family safety guide that are geared towards younger kids, such as asking them about the coolest and newest websites, or finding out if anything online has ever made them feel sad or uncomfortable. She also includes topics to discuss with older children as well. Parents should also check out the Internet Safety 101 quiz from Enough is Enough too. This 10 question test is designed to see how cyber savvy you really are.

Beyond these initial resources, SafeKids.com also provides a test designed to let kids show that they know what it takes to be safe online. Microsoft additionally offers an incredible amount of information, presentations and brochures that are meant to be shared with others, and can provide great discussion tools for parents and school administrators as well.

In summary, it's obvious that as your kids grow older, their interests and tastes will inevitably change. Maintaining ongoing and constructive dialogue will help everyone stay abreast of evolving concerns. But while creating open lines of communication about any and all technology-related issues is vital, it may be tough for some families to know where to start. Knowing this, with a tip of the hat to Anne Collier from ConnectSafely, we leave you with a few words from USC Professor Henry Jenkins on the subject.

"As a society, we have spent too much time focused on what media is doing to young people, and not enough time asking what young people are doing with media," Jenkins says. "[As responsible adults,] we need to embrace a [safety] approach based on media ethics. Specifically, one that empowers young people to take greater responsibility for their own actions and holds them accountable for the choices they make as media producers and members of online communities."

We sincerely wish you and your family the best as you begin to explore the digital world, and integrate technology into your household, classroom, or community. This guide is simply a starting point – the rest of the story is yours to write, as you and your kids start to get connected, get plugged in, and get to work making connected devices and solutions just another perfectly positive, healthy and normal part of growing up in children's lives.

PART VII:

ADDITIONAL ONLINE SAFETY TOOLS AND RESOURCES

ADDITIONAL ONLINE SAFETY TOOLS & RESOURCES

Center on Media and Child Health

www.cmch.tv

The Center on Media and Child Health at Children's Hospital Boston, Harvard Medical School, and Harvard School of Public Health is dedicated to understanding and responding to the effects of media on the physical, mental, and social health of children through research, translation, and education.

Common Sense Media

www.commonsensemedia.org

A non-profit organization dedicated to improving the lives of kids and families by providing trustworthy reviews of many types of media, as well as providing tips for online safety.

ConnectSafely.org

www.connectsafely.org

ConnectSafely is designed to give teens and parents a voice in the public discussion about youth online safety begun back in the '90s. ConnectSafely also provides all kinds of social-media safety tips for teens and parents, the latest youth tech news, and many other helpful resources.

CyberAngels

www.cyberangels.org

A resource focusing on safety matters. Offers guidance for parents and provides information and solutions to common Internet safety issues.

Cybersitter

www.cybersitter.com

Cybersitter is a monitoring and filtering program that allows parents to completely customize the content that they want to block or allow, and also protects against accidental clicks on malware links. The software can record Facebook chats and posts as well.

CyberTipline.com

www.cybertipline.com

The Congressionally-mandated CyberTipline is a means for reporting crimes against children including:

- Possession, Manufacture, and Distribution of Child Pornography
- Online Enticement of Children for Sexual Acts
- Child Prostitution
- Sex Tourism Involving Children
- Extrafamilial Child Sexual Molestation
- Unsolicited Obscene Material Sent to a Child
- Misleading Domain Names
- Misleading Words or Digital Images on the Internet

Embrace Civility in a Digital Age

www.embracecivility.org

Embrace Civility in a Digital Age promotes approaches that best ensure all young people become "Cyber Savvy" and address youth risks in a positive and restorative manner.

Enough is Enough

www.enough.org

Enough Is Enough aims to make the Internet safer for children and families by raising public awareness about the dangers of Internet pornography and sexual predators, and advances solutions that promote equality, fairness and respect for human dignity with shared responsibility between the public, technology, and the law.

Facebook Family Safety Center

http://www.facebook.com/safety

Provides tips for parents, law enforcement, kids and more about many aspects of maintaining safety and online privacy on today's most popular social network.

FamilyFriendlyVideoGames.com

www.FamilyFriendlyVideoGames.com

Provides detailed information about video games from a family perspective, with an emphasis on games that are fun to play together. The site categorizes games by age range and play style to make it easy to find games that are fun for your family.

Family Online Safety Institute

www.fosi.org

The Family Online Safety Institute (FOSI) works to make the online world safer for kids and their families by identifying and promoting best practices, tools and methods in the field of online safety that also respect free expression.

FBI Cyber Alerts Index

http://www.fbi.gov/news/stories/story-index/cyber-crimes

A place to see the latest alerts and news from the FBI about cybercrimes

GetNetWise.org

www.getnetwise.org

GetNetWise is a public service brought to you by Internet industry corporations and public interest organizations to help ensure that users have safe, constructive, educational and entertaining online experiences.

IamBigBrother

http://www.parentalsoftware.org/bigbrother.html

IamBigBrother is an online service that allows parents to examine everything that kids have done online. From websites viewed to messages sent, the digital monitoring solution further provides screen captures of e-mails if desired.

Internet Keep Safe Coalition

www.iKeepSafe.org

The site includes safety, security and ethics tools and resources for helping families and educators teach children to use the Internet safely and wisely.

McAfee's Internet Safety

www.InternetSafety.com

Contains useful tips and a frequently updated blog on issues that affect family online safety and security, and comes recommended.

Kaspersky

http://usa.kaspersky.com/

Offers online security products for families and businesses helping them maintain their safety and privacy on the Internet.

K-9

www.k9webprotection.com

K9 Web Protection is a free Internet filter and parental controls tool that allows users to block websites, force safe searches, set time restrictions, configure custom allow or lock lists, view activity reports and more.

Lookout

https://www.mylookout.com/

This leading smartphone security company helps protect mobile devices from malware, viruses, spyware and more.

Microsoft Safety & Security Center

http://www.microsoft.com/security/default.aspx

Provides resources and information on Microsoft products and happenings that affect families, as well as numerous articles on how to better protect your PC, router, operating system, and wireless network.

Microsoft YouthSpark Hub

http://www.microsoft.com/about/twc/en/us/default.aspx

Offers tips and articles about a broad range of online safety topics of relevance to computer and Windows users.

Microsoft Trustworthy Computing

http://www.microsoft.com/en-us/twc/default.aspx

Delivers a more technical view of cybersecurity and malware issues.

Mobicip

www.Mobicip.com

Mobicip software gives parents the ability to safeguard their children's mobile activities and devices. With three layers to its filtering technology, Mobicip does more than block website addresses... The software dynamically views the entire webpage to determine if there is offensive content, even on an allowed site, based on the parent's choice of one of three Mobicip-provided filtering levels.

Net Nanny

www.netnanny.com

Net Nanny's Internet filter software protects kids from things they don't need to see while still allowing them to freely search and browse online. With the parental control tools provided by this powerful filter, adults can rest easy knowing that their children's online experiences will be safe and inoffensive.

NetSmartz.org

www.netsmartz.org

An educational resource from The National Center for Missing and Exploited Children that ably discusses various Internet safety topics.

Norton Family Resource Center

http://us.norton.com/familyresources/

Designed to provide easy-to-understand insights into Internet safety issues. Led by Norton's family safety expert Marian Merritt, the site features a blog, video tips and other helpful links.

SafeKids.com

www.safekids.com

Contains information about the dangers that confront children using the Internet. Offers tips, advice and helpful rules relating to children's security and the Web.

Trend Micro Internet Safety

http://internetsafety.trendmicro.com/

Advice for families and schools from makers of the popular security software package. Features blogs and articles pertaining to emerging safety issues.

Web Watcher

www.webwatcherkids.com

Used by government and law enforcement agencies, WebWatcher software allows parents to block websites and record online and offline activity. The program even monitors keystrokes and allows parents to read all IM and e-mail messages. WebWatcher also has a feature that allows parents to securely keep track of their children's activity, even on a different computer.

WiredSafety

www.wiredsafety.org

WiredSafety is the largest online safety, education and help group in the world. They consider themselves a "cyber-neighborhood" watch group because the site is staffed by thousands of volunteers worldwide.

Zoodles

www.zoodles.com

Zoodles is an app that provides kids with a safe environment of child-friendly games, videos and activities, and allows parents to monitor what they've been playing. Parents can set time limits and restrict access to certain types of content too.

ABOUT SCOTT STEINBERG

Bestselling business author Scott Steinberg is one of the world's most celebrated professional speakers, futurists, and strategic innovation consultants, as seen in 600+ outlets from CNN to The Wall St. Journal. The author of Make Change Work for You: 10 Ways to Future-Proof Yourself, Fearlessly Innovate and Succeed Despite Uncertainty, the Fortune 500 calls him a "defining figure in business and technology" and "top trendsetter to follow." An internationally-renowned consumer and business trends expert, Fortune magazine recently named this leading trend forecaster and futurist the "master of innovation."

The CEO of management consulting and market research firm FutureProof Strategies, he helps clients create value and cultivate competitive advantage on the back of emerging innovations and trends. A top-rated provider of keynote speeches, workshops and seminars for Fortune 500 businesses, non-profits, associations and educational institutes, he's partnered with many leading organizations to deliver game-changing leadership, education, and change management programs. As a trusted advisor to the world's biggest and most well-known brands, he's consulted on dozens of innovative products, services, and marketing and social media campaigns.
Among today's most-quoted keynote speakers and trend experts, as seen by over one billion people worldwide, Scott's 10+ year track record for accurately predicting business, consumer and technology trends has made him a fixture in mainstream media. Today's #1-ranked technology expert according to Google, he's been a syndicated columnist on change and innovation for numerous outlets ranging from Fast Company, Inc. and Entrepreneur to Rolling Stone and The Huffington Post. An acclaimed entrepreneur who's built and sold several startups and divisions, recent works include Becoming Essential, The Crowdfunding Bible, Teaching Technology and the award-winning Business Expert's Guidebook. His motivational speeches, leadership seminars and training workshops are renowned for demonstrating thousands how to become more successful and effective in their life and career.
For more, see www.AKeynoteSpeaker.com.

"One of the best gurus on innovation and competitive advantage strategies to accelerate growth."
--European Commission

"If you really want to know about business, you should refer to Scott Steinberg."
 --Sir Richard Branson, Virgin Group

Popular Speeches Include

-- Leading with Innovation: How to Future-Proof Yourself + Succeed Going Forward

-- Change Management: Creating a Culture of Innovation

-- Becoming Essential: How to Build & Maintain Competitive Advantage

-- The New Rules of Marketing, PR and Social Media

-- The Relationship Economy - Reinventing Sales and Customer Service

-- Seeing Tomorrow Today: How to Stay Ahead of the Curve

ABOUT JOHNER RIEHL

Johner Riehl is your typical busy dad, juggling multiple work responsibilities and fulfilling family activities in a way that only parenthood can develop. He's worked in the video game industry for almost 20 years as a publicist, writer and reviewer, enjoying stints covering family-friendly games and apps and even hosting a nationally-recognized podcast aimed at new parents about the joys and challenges of parenthood. From Pokémon to parental controls to poopy diapers, Riehl has covered a vast number of digital and real-life parenting issues, which even included seeing his kids rack up hundreds of dollars buying worthless virtual goods. Still, Riehl marvels at the possibilities of the digital generation, and is working to not only be the best hi-tech parent possible, but also encourage others to embrace and educated themselves on the unique opportunities provided to this plugged-in generation.

ADDITIONAL RESOURCES

For more helpful resources, including free eBooks, tip sheets, training guides and videos, please visit us online at www.AKeynoteSpeaker.com.

Additional books and training guides by Scott Steinberg include:

• MAKE CHANGE WORK FOR YOU: 10 WAYS TO FUTURE-PROOF YOURSELF, FEARLESSLY INNOVATE, AND SUCCEED DESPITE UNCERTAINTY

• BECOMING ESSENTIAL: BUILDING GROWTH, VALUE AND COMPETITIVE ADVANTAGE THROUGH STRATEGIC INNOVATION

• SOCIAL MEDIA MARKETING AND MANAGEMENT

• CONTENT MARKETING: THE INSIDER SECRETS

• INFLUENCER MARKETING

• CUSTOMER SERVICE IS BROKEN

• PROFESSIONAL SPEAKERS, MEETINGS AND EVENTS MADE SIMPLE

• CROWDFUNDING AND KICKSTARTER: THE ULTIMATE GUIDE

• THE BUSINESS EXPERT'S GUIDEBOOK - #1 Bestseller

• THE CROWDFUNDING BIBLE - #1 Bestseller

• THE MODERN PARENT'S GUIDE: HIGH-TECH PARENTING - #1 Bestseller

• FACEBOOK FOR KIDS AND PARENTS - Bestseller

JUL -- 2018

CPSIA information can be obtained
at www.ICGtesting.com
Printed in the USA
LVOW03s1511150318
569990LV00002B/386/P